Violence
Against
Women

RESEARCH HIGHLIGHTS 56

Research Highlights in Social Work Series
This topical series examines areas of particular interest to those in social and community work and related fields. Each book draws together different aspects of the subject, highlighting relevant research and drawing out implications for policy and practice. The project is under the editorial direction of Professor Andrew Kendrick, Head of the School of Applied Social Sciences at the University of Strathclyde, Scotland.

other recent books in the series

Social Care, Service Users and User Involvement
Edited by Peter Beresford and Sarah Carr
Foreword by Simon Denegri
ISBN 978 1 84905 075 3
eISBN 978 0 85700 264 8
RESEARCH HIGHLIGHTS IN SOCIAL WORK 55

Social Work Education and Training
Edited by Joyce Lishman
ISBN 978 1 84905 076 0
eISBN 978 0 85700 262 4
RESEARCH HIGHLIGHTS IN SOCIAL WORK 54

Substance Misuse
The Implications of Research, Policy and Practice
Edited by Joy Barlow
ISBN 978 1 84310 696 8
eISBN 978 0 85700 219 8
RESEARCH HIGHLIGHTS IN SOCIAL WORK 53

Youth Offending and Youth Justice
Edited by Monica Barry and Fergus McNeill
ISBN 978 1 84310 689 0
eISBN 978 0 85700 195 5
RESEARCH HIGHLIGHTS IN SOCIAL WORK 52

Leadership in Social Care
Edited by Zoë van Zwanenberg
ISBN 978 1 84310 969 3
eISBN 978 0 85700 204 4
RESEARCH HIGHLIGHTS IN SOCIAL WORK 51

Public Services Inspection in the UK
Edited by Howard Davis and Steve Martin
ISBN 978 1 84310 527 5
eISBN 978 1 84642 830 2
RESEARCH HIGHLIGHTS IN SOCIAL WORK 50

Co-Production and Personalisation in Social Care
Changing Relationships in the Provision of Social Care
Edited by Susan Hunter and Pete Ritchie
ISBN 978 1 84310 558 9
eISBN 978 1 84642 721 3
RESEARCH HIGHLIGHTS IN SOCIAL WORK 49

Violence Against Women

Current Theory and Practice in Domestic Abuse, Sexual Violence and Exploitation

Edited by Nancy Lombard and Lesley McMillan

RESEARCH HIGHLIGHTS 56

Jessica Kingsley *Publishers*
London and Philadelphia

Figure 9.1 on p.161 has been reproduced with kind permission from Domestic Abuse Intervention Project (202 East Superior Street, Duluth, MN 55802, 218.722.4134, www.theduluth model.org).

First published in 2013
by Jessica Kingsley Publishers
73 Collier Street
London N1 9BE, UK
and
400 Market Street, Suite 400
Philadelphia, PA 19106, USA

www.jkp.com

Library of Congress Cataloging in Publication Data
Violence against women : current theory and practice in domestic abuse, sexual violence, and
exploitation / edited by Nancy Lombard and Lesley McMillan.
     p. cm.
  Includes bibliographical references and index.
  ISBN 978-1-84905-132-3 (alk. paper)
  1. Women--Violence against--Great Britain. 2. Girls--Violence against--Great Britain. 3. Sex crimes--
Great Britain. 4. Women--Crimes against--Lesotho. 5. Women--Violence against--Great Britain--
Prevention. 6. Abused women--Services for--Great Britain. I. Lombard, Nancy, 1977- II. McMillan,
Lesley, 1976-
  HV6250.4.W65V52167 2013
  362.88082'0941--dc23
                              2012027220
British Library Cataloguing in Publication Data
A CIP catalogue record for this book is available from the British Library

ISBN 978 1 84905 132 3
eISBN 978 0 85700 330 0

Printed by Bell & Bain Ltd, Glasgow

Contents

Introduction   7
Nancy Lombard and Lesley McMillan, Glasgow Caledonian University, UK

1.   Coercive Control   17
Evan Stark, Rutgers University, New Jersey, USA

2.   The 'Three Planet Model': Towards an Understanding of Contradictions in Approaches to Women and Children's Safety in Contexts of Domestic Violence   35
Marianne Hester, University of Bristol, UK

3.   Domestic Violence, Safety and Child Contact in England: Hiding Violent Men in the Shadows of Parenting   53
Lorraine Radford, independent violence prevention researcher, UK

4.   Sexual Victimisation: Disclosure, Responses and Impact   71
Lesley McMillan

5.   Violence Against Sex Workers in the UK   87
Alison Phipps, University of Sussex, UK

6.   Love, Power and Control: Girls' Experiences of Relationship Exploitation and Violence   103
Christine Barter and Melanie McCarry, University of Bristol, UK

7.   Older Women and Domestic Abuse: Where Ageism and Sexism Intersect   125
Nancy Lombard and Marsha Scott, Endgender, UK

8.   Intersecting Inequalities: Implications for Addressing Violence Against Black and Minority Ethnic Women in the United Kingdom   141
Aisha K. Gill, Roehampton University, UK

9. Domestic Abuse in the UK: Why We Need to Understand
    Perpetrators   159
    Elizabeth Gilchrist, Glasgow Caledonian University, UK

10. 'What About the Men?' Understanding Men's Experiences
    of Domestic Abuse Within a Gender-based Model
    of Violence   177
    Nancy Lombard

11. Effecting Operational Change Through Training:
    Challenges and Approaches   195
    Nel Whiting, Scottish Women's Aid, Edinburgh, UK

12. Partnership Working and Tackling Violence Against
    Women: Pitfalls and Possibilities   213
    Kirstein Rummery, University of Stirling, UK

13. Taking Stock: Theory and Practice in Violence
    Against Women   233
    Nancy Lombard and Lesley McMillan

    THE CONTRIBUTORS   245

    SUBJECT INDEX   249

    AUTHOR INDEX   251

Tables and Figures

Table 6.1 Ever experienced physical violence from partner   107

Table 6.2 Ever experienced sexual violence from partner   110

Table 6.3 Ever experienced emotional violence from partner   114

Figure 9.1 Range of abusing behaviours in intimate partner
           abuse: the Power and Control Wheel   161

Table 9.1 SARA items   176

Table 12.1 Mapping of some of the different potential partners
           involved in tackling violence against women   219

Introduction

Nancy Lombard and Lesley McMillan

Introduction

Violence against women is a pervasive problem in society and responding appropriately to those who experience such violence and those who perpetrate it is a constant challenge for social work, health and related professions today. Men's violence against women takes many forms including, but not restricted to, domestic abuse, rape and sexual violence, child abuse, sex work/prostitution and trafficking and so called 'honour' crimes. This violence affects adult women, young and teenage women and children and does not discriminate by ethnicity, sexuality or class. It is, however, the case that particular groups of women have particular needs in relation to the violence they experience and this volume will delineate the issues likely to be pertinent to women as a whole, and the issues that are specific to particular groups of women.

The volume provides those working in social work and related professions with up-to-date coverage of the major issues pertaining to violence against women and in doing so ensures practitioners have access to relevant evidence to inform practice. The book provides commentary on violence and motherhood, safety and parental contact in domestic abuse, partnership working and violence against women, training in domestic abuse awareness, working with men in violent relationships, and the response to and impact of sexual violence, and it addresses the particular experiences younger women, older women, BMER women and women in sex-work have of violence. The book discusses relevant research findings, policy developments and debates surrounding violence against women providing academics, practitioners and students with up-to-date knowledge that can be translated into practice. This is of paramount importance as statistics suggest the vast majority of women will have direct, or indirect, experience of violence in their lifetime and it is vital that social work and related professions are able to adequately respond to the needs of both victims/survivors and perpetrators. The book draws on contributors from academic research as well as those involved on the 'front line' in the public and third sector thus providing a variety of perspectives and experience.

This introduction outlines the theoretical importance of gender to any analysis of violence against women and the pervasiveness and persistence of violence against women. It then moves on to clarify the terminology used throughout the book and seeks to place in context the choice to use certain terms, for example domestic violence or domestic abuse and victim or survivor.

The importance of gender to the analysis of violence against women

A fundamental factor in any analysis of violence against women is that of gender, not least because violence against women both reflects and determines gendered social structures. Gender refers to the socially constructed roles, behaviours and expectations that are ascribed to men (and boys) and women (and girls). Gender is also understood as a social structure of norms and institutions. Women and men experience life differently because of the socially ascribed roles of gender. However, not all women share the same experiences simply because they are women. Therefore, locating gender within wider cultural and historical contexts enables the mediation of other social factors such as class, age, sexualities and ethnicity, thus conceptualising gender as a socially produced, continuously contested category that is perpetuated and negotiated at both ideological and institutional levels.

Violence is endemic within social interactions and structures. Certain demonstrations of men's violence are still considered 'understandable', 'defensible' and 'honourable', illustrating the endorsement of some expressions of men's violence. Not all men are violent but men are statistically the main perpetrators of violence against women, as well as against other men. As this volume will show, men and women use and experience violence differently, and it has a differential impact upon them.

A gendered analysis of violence views men's violence against women as a manifestation of male power that is replicated and endorsed through individual experiences and wider structural inequalities (Dobash and Dobash 1979; Radford and Kelly 1996; Rowland and Klein 1990). Using a gendered analysis to understand violence considers the different experiences, opportunities and resources that men and women have access to and how these may be limited because of their gender. The services and agencies available to men and women are not 'gender-neutral' because of the attitudes, assumptions and structures of power that are all highly gendered:

> Violence against women is not the result of random, individual acts of misconduct, but rather is deeply rooted in structural relationships of inequality between women and men... Violence constitutes a continuum across the lifespan of women, from before birth to old age. It cuts across both the public and the private spheres. (United Nations 2006)

The pervasiveness of violence against women

Violence against women is a salient and pervasive issue; it can affect women at any stage of their lives, and takes many forms, including physical, psychological, sexual and/or economic abuse (McMillan 2007). The range of behaviours that constitute violence against women are many (as evidenced in this volume), and Kelly (1988) has conceptualised this as the continuum of violence against women. According to Kenway and Fitzclarence:

> Violence is one of the major social problems of our time. (...) It is increasingly understood that violence occurs along a continuum and involves physical, sexual, verbal and emotional abuses of power at individual, group and social structural levels. (Kenway and Fitzclarence 1997, p.117)

Globally, nationally and locally violence against women is an endemic social problem and one that is increasingly being recognised as a human rights issue (Amnesty International 2004; Bond and Phillips 2000; McMillan 2011). Governments across the world have recognised women's human right to live a life free of violence (McMillan 2011) but unfortunately both incidence and prevalence statistics continue to tell us that this right is not a reality. Establishing the exact incidence and prevalence of violence against women is difficult, not least because of the hidden nature of much violence against women (which will be evidenced in this volume). Lifetime prevalence rates tend to offer us the most reliable indicator of the extent of the problem and these suggest one in four women will experience domestic abuse in her lifetime (Dominy and Radford 1996; Henderson 1997; McGibbon, Cooper and Kelly 1999) and between one in five and one in seven women will be raped or sexually assaulted (UNICEF 1997).

Establishing prevalence for other forms of violence against women is more difficult (and some chapters will address this issue specifically and provide what data are available) largely because the hidden nature of many of these forms of violence against women and the culture of silence that surrounds them make any attempt at measurement problematic. What is clear, however, given the range of abuses women are subjected to that fall on the continuum identified by Kelly (1988), is that most, if not all, women will experience some form of male violence, either directly or indirectly, in their lifetime. We also know that women are most at risk from the men they know and often from men they either currently have, or have previously had, an intimate relationship with. As Amnesty International (2004) highlight, 'At least one out of three women has been beaten, coerced into sex, or otherwise abused in her lifetime... Usually the abuser is a member of her own family or someone known to her.' This issue is highlighted throughout the book and is a recurring theme in almost every chapter.

Language and terminology

Throughout the book authors variously use terms relating to the area of violence against women such as violence or abuse, victim or survivor, prostitute or sex worker, and battering. There are often significant reasons for the choice of language and when placed in particular contexts, certain words have particular meanings and connotations. In this short section we seek to place in context the language used within chapters in the volume.

Throughout the volume some contributors use the term domestic violence and some use the term domestic abuse. This is in part a result of the geographical location of the researcher because (as will be explained by Lombard, Lombard and Scott, and Whiting, this volume) Scotland currently uses the term abuse in order to encapsulate the range of abuses women may suffer beyond physical violence. In contrast, nomenclature in England and Wales is the term violence, and it should be noted that contributors' use of this common policy language does not reflect a narrow understanding of the spectrum of abuses women may experience. Indeed, part of the endeavour of the violence against women movement has been to reconceptualise terms relating to domestic violence and to move away from the emphasis on the physical and to encapsulate the range of abusive behaviours perpetrated by men (Johnson 1995, 2005; Stark 2007; Yllo 1983, 1993).

Linked to this is Stark's use of the term 'battering'; a word that is in common usage in the USA but one which is regarded negatively in the UK because of its focus upon only physical actions. The many words used to describe domestic violence reflect changes in public perception and also legislation. It has changed from being viewed as an individual, rare, psychopathic phenomenon (wife battering) to a form of abuse that takes place within specific cultural, social and economic structures that perpetuate inequality.

The terms victim and survivor are also both employed in this volume. Whilst there has been a debate about the appropriateness of the term 'victim' within feminist discourse on violence against women, it is however the common term used within some agencies of the state, for example criminal justice. As such, within this volume some contributors may use the term victim in line with this criminal justice usage, whereas others may indicate the problematic nature of the term by placing it in inverted commas. In contrast other contributors may use the term survivor. A 'survivor' is someone who has suffered victimisation but at the same time the term recognises their agency in dealing with their experience and their ability to exercise that agency to make choices.

Outline of the book

The book addresses the issue of violence against women in relation to both current theory and practice in the areas of domestic abuse, sexual violence and exploitation, in many of their forms. The opening chapter by Stark sets the scene for an analysis of men's violence against women by providing a discussion and analysis of the history, theory and technology of coercive control. In doing so he challenges traditional understandings of domestic abuse as being primarily about physical violence and highlights that men's strategy for dominating women forms and reforms.

Chapter 2 by Hester and Chapter 3 by Radford address the issue of children and families in the context of domestic abuse. Hester details her three planet model which proposes a framework for collaboration for statutory and third-sector agencies to work concurrently with children, mothers and fathers in cases of domestic and child abuse. In doing so she discourages the tendency to blame mothers for the violence perpetrated by men in their lives and those of their children. Radford then goes on to address the issue of a child's relationship with a violent parent in the context of domestic abuse following the parents' separation or divorce. She provides an in-depth discussion of the impact of domestic abuse on children and young people and discusses policy and interventions aimed at making contact with the violent parent safe and in doing so promoting the child's wellbeing.

The book then goes on to address sexual violence in the chapter from McMillan. She discusses the reasons women may have to disclose rape to the police and other state agencies and the factors that influence that decision. Using recently conducted research on the criminal justice system's response to rape she provides an overview of the challenges for women of engaging in that process, particularly when judicial outcomes are likely to be poor. In Chapter 5, Phipps considers the issue of violence against sex workers. She provides an informative background to sex work in the UK looking at legal contexts, prevalence and the different forms of sex work including indoor and street work. She goes on to outline the types of violence sex workers experience, how they deal with this violence, and the impact it has, before concluding on the implications for social work practice.

The proceeding three chapters by Barter and McCarry, Lombard and Scott, and Gill move on to consider the issue of violence against women in relation to particular groups and communities of women. Barter and McCarry present data from the first UK-wide study of interpersonal violence in young people's intimate relationships. They outline incidence rates of physical, sexual and emotional violence in young people's relationships and evidence the gendered nature of both prevalence and impact. They conclude by reiterating the importance of challenging gender asymmetry discourses when developing appropriate interventions. Following this, Lombard and Scott address another aspect of the life course by looking at the issue of older women's experiences of domestic abuse. They argue that existing attitudes about gender and age have combined to make older women experiencing domestic abuse virtually invisible in both policy and service provision. The chapter outlines older women's experiences of domestic abuse, the theoretical and practical barriers to service access and new and more effective ways of meeting the needs of this particular group of women.

In Chapter 8, Gill continues to focus on specific communities of women by considering violence against women in black, minority ethnic and refugee (BMER)[1] communities. Using the South Asian community in the UK as an example, she looks at the impact of intersecting inequalities for this community of women. She addresses the issues of forced marriage and 'honour'-based violence in particular and argues that current state and public service actions only serve to marginalise BMER women and she concludes with a number of practical measures and policy recommendations to address these issues.

Chapters 9 and 10, by Gilchrist and Lombard respectively, address the issue of men. Gilchrist's chapter addresses the issue of male perpetrators of domestic abuse, specifically looking at how men's actions have been understood both in relation to theory and practice in the context of forensic psychology. She looks at what characteristics may be common or divergent in perpetrators, the effectiveness of risk assessment tools in the context of domestic abuse, as well as briefly examining perpetrator programmes. Lombard's chapter addresses the contentious issue of men as victims of domestic abuse and seeks to challenge arguments about gender symmetry. The chapter outlines research on men's experiences of victimisation in, and perpetration of, domestic abuse and in doing so problematises the current discourse of men as victims. She makes a case for a gender-based definition of violence that incorporates the meaning of violence, its context and impact.

The next two chapters of the book look specifically at issues of practice. In Chapter 11, Whiting provides a very informative outline of domestic abuse training and the importance of this training being theory-based. She argues that theory provides a framework in which practitioners can place their experience of working with survivors of domestic abuse and allows them to answer frequently recurring questions

1 Gill chooses to use the acronym BME to encapsulate refugee women too. See Thiara and Gill (2010) for a discussion of terminology.

such as 'Why doesn't she leave?' She draws on a range of active, reflective and experiential training techniques that ensure practitioners have a solid grasp of the dynamics of domestic abuse, which in turn leads to safe and effective intervention. In Chapter 12, Rummery extends this discussion of practice to look at the issue of partnership working. She addresses the theoretical, policy and practice issues around partnership working in the welfare state in relation to violence against women and critically assesses what facilitates and hinders partnership working. She discusses inter-agency, inter-professional, epistemological and ideological issues and concludes by outlining what practitioners can do to support partnership working and to support women who experience violence.

Finally, the book concludes with a chapter that seeks to draw out the key issues and themes present throughout the book in relation to theory and practice around violence against women. This concluding chapter will also draw out the key messages for social work in practice highlighted by the book's contributors.

References

Amnesty International (2004) *It's in our hands: Stop violence against women.* Oxford: Amnesty International Publications. Available at www.amnesty.org/en/library/asset/ACT77/001/2004/en/d711a5d1-f7a7-11dd-8fd7-f57af21896e1/act770012004en.pdf, accessed on 16 July 2012.

Bond, J. and Phillips, R. (2000) 'Violence Against Women as a Human Rights Abuse.' In C. Renzetti, J. Edleson and R. Bergen (eds) *Sourcebook on Violence Against Women.* London: Sage Publications.

Dobash, R.E. and Dobash, R.P. (1979) *Women, Violence and Social Change.* London: Routledge.

Dominy, N. and Radford, L. (1996) *Domestic Violence in Surrey: Developing an Effective Inter-agency Response.* London: Roehampton Institute.

Henderson, S. (1997) *Hidden Findings: The Edinburgh Women's Safety Survey.* Edinburgh: The City of Edinburgh Council.

Johnson, M. (1995) 'Patriarchal terrorism and common couple violence: Two forms of violence against women.' *Journal of Marriage and Family 57*, 283–294.

Johnson, M. (2005) 'Domestic Violence: It's not about gender – Or is it?' *Journal of Marriage and Family 67*, 5, 1126–1130.

Kelly, L. (1988) *Surviving Sexual Violence.* Cambridge: Polity Press in association with Basil Blackwell.

Kenway, J. and Fitzclarence, L. (1997) 'Masculinity, violence and schooling: Challenging "poisonous pedagogies".' *Gender and Education 9*, 1, 117–134.

McGibbon, A., Cooper, L. and Kelly, L. (1999) *What Support? Hammersmith and Fulham County Council Community Police Committee Domestic Violence Project.* London: Hammersmith and Fulham Community Safety Unit.

McMillan, L. (2007) *Feminists Organising Against Gendered Violence.* London: Palgrave.

McMillan, L. (2011) 'Sexual Violence Policy in Europe: Human Rights, Policies and Outcomes.' In M. Koch, L. McMillan and B. Peper (eds) *Diversity, Standardization and Social Transformation: Gender, Ethnicity and Inequality in Europe.* Farnham: Ashgate.

Radford, J. and Kelly, L. (1996) '"Nothing Really Happened": The invalidation of women's experiences of sexual violence.' In M. Hester, L. Kelly and J. Radford (eds) *Women, Violence and Male Power.* Buckingham: Open University Press.

Rowland, R. and Klein, R.D. (1990) 'Radical Feminism: Critique and Construct?' In S. Gunew (ed.) *Feminist Knowledge: Critique and Construct.* London: Routledge.

Stark, E. (2007) *Coercive Control: How Men Entrap Women in Personal Life.* Oxford: Oxford University Press.

Thiara, R. and Gill, A. (2010) 'Understanding Violence Against South Asian Women: What it Means for Practice.' In R. Thiara and A. Gill (eds) *Violence Against South Asian Women: Issues for Policy and Practice.* London: Jessica Kingsley Publishers.

Unicef (1997) *The Progress of Nations.* New York: UNICEF. Available at www.unicef.org/pon97/le4to48.htm, accessed on 16 July 2012.

United Nations (2006) *Ending Violence Against Women: from Words to Action, UN Secretary General's Report.* Available at www.un.org/womenwatch/daw/vaw/publications/English%20Study.pdf, accessed on 16 July 2012.

Yllo, K. (1983) 'Using a feminist approach in quantitative research: A case study.' In D. Finkelhor, R. J. Gelles, G. T. Hotaling, and M. A. Straus (eds) *The Dark Side of Families: Current Family Violence Research.* London: Sage.

Yllo, K. (1993) 'Through a feminist lens: Gender, power, and violence.' In R. J. Gelles and D. R. Loseke (eds) *Current Controversies on Family Violence.* London: Sage.

CHAPTER 1

Coercive Control

Evan Stark

Introduction: from domestic violence to coercive control

This chapter describes "coercive control," a model of partner abuse introduced to broaden the purview of social workers and other service providers in those cases beyond physical violence. In the l970s, feminist psychologists adapted the term "coercive persuasion" from the literature on "brain washing" to highlight parallels between POWs and what their victimized clients were experiencing (Okun 1986; Schein, Schneier, and Barker 1961). As the model evolved, the emphasis shifted from psychological manipulation to "control," a concept that subsumed the structural constraints perpetrators used to subjugate partners and make them dependent, including isolation, sexual and economic exploitation and the regulation of how they performed everyday activities (Johnson 2008; Jones and Schechter 1992; Okun 1986; Stark 2007). Evidence from both sides of the Atlantic shows that 60–80 percent of the abuse victims who seek outside assistance are experiencing coercive control rather than physical violence alone (Rees, Agnew-Davies, and Barkham 2006; Stark 2007; Tolman 1989).

I first became involved with domestic violence in the early 1970s, when I helped start a shelter for battered women. In both this work and the subsequent research Dr Anne Flitcraft and I conducted in a medical setting on the significance of abuse for women's health the focus was on physical violence and injury (Stark and Flitcraft 1996). But one unexpected finding in our health research was that violence alone could not explain why abused women developed alarming rates of medical, behavioral and psychosocial problems found among no other population of assault victims.

I got a more nuanced picture of abusive relationships after I finished my social work training and was asked to provide expert testimony on behalf of women who had killed their partners or committed other crimes in the context of being abused. Many of these women had suffered serious violence. But their typical experience involved frequent, but largely low-level, assaults combined with non-violent tactics that ranged from being deprived of basic necessities and being cut off from the outside world to rules about how they should dress, cook, or clean. I heard similar stories when my forensic social work practice expanded to custody disputes and child welfare. Moreover, my clients insisted that being isolated and controlled could be even more devastating than being beaten, in part because these tactics undermined their capacity for independent decision-making and inhibited effective resistance or escape. Some of my most fearful and subjugated clients had never been assaulted. I adapted the coercive control model of abuse because it captured the multi-faceted forms of oppression these women had experienced as well as the harms they described to their personhood, autonomy, dignity, and equality as well as to their physical integrity (Stark 2007).

There is now compelling evidence that the combination of coercion and control is the most devastating form of abuse as well as the most common. In a large, well-designed study, Glass, Manganello, and Campbell (2004) found that, along with a recent separation and the presence of a weapon, the level of control in an abusive relationship predicted a partner homicide far better than the severity or frequency of violence. This association also holds among couples involved in divorce or custodial disputes. Beck and Raghavan (2010) studied 2030 persons who had been separated for an average of six months and court ordered to attend mediation in Arizona. A majority of the women in their sample reported experiencing violence and/or coercive control in the past 12 months, with 25 percent reporting coercive control "a lot or all of the time" and 10 percent reported moderate or high physical abuse. Most importantly, more than 80 percent of the women who reported physically forced sex, escalating violence or threats to their life after separation were in the group reporting moderate/high coercive control during their marriage but little or no physical violence. A national survey of Finnish women found the highest levels of fear, anxiety, and other symptoms associated with abuse among a population of older women who had not been physically assaulted for an average of ten years (Piispa 2002). In the USA, meanwhile, Lischick (2009) reported that no assaults had occurred in 25 percent of the relationships where women scored in the highest risk categories for entrapment and other classic signs of abuse.

Despite evidence that social workers should identify, assess, and intervene to prevent the control tactics used by abusers as well as their violence, laws, policies, research, and practice in the field continue to emphasize physical violence almost exclusively. Among the dozens of instruments used to assess "dangerousness" in abuse cases, only a handful consider factors other than assaults and threats (Stark 2009). As a practical matter, services are often rationed based solely on the level of physical harm observed or inferred.

The problem with the violence definition of abuse

Violence is commonly defined as any "act carried out with the intention or perceived intention of causing physical pain or injury to another person" (Gelles 1997, p.14). When this definition is incorporated into law, policy, or social work, partner abuse is equated with discrete episodes of assault whose seriousness is measured by applying a calculus of physical or psychological harm. Perpetrators who repeat assaults are referred to as "recidivists," a term borrowed from criminal justice. Most interventions are predicated on the belief that there is sufficient time "between" assaultive episodes for victims and perpetrators to contemplate their options and make self-interested decisions to end their abuse or exit the abusive relationship.

In sharp contrast to what I will call the "violence model," research has consistently shown that the hallmarks of domestic violence are frequent, low-level assaults extended over a significant time-period (5.5–7.2 years on average) (Stark 2007; Stark and Flitcraft 1996). Indeed, even 95–97 percent of assaults reported to the emergency medical service or to police are non-injurious (ibid.). Meanwhile, over a third of abused women surveyed report "serial" abuse (once a week or more) (Klaus and Rand 1984; Mooney 1993; Stark and Flitcraft 1996; Teske and Parker 1983). These data suggest that abuse is typically a chronic rather than an acute problem, that the *pattern* is the appropriate target for assessment and intervention, not a discrete episode; and that the related harms are cumulative rather than incident-specific. A screen that assesses the seriousness of abuse by the level of injury will miss 95–97 percent of all cases.

Applying the violence model to the typical pattern has fragmented women's experience of abuse, made the multi-faceted nature of their oppression invisible, and elicited victim-blaming responses. Because abuse is ongoing, most victims seek help repeatedly. But if their help-seeking is linked to discrete episodes, these women seem to be "repeaters." The fear that accumulates over time can appear "exaggerated" when set against a relatively minor incident. Ironically, as abuse continues and a victim's entrapment becomes more comprehensive, the service response often becomes more perfunctory, a process I term "normalization" because even sympathetic providers conclude it is inevitable that this "type" of woman will continue to be abused.

The police response in England and Wales illustrates the tragic consequences of applying the narrow violence model. Research teams from the University of Bristol and the Home Office followed 692 offenders arrested between 2004–2005 in Northumbria (Hester 2006; Hester and Westmarland 2006). The ratio of arrests to calls was quite high (91%). But because the incidents were taken out of their historical context, arrests were primarily for breach of the peace and perpetrators were charged and convicted in only 120 (5%) of 2402 incidents of domestic violence reported, indicating an attrition rate from report to conviction of 95 percent. Even in the few cases of conviction, the most common penalty was a fine. Abuse in these relationships was chronic, an indication of its severity. Exactly half of the offenders were re-arrested for domestic abuse crimes within the three-year period covered by the study (2002–2004) and many were arrested multiple times.

Unsurprisingly, given the episode-specific response, there was no correlation between the likelihood that a perpetrator would be arrested and either the number of his domestic violence offenses or even whether he was judged "high risk." To assess the risk, police classified the target incident rather than the assailant. As a result, the same offender might be classified as "high risk" when he punched his wife and "low risk" a week later, when he slapped her. Neither the likelihood that offenders would be punished nor the punishment itself was related to previous offenses. Interviews confirmed that the absence of sanctions sent a clear message to the arrested men that their domestic assaults would not be taken seriously.

The technology of coercive control

I define coercive control as a strategic course of self-interested behavior designed to secure and expand gender-based privilege by establishing a regime of domination in personal life. This definition incorporates three facets of women's experience that are obscured by the violence model: that the oppression involved is "ongoing" rather than episodic (a "course of conduct") and resulting harms cumulative, that it is multi-faceted, and that it involves rational, instrumental behavior. Since "domination" is a political relationship, the definition points us towards the means used to establish and maintain "power" over a partner (such as isolation or control) and their consequence, an objective condition of subordination/ subjugation that is termed *entrapment* in the coercive control model. Entrapment has more in common with the predicament faced by hostages than a psychological state of *dependence*, for instance. The definition also highlights the gendered benefits of domination, to preserve privileges that accrue to men because of sexual inequalities simply because they are male. The model expands on this point by emphasizing that the most common targets of control are women's default roles as mothers, home-makers and sexual partners. By routinely deploying the *technology* of coercive control, a significant subset of men "do" masculinity (Connell 2005) in that they represent both their individual manhood and the normative status of "men."

Coercive control has identifiable temporal and spatial dimensions, typical dynamics and predictable consequences. To assess coercive control, I find it useful to subdivide its tactical dynamics into those used to hurt and intimidate victims and those designed to isolate and control them. Perpetrators adapt these tactics through trial and error based on their relative benefits and costs. The *generality* of coercive control refers to the features it shares with other forms of subjugation and constraint. Isolation and intimidation are features of hostage taking as well as coercive control, for instance. The *particularity* of coercive control refers to the unique tactical combination an individual abuser deploys in a given relationship. Rooted in the privileged access intimacy affords to personal information about a partner, the configuration of the four tactics depends on the personalities involved, their culture, the relative share of resources available to the parties, and situational factors such as their visibility to a larger community. For example, a husband who depends on income from his wife's high profile job may be less likely to inflict visible injuries than to use means of control. Obviously, this information can only be gleaned from interviews that include a complete history of abuse.

The following sections catalogue the four major tactics that comprise coercive control—violence, intimidation, isolation and control. My major focus in these sections is on what abusive men do to the women they victimize. But social workers should recognize that the major effects of coercive control arise because of what abusive men prevent women from doing for themselves. David Adams, a founder of one of the first perpetrator programs in the USA, defined abuse as "controlling behavior" and included any act "that causes the victim to do something she does not want to do, prevents her from doing something she wants to do, or causes her to be afraid...regardless of whether assault is involved" (1988, p.191). This definition highlights that "controlling behavior" harms individual autonomy and liberty as well as a person's sense of security and suggests, by implication, that restoring a person's capacity for independent decision-making is as important a goal of social work intervention as is safety.

Coercion

Coercion entails the use of force or threats to compel or dispel a particular response. In addition to causing immediate pain, injury, fear, or death, coercion can have long-term physical, behavioral, or psychological consequences.

Violence

Partner assaults frequently involve extreme violence, "beatings," choking, burning, rape, torture, and the use of weapons or other objects that cause severe injury, permanent disfigurement, even death. In a British survey of 500 women who sought help from Refuge UK (referred to below as "the UK Refuge study"), 70 percent had been choked or strangled at least once, 60 percent had been beaten in their sleep, 24 percent had been cut or stabbed at least once, almost 60 percent had been forced to have sex against their will, 26.5 percent had been "beaten unconscious," and 10 percent had been "tied up." As a result of these assaults, 38 percent of the women reported suffering "permanent damage" (Rees *et al.* 2006).

The frequency of severe violence does not mitigate the fact that well over 95 percent of the physical violence in relationships is low-level. Assault appears to be more frequent when it is part of the pattern of coercive control than when it is not. Johnson (2008) reported that men using coercive control assaulted women six times more often on average than men who used physical violence alone. In the Refuge UK sample, 58 percent of the women reported they were "shook or roughly handled" often or all the time; 65.5 percent were pushed, grabbed, shoved, or held "too hard"; 55.2 percent were slapped, smacked, or had their arm twisted; and 46.6 percent were kicked, bit, or punched with this frequency (Rees et al. 2006). Contrary to a common stereotype, violence in coercive control is typically used to keep any challenges from surfacing rather than to resolve conflicts, with 10 percent of victims reporting they were beaten in their sleep. Many abusers use violence so frequently that it becomes a routine, more like using the toilet or eating than the angry outbursts we may imagine.

Intimidation

As part of coercive control, intimidation is used to complement or in lieu of assault to keep abuse secret and to instill fear, dependence, compliance, loyalty, and shame. Offenders induce these effects in three ways primarily—through threats, surveillance, and degradation. Intimidation succeeds because the offender's threats are made credible by what he has done in the past or his partner believes he can or will do if she upsets or disobeys him (what is termed the "or else" proviso). If violence raises the physical costs of resistance, intimidation deflates the victim's will to resist.

In the UK Refuge study, 79.5 percent of the women reported that their partner threatened to kill them at least once, and 43.8 percent did so "often" or "all the time." In addition, 60 percent of the men threatened to have the children taken away at least once, 36 percent threatened to hurt the children, 32 percent threatened to have the victim committed to a mental institution, 63 percent threatened their friends or family, and 82 percent threatened to destroy things they cared about (Rees et al. 2006). Although credible threats are criminal offenses, few are reported to police and almost none result in arrest.

Intimidation extends to subtle warnings that are transparent to the victim but whose meaning eludes outsiders. One husband had a rule that my client would not make him jealous. A star athlete, when the woman made an outstanding play, her husband would come onto the field with her sweatshirt. He would instruct her softly to "Put this on. You're cold." While the teammates saw the husband's offer as affection, the woman recognized the implied warning that she would have to "cover up" the bruises he would inflict when they got home, and broke into a cold sweat. Her doing well had made him jealous and broken their "rule."

Offenders often use violence against others or destroy property to demonstrate what they can do to a partner. One of my clients reported: "Once, when he was angry about my buying a dress, he just turned and put his fist through the car windshield. All I could think was 'I'm glad that isn't me.'" Partners may also destroy objects that have special meaning to the victim and connect her to her family, her past, or the outside world. At the other extreme, when they are displeased or threatened with disclosure, abusers may give a certain look or gesture that sends a warning that is invisible to outsiders, making a client seem "over-wrought."

A variant on the commonplace threats abusers make to hurt the children or have them removed involves the "battered mother's dilemma." In this dynamic, an abusive man forces the mother to chose between protecting her child from his abuse, thus risking harm to herself, or doing nothing, allowing her child to be hurt. I have had several cases where women were killed after returning to the house to protect children whom their husband held as hostages. In another common scenario, women are compelled to discipline children in inappropriate ways to protect the children from their partner doing something worse. Unfortunately, social workers can aggravate this dilemma when we convey that parental custody may be jeopardized if women disclose their own abuse.

Many of the same tactics used to extract information or compliance from hostages are deployed in coercive control. These include withholding or rationing food, money, clothes, medicine, or other things on which a woman depends. Thirty-eight percent of the men in the UK Refuge sample stopped their partner from getting medicine or treatment they needed, and 29 percent of the US men did so (Rees *et al.* 2006; Tolman 1989, 1992). Passive-aggressive threats such as emotional withdrawal or the "silent treatment" can be equally devastating. Eighty-seven percent of the battered women in a US sample reported that their partners used the silent treatment to frighten them, and half of the men in the UK Refuge sample did so (Rees *et al.* 2006; Tolman 1989). Abusive men in my social work practice "disappeared" without notice for days or even weeks, "lost" the dog, stopped taking their antidepressants, stopped talking to their wives (in one case for two years), quit alcohol or drug treatment, "forgot" to pick up or feed the children, and threatened or attempted suicide if their partner failed to comply with their wishes. In the UK Refuge sample, more than half of the men threatened to hurt or kill themselves if the woman left, and 35 percent used the same threat to get her to obey (Rees *et al.* 2006). Withdrawal, threatening to leave, or withholding affection or sex (60% in the UK Refuge sample) is particularly devastating when a partner is already isolated from other sources of adult social interaction, is financially dependent, relies on her partner for child care or other vital services, draws her sense of safety/ danger from his verbal cues, or relies on making him "happy" to be safe. Anxiety may actually increase when a victim is separated from her abusive partner, particularly if no effective means are in place to sanction any contact.

Another class of threats, illustrated by the meticulously organized cabinets in the American film *Sleeping with the Enemy* (1991), involves anonymous acts whose authorship is never in doubt. Men in my caseload have left anonymous threats on answering machines, removed pieces of clothing or other memorabilia from the house, cut telephone wires, stolen their partner's money or their mail, removed vital parts from their cars, or left subtle signs that they have entered a home from which they are excluded by court order. At the other extreme, abusers exploit secret fears to which they alone are privy. A variant on these acts are "gaslight" games, named after the 1944 film *Gaslight* in which Charles Boyer created various visual and auditory illusions to convince his wife she was insane. Examples include stealing things from a woman's handbag that mysteriously reappear after a desperate search or re-parking her car during the night. In the UK Refuge sample, 75 percent of the women reported that their partners had tried to make them feel crazy "often" or "all the time" (Rees *et al.* 2006).

Perpetrators will also threaten their partners by telling transparent or outrageous lies, having affairs they deny but make sure their partners know about (30% of the men in the UK Refuge sample), or saying or doing things in a public setting that insult or embarrass them. The intent is to remind victims that confrontation is dangerous and that their wellbeing depends on accepting the abuser's view of reality, however irrational.

Stalking is the most dramatic form of surveillance used in coercive control and far and away the most common. Partner stalking is distinguished by its duration—lasting 2.2 years on average, twice the typical length of stalking by strangers—its link to physical violence, and its combination with complementary forms of intimidation and control. Of the 4.8 million women who reported being stalked by present or former partners to a US study, 81 percent were physically or sexually assaulted (31%), 61 percent received unsolicited phone calls, 45 percent were also threatened verbally or in writing, and roughly 30 percent had their property vandalized or received unwanted letters or other items (Tjaden and Thoennes 2000). Stalking falls on a continuum with a range of surveillance tactics whose aim is to convey the abuser's omnipotence and omnipresence and to let his partner know she is being watched or overheard. Abusive men time their partners on the phone; closely monitor their coming and going as well as their time away from the house; insist on "check-ins"—making intimidation portable; listen to their messages; go through their mail, hand-bags, bank records, and email or Facebook pages; and set up global positioning devices (cyber-stalking) or video cameras that track a partner's movements. Eight-five percent of the women in the US study and over 90 percent of the UK Refuge women reported that their abusive partner monitored their time (Rees *et al.* 2006; Tolman 1989, 1992). Fear that even a minor infraction will be discovered and lead to punishment causes many victims to severely curtail their social activity and is a major source of depression among abused women.

Degradation establishes the abuser's moral superiority by denying self-respect to their partners, a violation of what Cornell (1995) calls "the degradation prohibition." Virtually all of the women in the UK Refuge survey reported that their partners called them names (96%), swore at them (94%), brought up things from their past to hurt them (95%), "said something to spite me" (97%), and "ordered me around" (93%) and in more than 70 percent of these cases, this happened "often" or "all the time" (Rees *et al.* 2006). The insults used in coercive control target areas of gender identity from which the woman draws esteem (looks, cooking, etc.) and/or which she may no longer control because of abuse. Insults can be devastating in the context of coercive control because the woman cannot respond or walk away without putting herself at risk. One of my clients was sent to Weight Watchers by her husband, which she liked because it got her out of the house. But she also ate in response to the chronic stress created by the abuse. He would put her on the scale after a meeting and beat her if he discovered any weight gain.

Common shaming tactics involve using a tattoo, burns, or bites to "mark ownership"; forcing a partner to submit to sexual inspections or participate in sexual acts she finds offensive; or demanding she engage in other rituals around personal hygiene, toileting, eating or sleeping she finds degrading. In the UK Refuge sample, 24 percent of the women reported being forced to engage in anal intercourse at least once (Rees *et al.* 2006). Clients in my practice have been denied toilet paper or the right to cut their hair (in one case, for two years); forced to use the bathroom with a timer or with the door open; made to sleep standing up; or to steal money from their boss or their children. Other abusers force partners to obey rules that would be used to discipline a child, such as staying at the table until they've eaten all their food. One husband tied my client, naked, to a tree in the back yard for 24 hours to show her "what it felt like to be cold" because she had not heated the shower to the temperature he demanded. Shaming inhibits reporting because victims fear their humiliation will be exposed.

Control

In contrast to coercion, which is administered directly, perpetrators use control tactics to compel obedience indirectly by depriving victims of vital resources and support systems, exploiting them, dictating preferred choices and micro-managing their behavior by establishing explicit rules for everyday living. These rules remain in play even when the perpetrator is not present and so can be extended to work, school, or the shopping centre, for instance. Because of their portability, control tactics make victims feel their abuse is all-encompassing and their partner is omnipresent. Like the wife's "agreement" not to make her husband jealous, when control is embedded in rules, its underlying power dynamic is masked. This allows abusers to assume the role of a benevolent dictator and to punish a partner "for her own good." It is easy to blame victims for the observed results of control tactics whose authorship is invisible. Without knowing that these were her husband's demands, one of my clients was diagnosed as "obsessive" when she reported that she measured the size of each dish against the space in the fridge before she made it.

Isolation

Controllers isolate their partners to prevent disclosure, instill dependence, express exclusive possession, monopolize their skills and resources, and keep them from getting help or support. In a study of women in shelter, 36 percent had not had a single supportive or recreational experience during the previous month (Forte *et al.* 1996). By inserting themselves between victims and the world outside, controllers become their primary source of information, interpretation, and validation. Eighty-one percent of the UK Refuge sample reported they had been kept from leaving the house with almost half (47%) reporting this happened "often" or "all the time" (Rees *et al.* 2006).

As potential sources of support, family members and friends are major targets of isolation. Abusive men in my caseload have assaulted and threatened family members and friends; forbidden, timed, or listened in to their calls or visits; forced victims to choose between "them" and "me"; denied partners funds to travel for visits; stolen; moved their family to another town or state; stolen money or demanded their partner steal from family members or friends; showed up drunk or otherwise embarrassed their partner at family gatherings; and engineered situations guaranteed to alienate women from their families or friends. Over 60 percent of the women in the UK Refuge sample said their partners threatened their family or friends and 60 percent of the women in the US sample and 48 percent in the UK Refuge sample reported that partners kept them from seeing their families (Rees *et al.* 2006; Tolman 1989). When women cling to mementoes of family or friends such as photos, hand-me-downs, letters, or gifts, perpetrators search these out and destroy them.

Victims may isolate themselves to prove loyalty, protect friends or family, or in response to a partner's jealous accusations or disparaging comments. Isolation tactics also include denying women access to phones or cars—as in more than half of abusive relationships in the United States and UK Refuge samples. Abusers insist on "coming along," employ spies, lock their partners up, dictate behavior or conversation with friends (punishing them for "sharing our business"), and interrogate them after encounters. In one case, the husband listened to the messages on the answering machine when he returned home and then called anyone whose voice he didn't recognize. Among teens, a common isolating tactic, in my experience, is to sabotage birth-control and then use an unwanted pregnancy to force a girlfriend to drop out of school. Another involves demanding she leave the phone off the hook when she goes to bed at night so he knows "you are always there" (see also Barter and McCarry, this volume).

Isolation tactics are often designed to keep women from working or to isolate them at work, significantly impacting their employability as well as their performance or chances for promotion. More than a third of women in the US and UK Refuge samples were prohibited from working and over half were required to "stay home with the kids" (Rees *et al.* 2006; Tolman 1989). To keep women from going to work, men in my practice have blocked in their partner's cars, taken their keys or items of clothing, demanded sex just as they were going to work, blackened their eyes, forced them to call in sick, and suddenly said they could not babysit or transport a child to school or nursery. In cases where men depend on their wife's income, they try to keep partners from socializing with co-workers by driving them to work, picking them up, waiting outside at lunch or showing up unexpectedly, calling them repeatedly at work, and calling management or co-workers to verify their partner's whereabouts.

Isolation tactics extend to school, church, and to helping sites such as the hospital. Men in my practice have gone to class with their partners, left notes on or taken their car during church services, and sent family members, children, or friends to spy on their wives at the mall. To keep women from accessing professional help, my clients have ripped phones out of the wall, showed up at their psychiatrist's office, canceled their partner's appointments, refused to transport them to the hospital in an emergency, called police first, answered all questions on their behalf, and kept children at home as a warning of what could happen if they talk about the abuse.

Deprivation, exploitation, and regulation

In addition to isolation, control tactics foster dependence by depriving partners of the resources needed for independent living, exploiting their resources and capacities for personal gain and gratification, and regulating their behavior to conform to stereotypical gender roles.

What might be termed the "materiality of abuse" is rooted in a partner's control over the basic necessities of daily living, including money, food, sex, sleep, housing, transportation, routine bodily functions, communication with the outside world, and access to needed care. Seventy-nine percent of the UK Refuge sample and 58 percent of a US sample were denied access to money or had it taken from them through threats, violence, or theft (Rees et al. 2006; Tolman 1989). Among a population of men charged with assaulting their partners, 54 percent acknowledged they had also taken their partner's money (Buzawa and Hotaling 2003). Victims of coercive control are kept from carrying bank cards or opening their own accounts, forced to deposit their pay in accounts to which their husband alone has access, and forbidden to use their credit cards or forced to turn them over for safe-keeping. To complement this tactic, abusers insist partners provide detailed records or oral accounts of all expenditures or that all expenses be pre-approved, including the purchase of clothes. As Pahl (1989) showed some years ago, social workers cannot assume abused women can access "family" income or share its benefits.

Similar controls extend to other basic necessities. My clients have been strictly limited in their food purchases, made to sit at the table until intolerably hot food was consumed, forced to submit menus for pre-approval, made to eat off the floor or wait until their partner had "seconds" before eating, or to regularly prepare food on order for a partner's family or girlfriend. In one case, the physician husband would demand his dinner be ready by 8pm, return at 10pm and then throw the food in the garbage. Sex may be controlled directly through rules of how it must be provided. In an Iowa case that was widely publicized, Travis Frey forced his wife to sign a "Contract of Wifely Expectations" that exchanged "good behaviour days" (GBDs) for his wife's compliance with his sexual demands. Anal sex was worth 7 GBDs, for instance, and fellatio 3 (Frey 2006 cited in Stark 2007). Conversely, men withhold sex as punishment. In the UK Refuge sample, 30.6 percent of the women reported that their abusive partners "deliberately withheld affection or sex" often or all the time (Rees *et al.* 2006).

Perhaps the most significant facet of control is the extension of regulation to how women enact the already devalued domestic roles they inherit by default as well as to the micro-dynamics of everyday living. With varying degrees of explicitness, controllers micro-manage how women emote, dress, drive, wear their hair, clean, cook, eat, feed their children, the when, where and how of sleep, how they walk, talk, sit, or what they watch on TV. In the Frey contract, his wife was "not to argue (about anything with me or to me)," complain, cry, sob, whine, pout, show displeasure, raise her voice, be "condescending," ask for anything, or "be distracted from me by other things." A list given to a woman charged with embezzlement in my practice included rules for how she was to hang her clothes (colour coordinated), organize her CDs (alphabetize), how high the bedspread was to be from the rug, and which pictures she was allowed to put on the wall. The effort expended on micro-management can make abusive men seem crazy. But this misses its function, which is to exact obedience to the male's authority without regard to its substance and so to root out even the illusion of free will (and so of resistance/disobedience). As Mrsevic and Hughes (1997, p.123) put it in another context, "As men's control over women increases, the infractions against men's wishes get smaller, until women feel as if they are being beaten for nothing." So comprehensive can oppression become in coercive control that some women internalize the rules so that compliance becomes a means of self-esteem as well as safety. However, since the abuser's goal is domination, not achieving a particular end (such as a clean house), rules are continually being revised or reinterpreted, making it impossible for victims to satisfy their partner, leaving them in a state of chronic anxiety.

Conclusions: invisible in plain sight

Since the late 1970s, the absence of physical violence has become a litmus test for the integrity of relationships, a major achievement of the domestic violence revolution. There is no such consensus about the range of tactics deployed in coercive control. Although some of the tactics that comprise coercive control are already illegal, such as stalking, others, such as taking a woman's money, confining her in the house, or continually demeaning and harassing her, rarely prompt outside intervention when they occur in relationships, although they would be illegal if committed against a stranger. Regulating how a woman should dress, cook, clean, or care for their child may seem merely idiosyncratic, a sign of a "bad" marriage, but not particularly harmful. Indeed, because most women already perform these activities by default, their regulation in personal life is largely invisible. As we've seen, however, the micro-management of how women perform *as women* lies at the heart of coercive control and is emblematic of how coercive control violates their equal rights to autonomy, personhood, dignity, and liberty. Compliance with "rules" that extend to the trivia of daily life makes abusive men appear omnipotent and women like nothing.

Reframing partner abuse as coercive control begins when social workers and other providers place abuse in the historical context of a particular relationship, identify the major tactics used to establish and maintain women's subordination and dependence, and assess the relative significance and effect of each tactic. Once the elements of coercive control are identified and assessed, social work intervention shifts to redressing the particular harms it has caused as well as restoring a victim's capacity for free and independent decision-making, social connection, and self-direction, a process of helping her move from her "victim" to her "survivor" self. This work builds from a strengths perspective that starts when the social worker recognizes the courage it takes simply to survive coercive control, let alone to challenge or resist abuse, what I term "control in the context of no control." The next step is to harness this strength of character to the hopes and dreams that have been foreclosed by coercive control. Intervention concludes by reconnecting the woman's survivor self to the resources, supports, and opportunities needed to overcome the particular forms of coercion and control she has suffered. Provisions for safety are key if violence remains a serious risk; reconstructing support networks is the priority if isolation has been a key dynamic in her abuse. Recognizing the historical dimensions of abuse as well as the scope and depth of the oppression involved helps us to anticipate and even seek out repeat encounters with an abused client rather than fear them, respond proactively, and introduce protective, supportive, and empowerment strategies incrementally rather than in the context of a crisis or emergency response. Ultimately, of course, ending or preventing coercive control requires more than social work with individual victims or perpetrators. To treat the harms caused by coercive control as seriously as they merit, we must also advocate that women be given full status as persons. Ending coercive control and establishing sexual equality are inseparable.

References

Adams, D. (1988) "Treatment Models of Men Who Batter: A Pro-Feminist Analysis." In K. Yllo and M. Bograd (eds) *Feminist Perspectives on Wife Abuse.* Newbury Park, CA: Sage.

Beck, C.J.A. and Raghavan, C. (2010) "Intimate partner abuse screening in custody mediation: The importance of assessing coercive control." *Family Court Review 48,* 3, 555–565.

Buzawa, E. and Hotaling, G. (2003) *Domestic Violence Assaults in Three Massachusetts Communities: Final Report.* Washington D.C. National Institute of Justice.

Connell, R.W. (2005) *Masculinities* (2nd Edition). Berkeley: University of California Press.

Cornell, D. (1995) *The Imaginary Domain: Abortion, Pornography and Sexual Harassment.* London: Routledge.

Cukor, G. (dir.) (1944) *Gaslight.* Metro-Goldwyn-Mayer.

Forte, J.A., Franks, D.D., Forte, J.A. and Rigsby, D. (1996) "Asymmetrical role taking: comparing battered and non-battered women." *Social Work 41,* 1, 59–74.

Frey, T. (2006) "Marriage Contract: No Big Deal." *Omaha News.* Available at www.ketv.com/Bluffs-Man-Accused-Of-Creating-Marriage-Contract/-/9675214/10075354/-/owy7uj/-/index.html, accessed on 17 July 2012.

Gelles, R.J. (1997) *Intimate Violence in Families.* Newbury Park, CA: Sage.

Glass, N., Manganello, J. and Campbell, J.C. (2004) "Risk for intimate partner femicide in violent relationships." *DV Report 9* (2), 1, 2, 30–33.

Hester, M. (2006) "Making it through the criminal justice system: attrition and domestic violence." *Social Policy and Society 5,* 1, 1–12.

Hester, M. and Westmarland, N. (2006) "Domestic violence perpetrators." *Criminal Justice Matters 66,* 1, 34–35.

Johnson, M.P. (2008) *A Typology of Domestic Violence: Intimate Terrorism, Violence Resistance and Situational Couple Violence.* Boston: Northeastern University Press.

Jones, A. and Schechter, S. (1992) *When Love Goes Wrong.* New York: Harper Collins.

Klaus, P. and Rand, M. (1984) *Family Violence. Special Report.* Washington, DC: Bureau of Justice Statistics.

Lischick, C.W. (2009) "Divorce in the Context of Coercive Control." In E. Stark and E. Buzawa (eds) *Violence Against Women in Families and Relationships* (Vol. 2). Santa Barbara, CA: Praeger.

Mooney, J. (1993) *Domestic Violence in North London.* Middlesex: Middlesex University, Centre for Criminology.

Mrsevic, S. and Hughes, D. (1997) "Violence against women in Belgrade, Serbia: An S.O.S. hotline 1990–1993." *Violence against Women 3,* 2, 123.

Okun, L. (1986) *Woman Abuse: Facts Replacing Myths.* Albany: State University of New York Press.

Pahl, J. (1989) *Money and Marriage.* New York: St. Martin's Press.

Piispa, M. (2002) "Complexity of patterns of violence against women in heterosexual partnerships." *Violence Against Women 8,* 7, 873–900.

Rees, A., Agnew-Davies, R. and Barkham, M. (2006, June) "Outcomes for women escaping domestic violence at refuge." Paper presented at the Society for Psychotherapy Research Annual Conference, Edinburgh, Scotland.

Ruben, J. (dir.) (1991) *Sleeping With The Enemy.* Twentieth Century Fox.

Schein, E., Schneier, I. and Barker, C. (1961) *Coercive Persuasion.* New York: Norton.

Stark, E. (2007) *Coercive Control: How Men Entrap Women in Personal Life.* New York: Oxford University Press.

Stark, E. (2009) "Rethinking custody evaluations in domestic violence cases." *Journal of Child Custody 6,* 3–4, 287–321.

Stark, E. and Flitcraft, A. (1996) *Women at Risk: Domestic Violence and Women's Health.* Thousand Oaks, CA: Sage.

Teske, R.H. and Parker, M.L. (1983) *Spouse Abuse in Texas: A Study of Women's Attitudes and Experiences.* Huntsville, TX: Sam Houston State University, Criminal Justice Center.

Tjaden, P. and Thoennes, N. (2000) *Extent, Nature, and Consequences of Intimate Partner Violence: Findings from the National Violence Against Women Survey.* Washington, DC: U.S. Department of Justice.

Tolman, R. (1989) "The development of a measure of psychological maltreatment of women by their male partners." *Violence and Victims 4,* 3, 159–177.

Tolman, R. (1992) "Psychological Abuse of Women." In R. Ammerman and M. Hersen (eds) *Assessment of Family Violence: A Clinical and Legal Sourcebook.* New York: John Wiley.

CHAPTER 2

The 'Three Planet Model'

Towards an Understanding of
Contradictions in Approaches to
Women and Children's Safety in
Contexts of Domestic Violence

Marianne Hester

Introduction

In the past decade there has been increasing recognition in both policy and practice of domestic violence as a safeguarding issue for children. It is a feature in many of the most difficult cases being dealt with by social care services (Cleaver *et al.* 2007), and is a complex issue that requires work with all of those involved, including adult victims, perpetrators and children (Hester *et al.* 2007). Policy and practice has developed to reflect this, with emphasis on multi-agency approaches and responses. For instance, the past decade has seen development of a Co-ordinated Community Response (CCR) by the Labour government to provide a multi-agency approach to victim safety, there has been an increase in perpetrator programmes, and establishment of multi-agency children's safeguarding boards with domestic violence as one of the remits. A wide range of third sector as well as statutory provision, involving specialist domestic violence services, criminal justice, health and social care, has developed to tackle domestic violence and its impacts on families (Stanley 2011).

Yet despite the prolific and positive work of practitioners to tackle domestic violence, frustrations are often voiced by social care and other professionals – and echoed in women's and children's experiences – that it can be difficult to ensure and sustain safe outcomes for women and children in circumstances of domestic violence. This chapter takes as its starting point these frustrations and difficulties, and provides an attempt at understanding some of the systemic problems practitioners may be facing that undermine the effectiveness of their practice. Specifically, the chapter outlines the model of the 'three planets' as a way of conceptualising what is happening for practitioners on the ground.

Others have identified a variety of problems that may undermine particular aspects of work with families where there is domestic violence. For instance, the structures for assessment and intervention contribute to what Stanley *et al.* (2010) call a 'stop-start pattern of social work' that does not allow trust or engagement needed for domestic violence cases. Humphreys *et al.* (2010) suggest the need for social work professionals to be 'ready to change' in ways that are similar to those expected of mothers experiencing violence from partners. Or social workers may not always understand women's sense of responsibility and their feelings of loss of control in contexts of domestic violence (Lapierre 2010). In different ways these issues can play a part in undermining positive practice. However, I want to argue that we need a wider understanding of the approaches to domestic violence for women, children and men in different practice arenas in order to more fully understand the shifts needed to develop practice to a new level. In particular, we need to consider the unintended fragmentation and contradictions in practice that result from the use of different approaches across the three main areas of work with families experiencing domestic violence: in domestic violence work, in child protection work and in child contact work. The chapter explores systemic contradictions between these three areas of work, arguing that they are especially difficult to bring together into a cohesive and co-ordinated approach because they are effectively on separate 'planets' – with their own separate histories, culture, laws and populations (sets of professionals). The result is tensions and contradictions in professional discourses and practices which makes the effective tackling of domestic violence more difficult, and may result in outcomes that are likely to be contradictory for those individuals on the receiving end.

The notion of separate 'planets' can perhaps be understood in light of what Bourdieu (1989) would call the 'habitus' of groups, where 'the mental structures through which they apprehend the social world, are essentially the product of the internalization of the structures of that world' (Bourdieu 1989, p.19). The particular structures, orientations and approaches in the work of a professional group may create divides between their own everyday and commonplace professional assumptions and practices and those of other professional groups, and render them less able to see practice from a different professional perspective. I have found through extensive involvement in multi-agency training and multi-agency meetings that, despite two decades of multi-agency working, practitioners from the three different areas of domestic violence, child protection and child contact work are continually surprised at the different approaches each uses, including their differential thresholds for defining 'harm' or providing intervention. The 'three planet model' provides a means for thinking through what practitioners are facing and the expectations of their roles.

Each of the three 'planets' of domestic violence work, child protection work and child contact work can be seen to have distinct 'cultural histories' underpinning practices and outcomes with different elements to the fore in each one. Organisations and agencies on the 'domestic violence planet' are those working specifically with domestic violence, such as refuges and providers of advocacy that have developed with the adult victim/survivor as their central focus, and criminal and civil justice agencies that intervene with domestic violence perpetrators. The work of child protection and safeguarding services on the 'child protection planet' have a very different history, with the child as the central focus of their work. The work on the third 'planet', the 'child contact planet', involves yet another approach, where Family Court Advisors and other professionals are focused on parents, and their residence and contact arrangements in relation to children.

Alongside the notion of the planets another important force is at work: the process of gendering resulting from the continual replication and reconstruction of gender-based social inequalities. The 'planets' provide a way of understanding some of the systemic problems across criminal and social welfare systems. However, the ways in which approaches to the different actors in domestic violence situations are played out, that is in relation to perpetrators, victims/survivors and children, is also underpinned by processes of gendering. Meanings attributed to, and expectations associated with, gender may impact on the actions of professionals to perpetrators and victims/survivors and contribute to decisions made.

In the remainder of this chapter the operation of the 'three planets' will be looked at in more detail and the implications for women's and children's safety considered. In so doing, the chapter draws on a range of research evidence to indicate some of the key practices and patterns that may be attributed to each of the 'three planets'.

Domestic violence planet

It is now more than 30 years ago that work to combat domestic violence was begun in the UK and elsewhere by respective women's movement and related organisations. The resulting developments on the 'domestic violence planet' have tended to be influenced by understanding of domestic violence as rooted in gender inequality, and gender-based. While both men and woman can be violent, research from a range of methodologies highlight gender differences in the extent, severity and impact of domestic violence, with men most likely to use the ongoing pattern of 'coercive controlling tactics along with systematic threats and use of violence' that enables the perpetrator to exert power, to induce fear, and to control the other partner (Miller and Meloy 2006, p.90). On the 'domestic violence planet' a key problem is that of (mainly) male perpetrator violence and abuse impacting on (mainly) female victims/ survivors.

As alluded to earlier, two main areas of work on the 'domestic violence planet' are the range of victim/survivor focused support that includes specialist third sector services, advocacy and re-housing; and the more perpetrator oriented interventions of the criminal and civil justice systems and perpetrator programmes (Home Affairs Select Committee 2008). Building on the Co-ordinated Community Response to tackling domestic violence there has been an increasing focus in policy and practice on high risk victims of domestic violence with funding from central government (Home Office 2006; Howarth et al. 2009). As part of this, developments in support and advocacy have involved the establishment of Independent Domestic Violence Advisors (IDVAs) and Multi-agency Risk Assessment Conferences (MARACs). The third sector specialist domestic violence services, such as refuges, as well as support and advocacy services such as IDVAs, have tended to use an approach that seeks to empower women and attempts to equalise women's position in relation to abusive male partners (Coy and Kelly 2011).

The criminalisation of domestic violence, so that it is seen as a crime like any other, has been especially important in symbolising the shift from domestic violence being perceived as merely a 'private' problem to it being seen as an issue of public concern. This has involved a shift away from emphasis on domestic violence as a woman's own problem, to solve or protect herself, towards a view of domestic violence as an unacceptable crime which all agencies should try to prevent (Skinner, Hester and Malos 2005). Initiatives aimed at developing and strengthening criminal justice approaches to domestic violence have involved pro-arrest policies and increases in prosecution and conviction. The English Domestic Violence, Crimes and Victims Act 2004, for instance, further emphasised criminalising of domestic violence by making it a criminal offence to breach a civil protective order. Other developments have been dedicated domestic violence courts, which are found to increase conviction rates (Cook *et al.* 2004). However, the use of a criminal justice approach deals with only a minority of domestic violence cases and is focused on individual (largely physically violent) incidents. Such an approach is therefore unable to adequately deal with or reflect the actuality of domestic violence: that is, ongoing coercively controlling behaviours by the perpetrator (Stark 2007). The emphasis on individual incidents has also meant that where women retaliate against violent male partners, it is the woman who may end up being arrested rather than the primary, male, perpetrator (Hester 2009). Women victimised by domestic violence have been found to view criminalisation as a positive approach if they feel it will enhance their safety, but are critical if their safety is not ensured (Hester 2006).

Generally, the work of the 'domestic violence planet' is focused mainly on adults. Interventions are geared to dealing with (mainly) male perpetrators impacting on (mainly) female victims/survivors, and supporting victims/survivors to overcome those impacts. On the 'domestic violence planet' a male perpetrator's behaviour may be recognised by the police and other agencies as abusive in relation to the female victim/survivor. His behaviour is seen as a potential crime and he may even be prosecuted for a criminal or public order offence. He might also have a restraining or protective order taken out against him. Crucially, on the 'domestic violence planet' the perpetrator is perceived as a violent male partner or ex-partner and the female victim/survivor deemed in need of protection and support.

Children are not so prominent on the 'domestic violence planet', although recognition of the impacts on children of living with domestic violence began in this context, and much of the early intervention work with children also began from here, in the women's refuges (Hester *et al.* 2007). A number of key examples point, however, to an apparent lack of cohesive approaches between the 'domestic violence planet' and 'child protection planet'.

There is evidence from the work of IDVAs, whose role is ensuring safety of high risk domestic violence victims, that, where victims are also mothers, such work may have a positive impact on the safety of their children (Howarth *et al.* 2009). Yet Howarth *et al.* (2009) also point out that the links between IDVAs and children's services are not clear, suggesting that 'there is a need to map out, in partnership with children's services, a clear definition of the remit of IDVAs' work as it affects children, along with referral policies and procedures which should be agreed and communicated nationally' (Howarth *et al.* 2009, p.95). Children's services may also be represented at MARACs and information regarding contacts with children's services may form part of the resulting discussions about safety of victims (Robinson 2006). However, little is known about further interventions by children's services resulting from MARAC involvement, with no research in this area.

The police is another agency which, while focused on the adults, is expected to identify and refer on to children's services any children living in households where domestic violence is taking place. However, the thresholds for referral by the police and the threshold for getting a service from children's services tend not to be the same, resulting in few children receiving any intervention and also increasing the pressure on children's services (Laming 2009; Stanley *et al.* 2010). This highlights further potential tensions between the 'domestic violence planet' and the 'child protection planet'.

Children's safety: the child protection planet

While the focus on the 'domestic violence planet' is on adults, the focus on the 'child protection planet' is on children and what is considered by the state to be in children's best interests. The legal framework on this 'planet' is provided by the laws on safeguarding and protecting children, which in England are the Children Act 1989 and 2004, the Adoption and Children Act 2002, and to a lesser extent the Domestic Violence, Crime and Victims Act 2004. Child protection (unlike domestic violence) is largely situated within public law, as the emphasis is on intervention in families by the state to ensure that a child does not suffer significant harm. The general approach is to attempt partnership with parents rather than prosecution, with removal of children from families of origin into public care and/or adoption to be considered as a last resort (Hester *et al.* 2007).

There has been increasing recognition on the 'child protection planet' of the impact of domestic violence on children, across policy, legislation and practice. For instance, in 2002 the Adoption and Children Act extended the definition of 'harm' to include 'impairment suffered from seeing or hearing the ill treatment of another' (section 120). This came into effect in January 2005, and there has since then been a steady increase in the use of 'emotional abuse' as a category for registering children with the child protection services as at risk of significant harm (DCSF 2007, 2009). Domestic violence was seen as an important issue in the policy document *Every Child Matters* (2004), which underpinned the Labour government's approach to safeguarding and protecting children. It is an item for consideration in the Common Assessment Framework (CAF) (2010) linked to *Every Child Matters*, listed as 'violence' in relation to 'family history, functioning and well-being'.

Stanley (2011) outlines a range of innovative and positive recent practice by children's services with children and families where there is domestic violence. She points out, however, that practice is often uneven. Echoing the problem identified in relation to the 'domestic violence planet', she points out that the current system of notifications of children to children's services is inefficient as they are unable to identify children needing a service in relation to domestic violence. For instance, 10 per cent of families of children referred from the police on the 'domestic violence planet' were already known to children's services, but only 5 per cent obtained a new service. Also, it was unclear how many more should have a social work intervention (Stanley *et al.* 2010).

Although the focus on the 'child protection planet' is children, there is an emphasis on mothers (as main carers) to protect children. Yet, as Farmer (2006), points out, it can be difficult for mothers experiencing violence from partners to function effectively, and it may thus be unrealistic to expect them to be able to protect without their own safety being ensured. The Family Law Act 1996 allows the courts to exclude from the home someone who is suspected of abusing a child within the home, including a domestic violence perpetrator. The underlying expectation is, however, that the carer, usually the mother, will eventually exclude the abuser either by using civil protection remedies or through the intervention of criminal justice agencies (Hester *et al.* 2007). Echoing the Family Law Act 1996, child social workers on the 'child protection planet' have increasingly seen separation of mother and child from the violent male perpetrator as the favoured approach. However, there is extensive evidence that separating from a violent man creates the most dangerous context for both women and children. The heightened risk of violence, abuse and homicide during separation and post-separation is not only well-documented, but also forms part of the CAADA-DASH risk assessment tool used by the police and IDVAs with adult victims (CAADA 2011; Povey 2004).

Research has found that in practice many women experience as punitive the emphasis on the 'child protection planet' on mothers protecting their children (Humphreys and Thiara 2002). The problem may be compounded by the difficulty faced by practitioners in seeing the gender inequalities and coercively controlling behaviours from the primary aggressors that underpin domestically violent relationships. The main social work approach on the 'child protection planet' has been to see the family, and in particular 'dysfunctional' families, as central to the problem of domestic violence, often involving complexities of alcohol misuse and mental health problems (Cleaver *et al.* 2007). However, such an approach can lead to a hidden gendering of the meanings and expectations associated with victims' behaviour, and un-gendered 'parents', without recognition of a primary (usually male) aggressor. Professionals have expressed frustration at why women 'don't just leave' without recognition that women may be staying for reasons related to fear and safety, and/or lack of resources. The interconnectedness of men's abuse of both children and women are also important considerations with regard to the conflicts and problems women may face as mothers (Lapierre 2010; Radford and Hester 2006). Professionals, whose prime focus is on protecting children, may respond by threatening removal of the children – partly as a means of 'pushing' women to leave violent relationship (Humphreys and Thiara 2002). Or they may decide that the woman is no longer able to parent effectively in the context of the violent relationship, and have therefore removed the children into care. These may appear sensible courses of action, but may in reality be counterproductive because they create fear for women that their children will be taken away if they disclose domestic violence, and because such an approach largely ignores the (primarily male) abuser (Farmer 2006). A range of studies indicate the problems associated with this 'failure to protect' approach. For instance, in Humphreys and Thiara's (2002) study of women using domestic violence outreach services in the UK, concerns of social workers about child protection issues led to a significant number of these women being coerced into leaving their abusive partners before they were ready, or without the support needed to carry through such a difficult and dangerous process.

Since the late 1990s, and especially in more recent safeguarding policy, there has been mention of providing support for mothers as a positive approach in creating safety from violent men for both mothers and children (Hester *et al.* 2007). For instance, the guidance for multi-agency Children's Safeguarding Boards and local commissioners of children's services states that:

> The most effective intervention for ensuring safe and positive outcomes for children living with domestic violence is usually to plan a package of support that incorporates risk assessment, trained domestic violence support, **advocacy and safety planning for the non abusing parent who is experiencing domestic violence** in conjunction with protection and support for the child. (Local Government Association 2005, p.2; bold in original)

However, there is little evidence that children's services practitioners have applied this approach to any extent (Stanley 2011).

Another aspect is violent fathers. Devaney (2008) concludes from research on children at risk of significant harm in contexts of domestic violence that there needs to be 'a clearer refocusing of professional effort on holding men accountable for their behaviour and in attempting to engage them as fathers in ways which meet the needs of children' (Devaney 2008, p.452). Indeed, recent research does indicate that social workers are beginning to take a more active approach in relation to domestic violence perpetrators, for instance urging them to attend perpetrator programmes for the sake of the children (Stanley 2011). However, the approach may none the less counter that applied on the 'domestic violence planet' and thus undermine women and children's safety overall, with contradictory messages and outcomes resulting for some mothers. Research from the North East of England, for instance, highlighted a case with a very physically and psychologically abusive male ex-partner who was attending a perpetrator programme. Child social workers had fears about a significant emotional impact of the man's behaviour on two of the children. The parents were separated and as part of a safety plan developed by children's services the mother was provided with an alarm with direct access to the police so that she could easily call for help if the ex-partner/father came to the house. But rather than seeing the woman's use of the alarm as her attempts to increase her own and her children's safety, children's services used evidence of her triggering as proof that she was 'failing to protect', and the children were removed into local authority care. As the mother explained:

> So every time he came round and kicked the door in…I'd hit the alarm. Or when he did something I hit the alarm. And [children's services] used it against us in court to prove how many times he'd been to the house and to take the children. (Interview with mother, in Williamson and Hester 2008, pp.37–38)

Previous research has shown that child social workers may avoid violent men or minimise their behaviour for a number of reasons that include their assumptions about parenting as well as concerns regarding their own safety. Farmer (2006) discusses the ways violent men may assist in deflecting the focus of social work attention away from themselves and on to mothers. For instance, by being absent when the social work visit takes place, refusing to discuss with the social worker issues concerning the child, or being intimidating to (often female) professionals. Stanley (2011) suggests that 'children's social care practitioners need to build their skills and confidence in work with violent fathers' (Stanley 2011, p.115). One way of doing that is to work more closely with and draw on the knowledge of practitioners on the 'domestic violence planet' – who have extensive experience of work with domestic violence perpetrators.

To summarise, on the 'child protection planet' the focus is on protecting children, not adults – even if the research evidence suggests that making mothers safe might actually provide a better way of also ensuring children's safety. Although domestic violence is recognised, practice with families experiencing domestic violence is largely carried out within 'planetary' boundaries, and links with the 'domestic violence planet' appear neither cohesive nor extensive. On the 'child protection planet' the father's abuse of the mother may lead to involvement in the family by social care services or other child protection agencies. In England this may result in a child protection plan being required for emotional abuse. In order to protect the children, social workers are likely to insist that the mother removes herself and her children from the male abuser's presence, and leaves the relationship if she has not already done so. If she does not, then it is she who is seen as 'failing to protect', and the children might be removed into the care of the local authority. It is highly unlikely that the father will be prosecuted for such abuse because a predominantly welfare, rather than criminalising, approach prevails. On the 'child protection planet', therefore, despite the violence to the mother being primarily from the male partner, it is the mother who is seen as responsible for dealing with the consequences. In effect the violent man disappears out of the picture and the mother is construed as the main problem.

Post-separation: the child contact planet

On both the domestic violence and child protection 'planets' the ethos is intervention to deal with risk of further violence and harm whether to an adult (the 'domestic violence planet') or a child (the 'child protection planet'). In contrast, the 'child contact planet' draws on a 'private law' framework, underpinned by the notion that the state does not normally need to intervene in families, and if parents find it difficult to agree on arrangements for their children post-separation then a negotiated or mediated approach is preferable. While the 'domestic violence planet' and 'child protection planet' are concerned with past behaviour and abuse, on the 'child contact planet' the focus is specifically on the future. Despite copious evidence that domestic violence is likely to continue post-separation, the future-focused approach of the family court professionals on the 'child contact planet' (CAFCASS – Children and Family Court Advisory Service) means that a history of domestic violence in the parents' relationship is deemed to be in the past and thus largely irrelevant to future arrangements for the children. Drawing on the UN Convention on the Rights of the Child (1989), the overarching ethos is one of children having two parents even if the parents are no longer living together. The presumption is that contact between a child and the non-resident parent is the desired, and indeed inevitable, outcome of any court proceedings, whatever the history of the relationship (Radford and Hester 2006; Trinder *et al.* 2006).

Research has found that child contact is often the major flashpoint for post-separation violence and provides a context where (mainly male) domestic violence perpetrators may be able to continue to abuse and harass both woman and/or children (Radford and Hester 2006; Howarth *et al.* 2009). Contact may also provide the ultimate context for control by violent (male) perpetrators, that is, murder of their children, the mothers and/or themselves. Howarth *et al.*'s (2009) study of high risk domestic violence cases found that for 41 per cent of the

3600 children of mothers in contact with IDVAs there was significant conflict over child contact. Family court advisors have also indicated that domestic violence is a regular feature in contested contact cases, a court inspectorate report suggesting that CAFCASS practitioners placed the incidence of domestic violence in the region of 90 per cent or more of cases they dealt with (HMICA 2005). The arrangements made for contact with a violent parent (usually fathers) thus need to be considered in relation to the protection of children from abuse and harm.

Following pressure from women's organisations and evidence from research, the English judiciary, from the late 1990s, began to focus on the problems of children's contact in circumstances of domestic violence. A report from the Children Act Sub-Committee (CASC) of the Advisory Board on Family Law in May 2000 took a large step forward in acknowledging that there are links between domestic violence and possible harm to children, and that these need to be addressed in cases relating to children's contact with a violent parent. A notable set of appeal cases followed (Re: L (A Child), Re: V (A Child), Re: M (A Child) and Re: H (Children)) where the President of the Family Division supported the plea for courts to be more aware of the possible effects on children of domestic violence, 'both short-term and long-term, as witnesses as well as victims', and also the impact of violence on the residential parent, as identified in a range of research. However, this approach has since been found to be applied infrequently and inconsistently by the family courts (Radford and Hester 2006; Trinder et al. 2006; Ofsted 2008). Further legislation in 2005 (the Children (Contact) and Adoption Act 2005) re-emphasised the contact presumption and introduced enforcement of court orders for contact. The approach suggested an active facilitation via mediation/conciliation in such cases as well as the strengthening of legal enforcement. Thus despite attempts to shift policy and practice on the 'child contact planet' away from the contact presumption, the contact presumption has continued to be central.

Inspections of family courts in different parts of the country have been critical of a lack of attention to the impact of domestic violence on children, including the failure to obtain relevant information about criminal convictions. As exemplified by one of the reports:

> Whilst allegations of domestic violence were a common feature in cases, its impact on children was assessed adequately in only a minority of cases. One case involving domestic violence had such serious deficits in practice that

inspectors referred it to the regional director for immediate
review. (Ofsted 2008, p.11)

The 'habitus' of family court professionals, involving future focus and a
presumption of contact, appears almost impossible for the professionals
concerned to see, let alone to move beyond. A study of the family court
process, for instance, found that the contact presumption was in some
instances becoming 'a self-fulfilling prophesy' that would override any
allegations of risk arising from domestic violence (Trinder *et al.* 2006).
As exemplified by one of the judges interviewed:

> …I have to say I do try and steer the parties away from
> the past, I tend to say 'look, statistics show that there is a
> very high likelihood that there is going to be contact. At
> the end of the day the Court is going to order contact, so
> the more fruitful exercise is to concentrate on how that
> contact is going to progress.' (District Judge, in Trinder *et
> al.* 2006, p.96)

Other research looking in detail at different aspects of the family
proceedings process found that domestic violence, although increasingly
recognised, still 'disappears' within the family court process. Trinder *et
al.* (2010) examined the conversations between family court advisors
and parents during conciliation or mediation sessions, finding that
where mothers brought up the topic of domestic violence, this would
disappear by being ignored, reframed or rejected by family court
advisers. A further study (Macdonald 2010), involving analysis of
reports and recommendations to the courts from family court advisors
('section 7' reports), also showed how even extensive knowledge
about domestic violence tends to be deemed of minimal relevance in
recommendations for outcomes for children, and is overshadowed by
more 'hegemonic' discourses regarding presumption of contact and
future focus. That study also found that a failure to recognise the risks
of domestic violence to the safety of both the (usually) mother and the
child was at times compounded by an apparent lack of hard evidence
of previous or present violence to the mother or the child (e.g. from the
police or social care services) (Macdonald 2010). This itself may result
from a number of other problems, including lack of coordination of
information and evidence across 'planets', such as between the criminal
justice system and family proceedings; that women may not contact the
police; court pressure to reach agreement over arrangements for children;

inadequate legal representation leading to the full nature of the abuse being hidden or minimised; and the intrinsically private nature of the abusive behaviour itself (Radford and Hester 2006).

A Pilot Integrated Domestic Violence Court was set up in Croydon specifically to have one judge overseeing both criminal and family jurisdiction in relation to any one family, and might thus be expected to overcome some of the lack of cohesive practice across the child protection and domestic violence 'planets' referred to earlier. Evaluation of the court found, however, that there were contradictions regarding safety (Hester, Pearce and Westmarland 2008). While some female victims/survivors of domestic violence were provided with special measures in relation to criminal charges (that is, giving evidence behind a screen due to the perceived dangerousness of the ex-partner/perpetrator) such safety measures did not apply in relation to family matters. A similar disjuncture appeared in relation to outcomes. For instance, a female victim/survivor situated behind a screen during the criminal case, where her ex-partner was found guilty of assault, had no such protection during the child contact hearings where she had to sit on the same bench as her ex-partner and was reduced to tears as he attempted to communicate with her. Despite the perpetrator's denial of his criminally violent behavior and the victim/survivor's fear for her own and the child's safety, the judge in this case expressed strongly that contact should be occurring, and increasing, and that the parents should put aside their differences for the sake of the child.

To summarise, while the family court process on the 'child contact planet' has begun to take domestic violence into account in policy and case law, in practice the primary concern in the family courts is in getting women to overcome their fears of further abuse from ex-partners, rather than challenging the violence of men. On the 'child contact planet', a violent male perpetrator is most likely to be perceived as a good enough father. As Eriksson and Hester (2001) have argued, there is a distinct conceptual gap on the 'child contact planet' between a man being seen as a violent man, and the same man being seen primarily as a father. The family courts may order supervised contact or attach conditions to an order to keep parents apart, but the purpose and value of contact for the child is less likely to be considered. Keeping in contact with the non-resident father is almost always viewed as being in a child's best interests (Radford and Hester 2006).

For mothers and children the situation created by the approach on the 'child contact planet' is especially contradictory. The mother may, on the 'domestic violence planet', have attempted to curb her partner's violent behaviour by calling the police and supporting his prosecution. She may have left her violent partner following instruction from children's services on the 'child protection planet' that she leave to protect her children. However, the 'child contact planet', in effect, has the opposite approach, that families should continue to be families even if there is divorce and separation. On the 'child contact planet', therefore, she is ordered to allow contact between her violent ex-partner and the children, leaving her not only bewildered and confused but left to manage her ex-partner's violence, and yet again scared for the safety of her children, let alone herself.

Conclusion

This chapter has explored some of the systemic contradictions that appear to exist between the three areas of work on domestic violence, child protection and child contact, arguing that these can be perceived of as operating on separate 'planets' each with their own cultures, laws, policies and practices. The chapter has shown how such systemic contradictions are further compounded by gendered inequalities and associated processes of gendering. Mothers in particular may end up being subject to both formal and informal pressures from the separate 'planets', resulting in impossible choices about how they might or should be acting in order to ensure safety for themselves and their children. Moreover, children's welfare and interests are by no means achieved.

So what is the solution? In many respects the policies that exist in relation to the three 'planets' already take into account the issues and impacts of domestic violence and also attempt to overcome some of the 'planetary' problems between different sectors. For instance, following on from a series of child homicide serious case reviews there have been reports and policies outlining the crucial importance of multi-agency work in safeguarding and protecting children, including work on domestic violence (e.g. Laming 2009). Research has continually shown that co-ordinated and cohesive responses to domestic violence are more effective at creating safety for both adult victims and children. Sophisticated multi-agency approaches involving for instance MARACs and local safeguarding children boards (LSCBs) have been established, although these have tended to be situated within rather than across 'planets'. Practitioners have also been willing and keen to deal with domestic violence. However, as the chapter has indicated, the strength of the underpinning cultures and approaches on the three 'planets', and the separate professional 'habitus' on each 'planet', means that despite these developments the work of the 'planets' pull in different directions. The result is a 'black hole' that mothers and children may fall through. Tackling the 'three planet problem', and dealing more effectively with domestic violence as it impacts on adults and children, requires both a unified approach across the separate 'planet' areas and acknowledgement of the processes of gendering that are situating women as culpable victims. It requires much closer and coherent practices across the three areas of work, with understanding of professional assumptions and practices and those of other professional groups. For children's services it means not just taking into account that work on domestic violence requires intervention with victims, children and perpetrators, but that the most effective way of doing this is to team up with practitioners on the 'domestic violence planet' – who have extensive experience of work with both domestic victims and perpetrators, and with practitioners on the 'child contact planet' to integrate further a common response to women's and children's safety.

References

Bourdieu, P. (1989) 'Social space and symbolic power.' *Sociological Theory 7*, 1, 14–25.

CAADA (2011) The CAADA-DASH Risk Identification Checklist, available online at www.caada.org.uk/searchresult.html?sw=DASH, accessed on 8 October 2012.

Cleaver, H., Nicholson, D., Tarr, S. and Cleaver, D. (2007) *Child Protection, Domestic Violence and Parental Substance Misuse: Family Experiences and Effective Practice.* London: Jessica Kingsley Publishers.

Cook, D., Burton, M., Robinson, A. and Vallely, C. (2004) *Evaluation of Specialist Domestic Violence Courts/Fast Track Systems.* London: CPS/DCA/Criminal Justice System Race Unit.

Coy, M. and Kelly, L. (2011) *Islands in the Stream: An Evaluation of Four London Independent Domestic Violence Advocacy Schemes.* London: London Metropolitan University.

DCSF (2007) *Referrals, Assessments and Child and Young People Who are the Subject of a Child Protection Plan or are on Child Protection Registers, England – Year Ending 31 March 2007.* London: DCSF. Available at www.education.gov.uk/rsgateway/DB/SFR/s000742/sfr28-2007.pdf, accessed on 18 July 2012.

DCSF (2009) *Referrals, Assessments and Child and Young People who are the Subject of a Child Protection Plan or are on Child Protection Registers, England – Year Ending 31 March 2009.* London: DCSF. Available at www.education.gov.uk/rsgateway/DB/SFR/s000873/sfr22-2009.pdf, accessed on 18 July 2012.

Devaney, J. (2008) 'Chronic child abuse and domestic violence – children and families with long-term and complex needs.' *Child and Family Social Work 13*, 4, 443–453.

Eriksson, M. and Hester, M. (2001) 'Violent men as good enough fathers? – a look at England and Sweden.' *Violence Against Women 7*, 7, 779–798.

Farmer, E. (2006) 'Using Research to Develop Child Protection and Child Care Practice.' In C. Humphreys and N. Stanley (eds) *Domestic Violence and Child Protection*. London: Jessica Kingsley Publishers.

Hester, M. (2006) 'Making it through the criminal justice system: Attrition and domestic violence.' *Social Policy and Society 5*, 1, 79–90.

Hester, M. (2009) *Who Does What to Whom? Gender and Domestic Violence Perpetrators*. Bristol: University of Bristol and Northern Rock Foundation. Available at www.bris.ac.uk/sps/research/projects/reports/2009/rj4843/whodoeswhat.pdf, accessed on 18 July 2012.

Hester, M., Pearce, J. and Westmarland, N. (2008) *Early Evaluation of the Integrated Domestic Violence Court, Croydon*, Ministry of Justice Research Series 18/08. London: Ministry of Justice.

Hester, M., Pearson, C. and Harwin, N. with Abrahams, H. (2007) *Making an Impact – Children and Domestic Violence. A Reader* (2nd Edition). London: Jessica Kingsley Publishers.

HMICA (2005) *Domestic Violence, Safety and Family Proceedings: Thematic Review of the Handling of Domestic Violence Issues by the Children's Family Courts Advisory and Support Service (CAFCASS) and the Administration of Family Courts in Her Majesty's Courts Service (HMCS)*. London: Her Majesty's Inspectorate of Court Administration.

Home Affairs Select Committee (2008) *Domestic Violence, Forced Marriage and 'Honour'-based Violence*. Sixth report 2008. London: House of Commons.

Home Office (2006) *National Domestic Violence Delivery Plan*, Progress Report 2005/06. London: Home Office.

Howarth, E., Stimpson, L., Barran, D. and Robinson, A. (2009) *Safety in Numbers: A Multi-site Evaluation of Independent Domestic Violence Advisor Services*. London: The Hestia Fund and The Henry Smith Charity.

Humphreys, C. and Thiara, R. (2002) *Routes to Safety: Protection Issues Facing Abused Women and Children and the Role of Outreach Services*, Bristol: Women's Aid Federation of England.

Humphreys, C., Thiara, R.K. and Skamballis, A. (2011) 'Readiness to change: Mother–child relationship and domestic violence intervention.' *British Journal of Social Work 41*, 1, 166–184.

Laming, H. (2009) *The Protection of Children in England: A Progress Report*. London: The Stationery Office.

Lapierre, S. (2010) 'More responsibilities, less control: understanding the challenges and difficulties involved in mothering in the context of domestic violence.' *British Journal of Social Work 40*, 5, 1434–1451.

Local Government Association (2005) *Vision for Services for Children and Young People Affected by Domestic Violence – Guidance to Local Commissioners for Children's Services*. London: Local Government Association.

Macdonald, G.S. (2010) *Domestic Violence, Children's Voices and Child Contact: Exploring Cafcass Section 7 Reports*. Unpublished PhD thesis, University of Bristol.

Miller, S.L. and Meloy, M.L. (2006) 'Women's use of force: voices of women arrested for domestic violence.' *Violence Against Women 12*, 1, 89–115.

Ofsted (2008) *Ofsted's Inspection of Cafcass South East Region: An inspection of service provision by the Children and Family Court Advisory and Support Service (Cafcass) to children and families in the south east*. London: Ofsted. Available at www.ofsted.gov.uk/reports, accessed on 18 July 2012.

Povey, D. (ed.) (2004) *Crime 2003: Supplementary Volume 1 – Homicide and gun crime*. London: Home Office.

Radford, L. and Hester, M. (2006) *Mothering through Domestic Violence*. London: Jessica Kingsley Publishers.

Robinson, A.L. (2006) 'Reducing repeat victimization among high risk victims of domestic violence. The benefits of a coordinated community response in Cardiff, Wales.' *Violence Against Women 12*, 8, 761–788.

Skinner, T., Hester, M. and Malos, E. (2005) 'Methodology, Feminism and Gender Violence.' In T. Skinner, M. Hester and E. Malos (eds) *Researching Gender Violence*. Cullompton: Willan Press.

Stanley, N. (2011) *Children Experiencing Domestic Violence: A Research Review*. Dartington: Research in Practice.

Stanley, N., Miller, P., Richardson Foster, H. and Thomson, G. (2010) 'A stop–start response: Social services, interventions with children and families notified following domestic violence incidents.' *British Journal of Social Work 40*, 1, 1–18.

Stark, E. (2007) *Coercive Control*. Oxford: Oxford University Press.

Trinder, L., Connolly, J., Kellet, K., Notley, C. and Swift, L. (2006) *Making Contact Happen or Making Contact Work? The Process and Outcomes of In-court Conciliation*, DCA Research Series 3/06. London: Department of Constitutional Affairs.

Trinder, L., Firth, A. and Jenks, C. (2010) '"So presumably things have moved on since then?" The management of risk allegations in child contact dispute resolution.' *International Journal of Law, Policy and the Family 24*, 1, 29–53.

Williamson, E. and Hester, M. (2008) *Evaluation of STDAPP*. Bristol: University of Bristol.

CHAPTER 3

Domestic Violence, Safety and Child Contact in England

Hiding Violent Men in the Shadows of Parenting

Lorraine Radford

Introduction

In the UK and in many other countries across the world from the 1990s onwards there were significant changes in family law and social policy that redefined parental responsibilities and the role of fathers in families after separation or divorce. The expectation that children should have contact with both parents/fathers after parental separation became entrenched in family courts creating additional difficulties for women and children leaving violent men. It is now 12 years since an important review of expert opinion and legal principles by the English Court of Appeal, which at the time was heralded as a watershed change towards safer contact (Kaganas 2000). This chapter will initially review the developments from research about the risks and benefits of children having contact with fathers who are perpetrators of domestic violence.

It will then go on to consider developments in policy and practice aimed at making contact safe and promoting children's wellbeing.

Fathers and child contact: two approaches

Two oppositional discourses have been present in debates about post-separation child contact: the pro-contact stance, found among family law reformers and fathers' rights campaigners, and the more contingent safety approach, advocated by domestic violence and children's services. Both attract a range of views. The key elements of each will be briefly described before discussing recent findings from research and trends in policy and practice.

The pro-contact stance

The pro-contact stance is rooted in a vision of the 'broken family', which has recently resurfaced in UK politics (Conservative Party 2010). It is assumed that fixing the 'broken family' involves getting parents (in practice mothers) to 'agree' that the non-resident parent (most often fathers) have as much contact as possible with children after separation or divorce. It has a 'common sense' appeal often presented in terms of children's rights and the wellbeing of future generations (Featherstone and Peckover 2008). This means fathers staying involved in children's lives, but only if they wish to do so as there are no powers to force the non-resident parent to maintain contact, even though there are powers to force compliance from the parent living with the child. To varying degrees, there exists a belief there is 'injustice' to, or discrimination against, fathers. This includes claims that biased family courts collude with hostile mothers who make false allegations of abuse or who obstruct the child's contact (Turkat 1995; Weir 2006), as well as the more moderate belief that men are not always supported in their efforts to play a bigger part in their children's lives (Fatherhood Institute 2007). Some fathers groups have promoted an ideal of 'equal parenting', 50/50 shared care where the child spends half his/her time with the father and half with the mother (Equal Parenting Alliance 2010; Flood 2010).

From the pro-contact stance domestic violence affects few families and stops on separation. Some take the view that domestic violence will not necessarily be relevant to child contact (as in Re: L, V, M and H [2000]), while others argue that men are equally victimised by female partners (Archer 2007) and claims made by women about abuse need to be treated more sceptically (Basile 2005).

Contact and the risk of further abuse: the safe contact approach

By contrast, the safe contact approach challenges the notion that any father is better than none, pointing towards the high prevalence of domestic violence and the impact this has on children and their mothers (Rivett 2010). As much goes unreported, it is not possible to exactly estimate the prevalence of domestic violence in the UK population. Although both men and women report experiencing abuse in intimate relationships, domestic violence is highly gendered (Walker *et al.* 2009). The pattern of physical, sexual, psychological, financial abuse and controlling behaviour that is repeated and harmful (resulting in injuries) is overwhelmingly perpetrated by males against females. Indeed, the greatest risk factor for experiencing domestic violence is being female (Walby and Allen 2004).

Half of the women who have experienced domestic violence in the last 12 months have children (Povey *et al.* 2009). Recent research by the NSPCC on the maltreatment experiences of a nationally representative sample of 6196 children, young people and young adults found that 1 in 7 (14.2%) children and young people under 18 years had been exposed to domestic violence during childhood, and 2.9 per cent (equivalent to 380,623 children and young people in the current UK population) had witnessed this in the past year (Radford *et al.* 2011a). Research similarly with a nationally representative sample of 7865 children in the UK population by Meltzer found 4 per cent of children and young people had witnessed 'severe' domestic violence during childhood (Meltzer *et al.* 2009). These figures are likely to underestimate the extent of the problem (because those living with domestic violence may be less able to take part in a household survey) but they show that a substantial minority of children and young people in the UK will be facing parental separation in the context of domestic violence.

Domestic violence is a common concern in contested contact and residence cases in the family courts. A recent review for the Ministry of Justice found 53 per cent of family law cases have allegations of domestic violence or harm to a child (Cassidy and Davey 2011). Where there has been domestic violence the possibility of harm to a parent or child from continued contact should always be considered. According to the Home Office, 77 per cent of women who reported experiences of domestic violence said this ceased on separation but for 22 per cent the violence continued or escalated (Povey *et al.* 2009). At the most extreme end of the range of risks is the possibility that a parent or a child might be killed. Domestic violence is a factor in the majority of serious case reviews of child deaths (Brandon *et al.* 2008; Sidebotham *et al.* 2011). Violent men's murders of women and children on contact visits raise questions about whether or not these deaths could have been prevented if recommended steps to ensure safe contact had been taken. In a review of homicide cases where 29 children had been killed in 13 families, Saunders found that in 11 out of the 13 families, domestic violence had been a factor of the relationship. In five cases the killings were 'revenge' killings, and in three cases children were killed after unsupervised contact with violent fathers had been ordered by a court against professional advice (Saunders 2006).

Serious case review research suggests that domestic violence is *one*, but not the only, factor in an accumulation of risk factors associated with child abuse related deaths (Brandon *et al.* 2008). Some contact-related child deaths might be more preventable than others. The context and circumstances in which women and children are killed vary. Domestic violence may have a greater influence in the proportion of mother and child homicides which occur at the point of, or after, separation and could be categorised as 'revenge' killings. These killings often involve a man's murder of the children followed by his suicide, or his murder of the mother and the children. They occur after a history of domestic violence or controlling behaviour where the family have recently separated or tried to leave the violent partner (Cavanagh, Dobash and Dobash 2007). It is very rare for women to kill their partners or their children in the same circumstances (Cavanagh *et al.* 2007; Wilson and Daly 1999) although this may have happened in some cases.[1]

The estimated co-occurence of child maltreatment and domestic violence ranges from 30 per cent to 60 per cent depending on how the maltreatment is defined and measured and where survey samples are selected (Edleson 1999). Up to two-thirds of children on child protection registers (now these would be children with a child protection plan in England) live with domestic violence (Hester and Pearson 1998). Hamby *et al.* (2010) telephone-interviewed 4549 caregivers and young people in the USA and found 33.9 per cent of under 18-year-olds who had seen

---

1   In October 2009 three-year-old Bethany Kennerley was smothered by her mother. In August 2010 Gianluca and Augustino Riggi, eight-year-old twins, and Cecilia Riggi, aged five, were killed by their mother. In both these cases the murders occurred in the context of a dispute with the ex-partner over contact and residence.

or overheard domestic violence had also experienced maltreatment in the past year. Research in the UK by the NSPCC with a sample of 6196 parents, children and young people and young adults found that of the 2.9 per cent of children and young people under the age of 18 who had been exposed to domestic violence in the past year, nearly 1 in 3 (27.2%) of them had also been physically or sexually abused and/or neglected in the past year (Radford et al. 2011a).

The possibility that contact will be part of a domestic violence perpetrator's efforts to maintain coercive control (Stark 2007) over an ex-partner needs to be considered. Where this happens the child may be in a worse position than when the parents were living together. Domestic violence perpetrators may psychologically and emotionally abuse children by trying to draw them into the abuse of mothers by: forcing them to join in the denigration, violence or harassment; pumping them for information about the mother's movements and activities, so they can monitor or track down women who have moved away; getting the children, sometimes unwittingly, to relay threats to the mother; and influencing the children's beliefs or behaviour in order to undermine the mother's parenting.

Children can feel overwhelmingly responsible and try to manage the father's behaviour and act as protectors for their mothers and siblings. Children can feel confused, alienated or have divided loyalties, especially if the violent parent undermines their relationship with the mother and emotionally manipulates them (Radford and Hester 2006). The safe approach to contact recognises that children benefit most from contact that is conflict-free (Rodgers and Pryor 1998).

The pro-contact stance reframes the child safety issues in terms of mothers overcoming their fears and agreeing to unregulated contact. The safe contact approach instead demands different treatment for domestic violence cases, so that the safety of the child and parent, rather than agreement, is the priority. This requires identification of domestic violence, adequate assessment of safety and risk, differentiated responses targeted at differing levels of need, better working together among services and the provision of resources and practical support such as supervision services (Jaffe et al. 2008).

Child contact and wellbeing

Relationships break down for a number of reasons, including domestic violence. Parental separation affects a significant number of children and young people living in the UK. Out of 11 million children in England and Wales, 25 per cent are likely to experience their parents' divorce before the age of 16, while 150,000 to 200,000 are estimated to be affected by parental separation each year (ONS 2004). On a range of outcomes, including educational achievement, behaviour, mental health, self-concept, social competence and long-term health, children who experience parental separation fare less well than children from intact families (Mooney, Oliver and Smith 2009). However, few children and young people have lasting adverse consequences following parental separation and for some, especially those who experience abuse or a high level of parental conflict, the family breakdown may be beneficial (ibid.). Children in the public care system have considerably better outcomes if they *are not* returned to live with an abusive or neglectful parent (Davies and Ward 2011; Farmer and Lutman 2010; Wade *et al.* 2010). Child welfare research findings do not show that being separated from a parent will inevitably harm a child.

Sustaining a *meaningful relationship* with the non-resident parent is important for meeting a child's emotional needs for warmth, security and approval and the majority of children want to preserve contact with both parents after separation (Hunt and Roberts 2004). Article 9 of the United Nations Convention on the Rights of the Child (UNCRC) set out the principle that a child has the right to know and have contact with parents and family *unless it is contrary to the child's best interests*. Ninety per cent of children in England and Wales live with one parent after their parents separate and this is usually the mother. It is estimated that 30 per cent of separated children have no contact at all with the non-resident parent (Peacey and Hunt 2009). Contact tends to decline over time (Giovanninni 2011). In contrast to father's rights and equal parenting lobbyists' views, it seems that practical difficulties, such as long working hours, other demands on the child's time or geographical distance, are the main factors influencing the decline in contact over time (Peacey and Hunt 2009).

There is very little research that considers the wishes and feelings of children and young people who have separated from fathers who are domestic violence perpetrators (Giovanninni 2011). The most relevant studies from the UK suggest that some children and young people feel ambivalent about violent fathers, wanting to preserve a relationship after separation if this can be done safely but also hating and being fearful of the violence (McGee 2000; Morrison 2009). Others are clear that they do not want to see their father and complain about feeling pressurised into doing so by the family courts (Mullender *et al.* 2002).

Women who have experienced domestic violence often support the child's continued contact with the father after separation (Peacey and Hunt 2009; Radford, Sayer and AMICA 1999). The reasons given include:

- Despite the domestic violence, the partner was a 'good father'.

- The children want to see the father.

- Women believe their children need to know their father – they have 'blood ties'.

- Contact is seen as a way of ensuring fathers take some responsibility for their children, especially if the father has not been married or has denied the paternity of the child.

- Having left the father, some women do not want to be in the position of also preventing contact and having to cope with a child's resentment.

- Preserving cultural or religious links with the father, his family and/or community.

(Thiara and Gill 2012)

Many mothers take active steps to try to make contact work for the children, facilitating or regulating contact between the children and the non-resident father (Trinder 2008). Many also say they want contact to be worthwhile, to be safe, 'quality contact' for the child (Radford and Hester 2006).

Research on children's welfare suggests that it is indeed the quality of contact rather than the quantity that is most significant for children (Hunt and Roberts 2004). Contact that starts with problems tends to deteriorate as time goes by (Trinder, Beek and Connolly 2002). A large study of children and their parents, who were subjects of a welfare report for the court following parental separation, found very high levels of distress amongst the children involved. Fifty-two per cent of boys and 48 per cent of girls had significant adjustment problems[2] immediately after the proceedings, and a year later 62 per cent of boys and 32 per cent of girls were still maladjusted. Children were more likely to have problems where parents were also distressed and where there was

---

2   As measured by the Strengths and Difficulties Questionnaire (SDQ).

domestic violence. Where domestic violence had been an issue in the proceedings, children were three times more likely (than the general population) to have borderline or abnormal scores on the SDQ (Bream and Buchanan 2003). The distress of the main carer caused by domestic violence after separation is therefore an important factor for professionals to address when considering whether or not contact is in a child's best interests.

Getting the contact right for the child should involve considering the purpose of contact, which is to promote the child's wellbeing. Where there has been violence or abuse it is much more difficult to establish worthwhile contact for the child, although direct visiting contact may not be the only option to consider (Jaffe *et al.* 2008). Sturge and Glaser (2000) have recommended that courts start by understanding that direct visiting contact is less likely to work and benefit the child if there has been domestic violence. Post-separation contact between a child and a non-resident parent needs proactive efforts and good communication between the parents to make it work. The child is much less likely to have had a beneficial relationship with a violent parent and it is difficult to repair a relationship based upon fear if the violent parent is unwilling to accept his responsibility to change. Safety should include thinking about the perpetrator's capacity to change, the practical arrangements needed to support safe contact and what needs to be done to restore the child's emotional security, healthy development and peace of mind.

Making contact happen and making contact safe?

There have been considerable changes in policy since 2000 but practice has seemed stubbornly stuck. Less effort has been put into making contact *safe* than making contact *happen*, either by getting an 'agreement' with renewed emphasis on mediation, or by finding more ways to enforce contact. Resources in the community or family court that might help to make contact safe and worthwhile for children have been woefully short of what is needed (see Hunt and Macleod 2008).

There is no evidence of gender bias against fathers in the family courts (MOJ 2011). Nor is there, technically, any presumption for or against contact, but it is viewed by the family courts and associated professionals as being 'almost always' in the best interests of a child and this allows a huge scope for it to happen when it should not. Steps taken towards safe contact have lacked substance, proliferating guidance but not the resources to implement change. The first guidance on safe contact for the courts came from the Children Act Sub-Committee[3] (CASC 2000) following the Court of Appeal hearing Re: L, V, M and H (2000). The guidance, reissued as reminders in Practice Directions in 2008 and 2009, *recommended*, rather than required, courts to consider domestic violence and its impact on children when making decisions in child contact cases. Courts were also advised to make findings of fact where allegations of domestic violence were made, to establish the extent of the domestic violence, its effect on the primary carer and the children, and the ability and willingness of the perpetrator to change and make amends.

The Adoption and Children Act 2002 further endorsed the view that domestic violence posed risks to children's wellbeing but again no new resources were provided to enable the police or children's social care to cope with increased notifications that resulted (Radford *et al.* 2011b; Stanley *et al.* 2010). Domestic violence guidance was produced for CAFCASS in 2005 and revised as a domestic violence toolkit in 2007 (CAFCASS 2007) to incorporate the new safeguarding framework. The guidance and toolkit gave advice to family court advisers (who work with children and parents in the family court system) on how to do assessments and look at risk.

Potentially more scope for change came with the Children and Adoption Act 2006 which further amended the Children Act 1989 to allow greater flexibility for courts facilitating contact and ensuring safety. CAFCASS officers' roles under the 2006 Act shifted from writing reports for the court to include doing risk assessments and more directly assisting and monitoring contact. Courts gained new powers to require parents to undertake a 'contact activity' such as attending a parenting programme or information session (a PIP) before a contact order is made, a mediation information and assessment meeting (MIAM) and referral to a domestic violence perpetrator programme (DVPP). At the same time there were changes to make sure that contact happened. New enforcement options were introduced to deal with parents who breached court orders for contact. These included requiring the parent in breach to pay financial compensation or undertake unpaid work.

There is no evidence that any of the domestic violence guidance was followed consistently nor that it reduced the number of unsafe contact orders made in the courts. One senior judge said the guidance was

---

3 This was a committee of senior judges set up to review how well the Children Act 1989 was being implemented in the Family courts.

'more honoured in breach than observance' (Craig 2007, p.4). Masson's survey on lawyers' cases found only 4 per cent of domestic violence cases had any findings of fact (Masson 2007). Family courts 'bend over backwards' to get contact as an outcome (Hunt and Macleod 2008). Contact is almost never refused with 93 per cent of applications being granted (Giovanninni 2011) and orders made very rarely adequately supervised. In 60 per cent of court cases with serious welfare concerns about a child, staying or unsupervised contact was the outcome (Hunt and Macleod 2008). Even where resident parents came to proceedings initially opposed to contact, 85 per cent of contact orders were settled by parental agreement (Hunt and Macleod 2008). Domestic violence had a greater than expected impact on initiatives set up to resolve conflict and bring about agreement (Trinder *et al.* 2007). Pressures put on parents to agree are likely to discourage the parent living with domestic violence from bringing this up even when there may be evidential support available. A study of C1A court screening forms found that while in the majority of applications where there was a history of domestic violence the forms helped bring disclosures, in almost a third of cases (29.3%) the trigger question on domestic violence was answered negatively even though the case files showed a high level of previous abuse (Aris and Harrison 2007).

Worryingly, Trinder *et al.*'s recent research, which compared outcomes for parents who attended PIPs with outcomes for parents who did not, found almost 1 in 5 (18%) of PIPs parents had cases concerning a child at risk of harm from maltreatment or domestic violence. For a significant number of these parents, attending the PIP had made things worse. There was also evidence to suggest that parents might have been referred to a PIP in an effort to do something about the perpetrator where there was no programme in the family court locality working with domestic violence perpetrators (Trinder *et al.* 2011).

Inspections by HMICA (2005), research on contact centres (Humphreys and Thiara 2003) and more recently on high-risk cases handled by IDVAs (Independent Domestic Violence Advisers) (Howarth *et al.* 2009) have all highlighted the problems with getting safe contact arrangements and CAFCASS's shortcomings in identifying and investigating domestic violence to safeguard children:

> The family legal system will insist on sending him (child)
> to his violent bully of a father. The family courts are
> still failing our children and something has to be done

to protect everyone from domestic violence. (House of Commons 2008, p.93)

Post-separation violence especially around child contact was found to be a factor in about half the calls to the police in one recent research study (Stanley *et al.* 2010), for 30 per cent in another (Hester 2009).

There are findings from research done directly with children which suggest that, although many children are content with their contact arrangements, there are a sizeable minority who feel 'pestered' by the courts or feel they have been pushed into having contact they do not want. Timms, Bailey and Thoburn's research with children found over half who were living with their mothers said they did not want to see their fathers. Some of these young people felt pressurised into contact as illustrated in the following quotation from a young person from the research:

> When I said I didn't want to see my Dad I should have been able to do that. I told CAFCASS I didn't want to see him, but they still kept wanting to talk to me. I think the court shouldn't push children to see their Dad if they don't want to. (Timms *et al.* 2007, p.33)

There may be an element of optimism about the importance of continued contact and parents' capacity to change within child protection practice that has a detrimental impact on children's wellbeing, as suggested by the research on family reunification (Farmer and Lutman 2010; Wade *et al.* 2010).

From 2008 onwards after the measures introduced by the Children and Adoption Act 2006 came into force, the contradictory pressures on the family courts to work proactively towards safety *as well as* get parents to agree to contact were aggravated by over-workload pressures put on courts and child protection (Rivett 2010). Following the murder of baby Peter Connelly in Haringey in London, applications for child protection in 'public law' and child contact or residence in 'private law'[4] increased. By 2009–2010 the family justice system was seen to be failing badly, to be costly, with long delays, lack of regard to children's wishes and dogged by low staff morale (MOJ 2011). CAFCASS officers were told to

---

4   'Public' law refers to cases involving children brought by local authorities (adoption, child protection). 'Private' law cases involving children are cases brought by an individual, usually a family member such as a parent. Examples are contact cases linked with the parent's separation or divorce.

do an initial 'safeguarding analysis' of child protection cases, criticised for being 'an arms length paper risk assessment exercise' (Lepper 2010), to support private law cases to first hearing and then allocate resources according to need of the child and the resource availability. Critics felt CAFCASS had lost its focus. Rather than seeing children, it had become obsessed with form filling and safeguarding procedures that had dubious, unproven impact upon outcomes (NAGALRO 2010). The organisation was no longer 'fit for purpose' (House of Commons 2010). Despite some valiant efforts to do so (Harne 2011) the likelihood that CAFCASS could implement policies of proactive support for safe contact in this context looked slim. It is difficult to bring about safer outcomes if the options for working with perpetrators of domestic violence in the family court system are so limited, services in the community are too scarce to respond and courts remain steadfastly against the idea of stopping contact.

Next steps

The Family Justice Review made organisational recommendations for change as well as suggesting that conflict could be avoided by abolishing orders for 'contact' and 'residence' and replacing these with 'child arrangement orders' (MOJ 2011). In 1989, the Children Act similarly attempted to curb conflict by renaming 'custody' and 'access' as 'residence' and 'contact' although in 2011 it was recognised many people still commonly used the former terms (MOJ 2011). Time will tell whether the rebranding and other changes happen and whether they will bring safer outcomes for children and their mothers.

In the USA, Canada, Australia and New Zealand there have similarly been a range of initiatives aimed at improving the lives of children affected by domestic violence and also, to date, not a lot of evidence of their success (Chisholm 2009; Jaffe et al. 2008; Kaspiew et al. 2009; Wasoff 2007). In the USA an integrated programme called the 'Greenbook' is perhaps one of the most resource-intensive, coordinated projects so far evaluated (Edleson and Malik 2008). The Greenbook Initiative aimed to improve working together between the juvenile, family and dependency (child protection) courts. It involved setting up joint courts, training specialists, sharing information on the child's circumstances and working together closely to coordinate actions to provide the differentiated safe responses needed for children. Key lessons to emerge from an evaluation five years on of the Greenbook were that: change takes time; training needs to be frequently repeated to reinforce core knowledge especially where this is lacking in professionals' mainstream curriculum; there is resistance to change and in the judiciary this presents a considerable challenge (Edleson and Malik 2008). Judges could take a firmer stand to join up with other professionals to push forward evidence-based change and stop contact when it has no value for children.

The belief that children's safeguarding needs can be assessed without a child being seen is dangerous. So too is the belief that all parents will eventually sort things out themselves. Where power differences exist between parents, because of domestic violence, the abused parent needs protection from violence and support from services. It is worth remembering that although children may have very mixed views about contact with a violent parent, there are some who most want the abuser to be dealt with promptly, to be taken away and kept away (Radford *et al.* 2011b).

Approaches to children living with domestic violence in Wales and in Scotland have taken different routes, emphasising more the need to challenge and engage with perpetrators and provide services so that children can be safe. The Caring Dads programme currently being rolled out in Wales has been evaluated on behalf of the Welsh Assembly. In England there are very few programmes specifically focused on violent fathers, with only 15 programmes sponsored by CAFCASS which work with men referred by family courts. While not enough is known about whether or not programmes that focus on violent fathers are effective (Bancroft and Silverman 2002) these do open the door to developing practice in this area.

In Scotland, the *National Domestic Abuse Delivery Plan for Children* (Scottish Government 2008) had safe contact for children as one of the priorities and work with perpetrators as parents included in the Caledonian programme. The Family Law (Scotland) Act 2006 requires courts to consider the need to protect a child when looking at contact. The Children's Hearing (Scotland) Act 2011 makes domestic abuse for the first time grounds for referral to a children's hearing. In Scotland services for children in contact with domestic violence agencies such as Women's Aid were also funded as part of the Scottish government's domestic violence delivery plan. We need to carefully consider where adequate assessment, which includes directly seeing and talking with children, and community support provided directly to children and to the non-abusive parent would be a more effective and appropriate way to reach out to and meet the needs of children living with domestic violence.

References

Archer, J. (2007) 'A cross cultural perspective on physical aggression between partners.' *Issues in Forensic Psychology 6*, 124–131.

Aris, R. and Harrison, C. (2007) *Domestic Violence and the Supplemental Information Form C1A.* Ministry of Justice Research Series 17/07. London: Ministry of Justice.

Bancroft, L. and Silverman, J. (2002) *Assessing Risk to Children from Batterers.* Available at http://new. vawnet.org/Assoc_Files_VAWnet/RisktoChildren.pdf, accessed on 9 October 2012.

Basile, S. (2005). 'A measure of court response to requests for protection.' *Journal of Family Violence 20*, 3, 171–181.

Brandon, M., Belderson, P., Warren, C., Howe, D., Gardner, R., Dodsworth, J. and Black, J. (2008) *Analysing Child Deaths and Serious Injury Through Abuse and Neglect; What Can We Learn? A Biennial Analysis of Serious Case Reviews 2003-2005.* Research Report DCSF RR023. London: DCSF. Available at www.education.gov.uk/publications/eOrderingDownload/DCSF-RR023.pdf, accessed on 9 October 2012.

Bream, V. and Buchanan, A. (2003) 'Distress among children whose separated or divorced parents cannot agree arrangements for them.' *British Journal of Social Work 33*, 2, 227–238.

CAFCASS (2007) *Domestic Violence Toolkit.* London: CAFCASS. Available at www.cafcass.gov.uk/pdf/Domestic_Violence_toolkit_(Version_2_-_August_2007).pdf, accessed on 18 July 2012.

Cassidy, D. and Davey, S. (2011) *Family Justice and Children's Proceedings: A Review of Public and Private Law Case Files.* Research Summary 51/1. London: Ministry of Justice. Available at www.justice.gov.uk/downloads/publications/research-and-analysis/moj-research/family-justice-childrens-proceedings.pdf, accessed on 18 July 2012.

Cavanagh, K., Dobash, R. and Dobash, R. (2007) 'The murder of children by fathers in the context of child abuse.' *Child Abuse and Neglect 31*, 7, 731–746.

Children Act Sub-Committee (2000) *A Report to The Lord Chancellor On The Question of Parental Contact in Cases Where There is Domestic Violence.* London: Lord Chancellor's Department.

Chisholm, R. (2009) *Family Courts Violence Review.* Canberra: Australian Government. Available at www.ag.gov.au/Documents/Chisholm_report.pdf, accessed on 9 October 2012.

Conservative Party (2010) *Invitation to Join the Government of Britain: Conservative Party Manifesto.* London: Conservative Party. Available at www.conservatives.com/~/media/Files/Activist%20Centre/Press%20and%20Policy/Manifestos/Manifesto2010, accessed on 9 October 2012.

Craig, J. (2007) *Everybody's Business: How Applications for Contact Orders by Consent should be Approached by the Court in Cases Involving Domestic Violence. The Family Justice Council's Report and Recommendations to the President of the Family Division.* Family Justice Council.

Davies, C. and Ward, H. (2011) *Safeguarding Children Across Services: Messages on Research on Identifying and Responding to Child Maltreatment.* London: Department for Education. Available at www.education.gov.uk/publications/eOrderingDownload/DFE-RR164.pdf, accessed on 18 July 2012.

Edleson, J. (1999) 'Children's witnessing of adult domestic violence.' *Journal of Interpersonal Violence 8*, 14, 839–871.

Edleson, J. and Malik, N. (2008) 'Collaborating for family safety: Results from the Greenbook multi-site evaluation.' *Journal of Interpersonal Violence 23*, 871–875.

Equal Parenting Alliance (2010) *Shared Residence.* Available at www.equalparentingalliance.org, accessed on 18 July 2012.

Farmer, E. and Lutman, E. (2010) *Case Management and Outcomes for Neglected Children Returned to their Parents: A Five Year Follow-up Study.* Research Brief DCSF RB214. London: DCSF.

Fatherhood Institute (2007) *Research Summary: Separated Families.* Available at www.fatherhoodinstitute. org.uk, accessed on 18 July 2012.

Featherstone, B. and Peckover, S. (2008) 'Letting them get away with it: Fathers, domestic violence and child welfare.' *Critical Social Policy 27*, 2, 181–202.

Flood, M. (2010) '"Fathers' rights" and the defense of paternal authority in Australia.' *Violence Against Women 16*, 3, 328–347.

Giovanninni, E. (2011) *Outcomes in Family Justice and Children's Proceedings – A Review of the Evidence.* London: Ministry of Justice. Available at www.justice.gov.uk/downloads/publications/research-and-analysis/moj-research/outcomes-family-justice-childrens-proceedings.pdf, accessed on 18 July 2012.

Hamby, S., Finkelhor, D., Turner, H. and Ormrod, R. (2010) 'The overlap of witnessing partner violence with child maltreatment and other victimizations in a nationally representative sample of youth.' *Child Abuse and Neglect 34*, 10, 734–741.

Harne, L. (2011) *Violent Fathering and the Risks to Children: The Need for Change.* London: Policy Press.

Hester, M. (2009) *Who Does What to Whom?* Bristol: University of Bristol/Northern Rock Foundation. Available at www.bristol.ac.uk, accessed on 18 July 2012.

Hester, M. and Pearson, C. (1998) *From Periphery to Core.* Bristol: Policy Press.

HMICA (2005) *Domestic Violence, Safety and Family Proceedings: Thematic Review of the Handling of Domestic Violence Issues by the Children's Family Courts Advisory and Support Service (CAFCASS) and the Administration of Family Courts in Her Majesty's Courts Service (HMCS).* London: Her Majesty's Inspectorate of Court Administration. Available at www.hmica.gov.uk, accessed on 18 July 2012.

House of Commons (2008) *Domestic Violence, Forced Marriage and Honour Based Violence.* Sixth report of the Home Affairs Committee Session 2007-8 HC 263. London: Stationery Office.

House of Commons (2010) *Public Accounts Committee Minutes of Evidence: CAFCASS's Response to Increased Demand for its Services*, 7 September. London: House of Commons, UK Parliament. Available at www.publications.parliament.uk/pa/cm201011/cmselect/cmpubacc/439/43902.htm, accessed on 20 November 2012.

Howarth, E., Stimpson, L., Barran, D. and Robinson, A. (2009) *Safety in Numbers: A Multi-site Evaluation of IDVA Services.* London: Henry Smith Charity. Available at www.caada.org.uk/policy/Safety_in_Numbers_full_report.pdf, accessed on 9 October 2012.

Humphreys, C. and Thiara, R. (2003) 'Neither justice nor protection: women's experiences of post-separation violence.' *Journal of Social Welfare and Family Law 25*, 3, 195–214.

Hunt, J. and Roberts, C. (2004) *Child Contact and the Non Resident Parent.* University of Oxford, Department of Social Policy and Social Work Policy Briefing 3.

Hunt, J. and Macleod, A. (2008) *Outcomes of Applications to Court for Contact Orders After Parental Separation or Divorce.* London: Ministry of Justice.

Jaffe, P., Johnston, J., Crooks, C. and Bala, N. (2008) 'Custody disputes involving allegations of domestic violence: Toward a differentiated approach to parenting plans.' *Family Court Review 46*, 3, 500–522.

Kaganas, F. (2000) 'Re L: Contact and domestic violence.' *Child and Family Law Quarterly 12*, 311–324.

Kaspiew, R., Gray, M., Weston, R., Moloney, L., Hand, K. and Qu, L. (2009) *Evaluation of the 2006 Family Law Reforms.* Australian Institute of Family Studies, Canberra: Australian Government. Available at www.aifs.gov.au/institute/pubs/fle, accessed on 18 July 2012.

Lepper, J. (2010) 'CAFCASS caseload system criticized by children's guardians.' *Children and Young People Now*, 21 Jan.

Masson, J. (2007) 'A Detailed Report by Judith Masson on the Family Justice Council's Survey of Resolution Members.' In J. Booth (ed.) *Report of the President to the Family Division on the Approach to be Adopted by the Court When Asked to Address Contact Orders by Consent Where Domestic Violence is an Issue.* London: Family Justice Council.

McGee, C. (2000) *Childhood Experiences of Domestic Violence.* London: Jessica Kingsley Publishers.

Meltzer, H., Doos, L., Vostanis, P., Ford, T. and Goodman, R. (2009). 'The mental health of children who witness domestic violence.' *Child and Family Social Work 14*, 4, 491–501.

Ministry of Justice (2011) *Family Justice Review Final Report.* London: Ministry of Justice. Available at www.justice.gov.uk/downloads/publications/moj/2011/family-justice-review-final-report. pdf, accessed on 9 October 2012.

Mooney, A., Oliver, C. and Smith, M. (2009) *Impact of Family Breakdown on Children's Well-Being Evidence Review. Research Report No DCSF-RR113.* London: DCSF. Available at www.education. gov.uk/publications/eOrderingDownload/DCSF-RR113.pdf, accessed on 18 July 2012.

Morrison, F. (2009) *After Domestic Abuse: Children's Perspectives on Contact with Fathers.* Briefing 42. Edinburgh: Centre for Research on Families and Relationships. Available at www.crfr.ac.uk/reports/rb42.pdf, accessed on 18 July 2012.

Mullender, A., Hague, G., Iman, U., Kelly, L., Malos, E. and Regan, L. (2002) *Children's Perspectives on Domestic Violence.* London: Sage.

NAGALRO (2010) *Time for Children Cafcass Public Law Work – a Survey of Nagalro Members.* London: NAGALRO. Available at www.pfjc.org.uk/images/stories/time_for_children_report_of_ nagalro_survey_january_2010.pdf, accessed on 18 July 2012.

Office of National Statistics (2004) *Children's Needs, Parents' Responsibilities: Supporting Evidence for the Consultation Paper.* London: ONS.

Peacey, V. and Hunt, J. (2009) *I'm Not Saying it was Easy… Contact Problems in Separated Families.* London: Gingerbread.

Povey, D., Coleman, K., Kiazo, P. and Roe, S. (2009) *Homicides, Firearm Offences and Intimate Violence 2007-8 Supplementary Volume 2 to Crime in England and Wales 2007-8.* London: Home Office.

Practice Direction (2008) *Residence and Contact Orders: Domestic Violence and Harm.* 9 May 2008, Family Division.

Practice Direction (2009) *Residence and Contact Orders: Domestic Violence and Harm.* 14 January 2009, Sir Mark Potter, President of the Family Division.

Radford, L., Corral, S., Bradley, C., Fisher, H., Bassett, C., Howat, N. and Collishaw, S. (2011a) *Child Abuse and Neglect in the UK Today.* London: NSPCC. Available at www.nspcc.org.uk/childstudy, accessed on 18 July 2012.

Radford, L., Aitken, R., Miller, P., Ellis, J., Roberts, J. and Firkic, A. (2011b) *Meeting the Needs of Children Living with Domestic Violence in London.* London: NSPCC/Refuge. Available at www. nspcc.org.uk/Inform/research/findings/domestic_violence_london_pdf_wdf85830.pdf, accessed on 18 July 2012.

Radford, L. and Hester, M. (2006) *Mothering Through Domestic Violence.* London: Jessica Kingsley Publishers.

Radford, L., Sayer, S. and AMICA (1999) *Unreasonable Fears? Child Contact in the Context of Domestic Violence: A Survey of Mothers' Perceptions of Harm.* Bristol: Women's Aid Federation.

Rivett, M. (2010) 'Working with Violent Male Carers (Fathers and Stepfathers).' In B. Featherstone, C. Hooper, J. Scourfield and J. Taylor (eds) *Gender and Child Welfare in Society.* London: Wiley/ Blackwell.

Rodgers, B. and Pryor, J. (1998) *Divorce and Separation: The Outcomes for Children.* York: Joseph Rowntree Foundation.

Saunders, H. (2006) *Twenty-nine Child Homicides: Lessons Still to be Learnt on Domestic Violence and Child Protection.* Bristol: Women's Aid Federation.

Scottish Government (2008) *National Domestic Abuse Delivery Plan for Children and Young People.* Edinburgh: Scottish Government.

Sidebotham, P., Brandon, M., Bailey, S., Belderson, S. and Hawley, C. (2011) *Serious and Fatal Child Maltreatment: Setting Serious Case Review Data in the Context with Other Data on Violent and Maltreatment Deaths in 2009-10.* Research Report DFE-RR167. London: Department for Education. Available at www.education.gov.uk/publications/eOrderingDownload/DFE-RR167.pdf, accessed on 18 July 2012.

Stanley, N., Miller, P., Richardson Foster H. and Thomson, G. (2010) *Children and Families Experiencing Domestic Violence: Police and Children's Services Responses.* London: NSPCC. Available at www.nspcc.org.uk/Inform, accessed on 18 July 2012.

Stark, E. (2007) *Coercive Control: How Men Entrap Women in Personal Life. Interpersonal Violence.* New York: Oxford University Press.

Sturge, C. and Glaser, D. (2000) 'Contact and domestic violence the experts' court report.' *Family Law 30,* 615–629.

Thiara, R. and Gill, A. (2012) *Domestic Violence Child Contact: Issues for South Asian and African Caribbean Women and Children: A Report of Findings.* London: NSPCC. Available at www.nspcc. org.uk/Inform/publications/new/newpublications_wda47986.html, accessed on 18 July 2012.

Timms, J., Bailey, S. and Thoburn, J. (2007) *Your Shout Too! A Survey of the Views of Children and Young People Involved in Court Proceedings When their Parents Divorce or Separate.* London: NSPCC.

Trinder, L. (2008) "Maternal gate closing and gate opening in postdivorce families." *Journal of Family Issues 29,* 10, 1298–1324.

Trinder, L., Beek, M. and Connolly, J. (2002) *Making Contact: How Parents and Children Negotiate and Experience Contact After Divorce.* York: Joseph Rowntree Foundation.

Trinder, L., Bryson, C., Coleman, L., Houlston, C., Purdon, S., Reibstein, J. and Smith, L. (2011) *Building Bridges? An Evaluation of the Costs and Effectiveness of the Separated Parents Information Programme (PIP).* Research Report DFE-RR149. London: Department for Education. Available at www.education.gov.uk, accessed on 18 July 2012.

Trinder, L., Kellett, J., Connolly, J. and Notley, C. (2007) *Evaluation of the Family Resolutions Pilot Research Report 720.* London: DCSF.

Turkat, I. (1995) 'Divorce related malicious mother syndrome.' *Journal of Family Violence 10,* 3, 253–264.

Wade, J., Blehal, N., Farrelly, N. and Sinclair, I. (2010) *Maltreated Children in the Looked After System: A Comparison of the Outcomes for Those Who Go Home and Those Who Do Not.* Research Brief DFE-RBX 10-06 August. London: Department for Education. Available at www.education. gov.uk/publications/eOrderingDownload/DFE-RBX-10-06.pdf, accessed on 18 July 2012.

Walby, S. and Allen, J. (2004) *Domestic Violence, Sexual Assault and Stalking: Findings from the British Crime Survey.* London: Home Office.

Walker, A., Flatley, J., Kershaw, C. and Moon, D. (2009) *Crime in England and Wales 2008/09 Volume 1: Findings from the British Crime Survey and Police Recorded Crime.* London: Home Office.

Wasoff, F. (2007) *Dealing with Child Contact Issues: A Literature Review of Mechanisms in Different Jurisdictions.* Edinburgh: Scottish Government. Available at www.scotland.gov.uk/Resource/ Doc/201147/0053739.pdf, accessed on 18 July 2012.

Weir, K (2006) 'Clinical advice to courts on children's contact with their parents following parental separation.' *Child and Adolescent Mental Health 11,* 1, 40–49.

Wilson, M. and Daly, M. (1999) 'Lethal and Non-Lethal Violence against Wives and the Evolutionary Psychology of Male Sexual Proprietariness.' In R. Dobash and R. Dobash (eds) *Re-Thinking Violence against Women.* London: Sage.

CHAPTER 4

Sexual Victimisation
Disclosure, Responses and Impact

Lesley McMillan

Introduction

This chapter addresses the area of sexual victimisation, and in particular rape and sexual assault. It will examine women's experiences of sexual violence and look at its prevalence and impact highlighting the pervasiveness of the problem and the very real individual and societal costs. It will draw on recently conducted research on the criminal justice response to sexual violence and examine reasons for disclosure and non-disclosure of sexual violence, how women experience the response of criminal justice agencies, and the particular challenges of that engagement for survivors and practitioners. It is the case that many improvements have been made in the criminal justice response to rape and sexual violence; however, challenges remain, some of which might compound the impact of such events for women. Given that social workers may encounter rape survivors in locations as diverse as hospitals, mental health centres, homeless facilities, drug and alcohol treatment centres, prisons and schools (McMahon and Schwartz 2011), it is important to be aware of the particular challenges survivors may face whether they choose to engage with the justice process or not.

Scale and impact of sexual violence

Rape and sexual assault, as with all violence against women, remains a significant social problem. The true prevalence and incidence of rape and sexual violence is very difficult to measure, largely because sexually violent acts most often happen in private spaces (Stanko and Williams 2009; McMillan 2011). It is also the case that rape is one of the most under-reported crimes, therefore statistics about reported crime betray the true prevalence of rape, which is likely to be much higher (Koss and Harvey 1991). Data that is available on the prevalence of rape and sexual violence clearly shows that women face a disproportionate risk. Kessler *et al.* (1995) found lifetime prevalence rates of rape for women of 9.2 per cent and rates of molestation of 12.3 per cent. In comparison, men experienced these same acts at a rate of 0.7 per cent and 2.8 per cent respectively. However, other research has estimated higher prevalence rates, suggesting between 1 in 5 and 1 in 7 women will experience rape in their lifetime (UNICEF 1997). Further, Russell's (1982, 1984) research found 44 per cent of women in the USA in her randomly generated sample had experienced rape or attempted rape. Given the high numbers of women who experience rape, it suggests that social workers in all settings are likely to encounter clients who are survivors of sexual violence (McMahon and Schwartz 2011).

Many scholars have documented the negative impact of rape and sexual assault on survivors in a number of areas of their lives, including the physical, mental, social, and the interpersonal (Bachar and Koss 2001; Campbell 2008; Koss, Koss and Woodruff 1991; Waigandt *et al.* 1990). The potential short-term and longer-term impacts of sexual violence are considerable (McMillan 2007) and women may suffer a number of physical and/or mental health symptoms in the immediate aftermath of a sexual assault, or many years after the event (Koss 1993; New and Berliner 2000; Plichta and Falik 2001). The World Health Organisation (2005) also highlights that sexual violence significantly increases chances of depression, anxiety, psychosomatic disorders and suicidal behaviour. Given this, women with experience of sexual violence involved with social work services may present in many ways, and may be struggling with the aftermath of their assault(s). The chapter will now move on to consider recent research findings about what influences women's decision to disclose sexual violence and their experiences of justice processes when they do.

Methodology

Data that informs this chapter comes from an ESRC-funded (RES-061-23-0138-A) project *Understanding Attrition in Rape Cases* that I conducted from 2007 to 2010. The project used a case study design within a county in the South East of England. The project used a mixed methods approach and had a number of methods of data collection, both quantitative and qualitative, with a variety of population groups, for example police officers, forensic medical staff, barristers, prosecutors and judges (see McMillan 2010). Data for the chapter is drawn from two aspects of the research project: from a review of reported rape case files; and from interviews with those who reported rape to the police, and those who did not.

The review of reported rape files involved examining all cases of reported rape in the police force area over one calendar year. This yielded a total sample of 408. Case files were analysed in full and data pertaining to 60 core variables was extracted for each case, and data for an additional 459 variables was extracted from a subsample (n = 156). Qualitative data was also extracted from notes and commentary included within the files, from, for example, police officers' comments in case reviews, victim statements, and other documentation in the files.

Interviews were conducted with 15 individuals who have experienced rape. Those who had reported rape to the police ('reporters') were accessed via the police force. In order to comply with Data Protection (1998) legislation the initial approach was made by the police force on the researcher's behalf. For ethical reasons only those over the age of 16 were approached for interviews, and survivors who were recorded as particularly vulnerable (e.g. mental health) or who were still living in a violent relationship were not approached for interview. This sampling approach yielded a final sample of five although a much larger number of women were approached. Those who did not report to the police ('non-reporters') were accessed through a general advertising approach (emails to large organisations such as universities), distribution of recruitment postcards for the research in local leisure facilities, pubs, clubs, sports centres etc. throughout the county, from snowball sampling (Bryman 2008) and word of mouth. Again, only those over 16 years of age were interviewed. This yielded a final sample of ten. Interviews were transcribed verbatim and analysed thematically.

Characteristics of reported rape

Analysis of one calendar year of reported rapes in the county provides a snapshot of the reality of reported rape.[1] The findings show that the vast majority (89.6%,[2] n = 366) of complainants were raped by men known to them, a finding which is consistent with existing research (Greenfield 1997; Koss 1993; Koss and Heslet 1992; Stanko 1984). Assailants included friends, relatives, parents, current and former partners or boyfriends, colleagues and family friends, highlighting that women are potentially at risk from any man in their lives. Only 10.4 per cent (n = 42) of complainants were assaulted by a stranger. Over a quarter were assaulted by a current or former intimate (25.9%, n = 105), a further 14.1 per cent (n = 57) by a relative, one-third (33.3%, n = 135) by someone known to them who they have known for more than 24 hours (including friends, colleagues, etc.), and lastly 16.3 per cent (n = 66) were assaulted by someone they had known for less than 24 hours, who they may have met at a social gathering or work function, for example.

The case review also reiterates that all women are at risk of sexual victimisation throughout the life course. The youngest survivor was two years of age and the eldest was 64. Similarly, it also restates that any men in women's lives can perpetrate sexual violence, as suspects ranged in age from as young as 9 years of age to as old as 74 years of age at the time of the incident. Those reporting rape come from varied backgrounds but there is a high prevalence of additional vulnerabilities in the sample. Slightly more than one-third of the sample were recorded in the case files as being considered vulnerable, which includes having a mental disorder (as defined by the Mental Health Act 1983), an impairment of intelligence or social functioning, and/or a physical disability or disorder. If other aspects of vulnerability are included, for example the consumption of alcohol or drugs, being under the age of 18, and/or being in an intimate relationship with the assailant (as in Stanko and Williams' [2009] research), then the numbers considered vulnerable are much higher. There are likely to be two factors at play here: firstly that those who are most vulnerable are at greater risk of sexual predation (Stanko and Williams 2009) and also at greater risk of repeat victimisation; but also that those with existing vulnerabilities are

---

1   This is not to suggest that this represents characteristics of rape *per se*, as we know only a small proportion of rapes are reported to the police.

2   All percentages used are valid percentages. That is, they represent the proportion of those for whom data was available, rather than a proportion of the whole research sample.

likely to already be engaged with agencies of the state, and may already have had dealings with the police in relation to previous victimisation or vulnerability, which might increase the chances of reporting the incident.

The case review also revealed a wide range of time frames in which survivors disclose sexual violence. Some survivors report the incident to the police immediately with 17.1 per cent (n = 67) reporting within an hour of the assault, and a further 24.5 per cent (n = 96) within 24 hours of the assault. This mirrors findings in earlier research that only a small number of survivors seek support or treatment from formal sources immediately post-assault (Ullman 2007). At the other end of the spectrum some survivors waited as long as 47 years to disclose to the police. In fact, for 23 cases in the sample the assault had occurred more than 10 years ago; in six cases it was more than 20 years ago, and for a further eight cases more than 40 years ago. In the most part, these cases represent rape in the context of child sexual abuse as most survivors were less than 12 years of age at the time of the assault. Analysis of the case files showed that delayed reporting of this length was often prompted by the return of the attacker into the survivor's life (e.g. they may have moved away but returned to the area), the discovery that the attacker was involved with other children or young people in the family or local area, or the disclosure of the incident for the first time to partners, family members, friends or other professionals, for example General Practitioners, counsellors and social workers. It may be that when survivors begin to disclose to one individual, it supports disclosure elsewhere, and subsequent engagement with stage agencies. However, it remains the case that disclosure of sexual violence to the police remains the exception rather than the norm, and the reasons for this will be examined below.

Disclosure

Existing research on sexual violence tells us that women are often reluctant to disclose sexual victimisation to anyone. For example, Painter's (1991) research found that 91 per cent of women in her sample had told no one prior to taking part in the research. More recent analysis of British Crime Survey data suggests that women are increasingly more willing to tell someone about incidents of rape and sexual assault (Myhill and Allen 2002; Walby and Allen 2004) but this disclosure is most likely to be to a friend or family member rather than a statutory body such as the police or social work. Given this, and what we know from prevalence rates discussed above, many women encountered in the day-to-day practice of social work may have experienced sexual violence but that is undisclosed. Research suggests a number of reasons for non-disclosure more generally, and in particular for non-disclosure – or non-reporting – to the police. Research provides compelling evidence that rape is one of the most under-reported crimes (Spohn and Trellis 2012) and reasons thought to influence women's decision not to report rape include: not naming the incident as rape; a fear of not being believed; fear of being blamed; and a lack of confidence in the justice process (Kelly and Regan 2003). Bachman (1998) also identified fear of retaliation from the rapist and feelings of shame and embarrassment. These findings were reiterated in my own research from a large proportion of the survivors interviewed, and are exemplified by 'Ella's' comments on her decision not to report to the police. We see her reluctance to identify or name the incident as rape, her concerns about self-blame and the attacker's retaliation, and also the shame she feels:

> Um, I didn't know how to, I didn't realise that was what I was actually upset about, I know that sounds really stupid but…no I was just stuck. … It took me a while to gather up the courage to say 'that's it', because I was worried, stupid worries like he'd come after me and stuff, which was totally unfounded but… And I wasn't really sure in my head what had happened, 'because we'd been going out for so long did I have the right to say no?', 'did he hear me say no?', 'was that right?', 'did I actually say it?', and then I started questioning myself. … Because I feel terrible, and I should have, but at the time I just couldn't, you know it took me a while to work out…'was I over reacting?', I still wonder if I am over reacting, and 'have I done the wrong thing?', and 'is it my fault?', 'how did I make it happen?', 'I should have got up then' and 'I should have done this' and the endless questioning…

Other respondents also highlight the difficulty women have in naming (Kelly 1988) an experience as rape and that this personal naming may take some time to happen, and may be some months, or even years, after the incident:

> Yes definitely, I just kind of, immediately I just went oh that didn't happen and kind of got on with my night, and

> then afterwards I told a couple of people, one of whom did
> kind of say to me look that was assault, what happened to
> you and I did go oh my god but then the shock kind of
> came back in again and I just didn't really engage with it
> for quite a few months after it happened.

Additionally, a common theme in interviews with survivors was the
feelings of guilt and embarrassment that characterise the aftermath
of sexual violence. Survivors often report feelings of guilt about the
incident, and a feeling they are somehow responsible, and many feel
embarrassed disclosing they have experienced rape. This is likely to be
exacerbated in circumstances where they have to provide details of what
happened, as the following two excerpts show:

> ...even though I have reported it now I still feel guilty, and
> I still feel embarrassed about it.

> It's such an embarrassment for me, I can't tell anyone. How
> can you tell anyone that stuff?

Part of the consequence of women's difficulty in naming sexually violent
experiences, and their experience of embarrassment, guilt and shame, is
that it reduces their likelihood of engaging with support agencies, not
just criminal justice agencies, and it therefore makes disclosure to other
'helping' professionals, such as social work, less likely. It also makes the
responses of professionals, including the police and social work, of vital
importance in order not to compound this shame and embarrassment, or
to question the naming women have attached to their experiences. This
need for sensitive response and intervention will be discussed in more
detail below.

Existing research also tells us that survivors are especially reluctant
to report if their abuser is known to them (Greenfield 1997; Koss 1993;
Koss and Heslet 1992; Stanko 1984), and as we have seen from this
current research project (above), this is most often the case. The findings
show that disclosure can be particularly problematic for survivors when
their attacker is a family member because any allegation of violence
within the family can challenge taboos that imbue families and lead
to stigma (McKie 2005). There are many potential consequences for
survivors when they disclose sexual violence from a family member and
social work practitioners may be called upon to intervene in such family
situations. Part of the reluctance of women to disclose familial assault
was that they did not want their family to find out what had happened

and a desire to protect other members of the family from distress. For example:

> Just I didn't want to hurt her (mother), still now I just feel,
> I think that's what part of the guilty feeling is, I feel guilty
> that I have hurt her, which I haven't hurt her at all.

It is also evident from this quote that survivors can also feel responsible for the feelings of others if they do think about disclosing, with this survivor highlighting her feelings of guilt. Another survivor indicated she felt reluctant to disclose her assault because she feared she would ruin the family's Christmas celebration:

> Just because it was Christmas and I didn't, I felt like I'd
> ruin Christmas...

Other complicating factors for women who are raped by family members is fear that they will not be believed by other members of the family and that rather than being supported they would be vilified. For example:

> And if I had actually made a complaint I would have been
> slapped down and told to just, oh stop, you're pathetic.

> I would not get support from the police or my family
> and to be honest with you if my family are not going to
> support me it's just my word against his.

> I have often thought the day my mum dies and she is
> buried I will go to the police. I cannot do it all the while
> my mum is alive.

Cohen (2001) also recognises the capacity of families to know about violence but fail to acknowledge it. He says that family members have an:

> astonishing capacity to ignore or pretend to ignore what
> happens in front of their eyes, whether sexual abuse, incest,
> violence, alcoholism, or just plain unhappiness... The
> family's distinctive self-image determines which aspects of
> shared experience can be openly acknowledged and which
> must remain closed and denied. (p.64)

This is aptly illustrated by the third quotation above where the survivor indicated that she could not disclose to the police until her mother has died; to do otherwise would violate these rules. It is very likely that feelings like these contribute to the delayed reporting of rapes that occur within the context of child sexual abuse, and the review of case files confirms that significant changes in a family structure, for example the death of a parent or the relocation of family members, can precipitate delayed reporting.

This leads us to survivors' fear of not being believed, which we know is a significant deterrent to reporting (Kelly and Regan 2003; McMillan and Thomas 2009). The research findings from this current project also highlight this (see excerpt below), and the importance to victims of being believed will also be discussed in more detail in relation to the challenges of engagement with state agencies, below.

> …he's absolutely charming as well my ex-husband, so that kind of, you know, he's much better at lying than I am or at putting on a good front of things than I am so I thought they are much more likely to believe him than they are to believe me.

Additionally, survivors who had experienced cumulative abuse in either the context of child sexual abuse, or in the context of an intimate relationship, were concerned that in disclosing, questions would be raised about why they had not reported earlier incidents. This was evident both from comments in the case files, and from interviews with survivors:

> Yeah, yeah or maybe impact on, how they, they, if they believed me or not. I don't know about how they treated me but certainly about if they believed me because if I had let it go so many times before why was I complaining now.

But it was also the case for some women that the accumulation of rapes from the same assailant actually precipitated disclosure:

> I couldn't take it anymore. I'd had enough.

It was evident from case files and from survivor interviews that whilst it was certainly not an easy decision to report their rape to the police, those who were assaulted by strangers were likely to experience it as a more 'clear cut' decision and more likely to identify and name it as rape, and as a criminal act. For example:

> I knew it had to be reported to the police so I didn't mind. It was a criminal offence what he did to me so…obviously had to let the police know, because someone who could do this was out in the public.

What these findings show is that the decision to disclose rape and to report to the police is a complex decision for most women and several things are likely to influence the decision. We also know from existing research that secondary victimisation in the justice system, that is, poor treatment by criminal justice personnel, deters reporting (Byrne and Kilpatrick 1999; Chesney-Lind 1999; Hudson 1998) and may make women reluctant to engage with state agencies (criminal justice or otherwise). But all agencies of the state are charged with addressing the causes and consequences of violence against women. This is particularly important because survivors may contact many agencies for support (Campbell 1998) before or after the police, and as noted above, the case review for this research revealed that many women disclosed to professionals other than the police in the first instance. In order to address the causes and consequences of violence, agencies of the state (including social work) have a duty to ensure practices are fit for purpose, and do not victimise or traumatise women further. It is to this issue I will now turn and examine women's engagement with criminal justice agencies and what we can learn from this for other aspects of practice.

Challenges of engagement with the justice process

The impact of sexual violence can be significant as was discussed above, but can also be worsened by the response survivors receive from their community and wider society. An increasing body of literature shows survivors often feel they are denied support and help by their communities, and what help they do receive can result in them feeling revictimised (Campbell 1998; Campbell and Bybee 1997; Frohmann 1991; Madigan and Gamble 1991; Martin and Powell 1994; Matoesian 1993; Williams 1984). This revictimisation can be particularly prevalent in the criminal justice process and social workers supporting women and/or their families going through this process should be aware of the challenges women are likely to face.

Research tells us that criminal justice personnel are likely to make judgements about women's behaviour at the time of the incident and to convey to survivors, either explicitly or implicitly, that they believe their behaviour may have been questionable (Frohmann 1991, 1997, 1998; Kerstetter 1990; LaFree 1989; Spohn, Beichner and Davis-Frenzel 2001). This experience for survivors can be very damaging and can make disclosure to other professionals, for example medical and mental health, less likely; services that survivors may already find it difficult to access (Campbell *et al.* 1999). The criminal justice system in England and Wales, and elsewhere, has been subjected to significant criticism for assessing the credibility and truthfulness of victims of rape and sexual violence using stereotypical assumptions about gender-appropriate behaviour and moral conduct (see Stanko and Williams 2009; McMillan 2010). It is the case that criminal justice personnel use a number of myths and stereotypes about women, and about rape and sexual violence, when making judgements about rapes reported to them.

These myths and stereotypes contribute to the reasons for low conviction rates and high attrition rates (see Harris and Grace 1999; Kelly, Lovett and Regan 2005; McMillan 2010), but also to the potential for secondary victimisation of those who report rape and sexual assault. We know from existing research that a fear of not being believed is a significant deterrent for women to engage with the justice process (Bachman 1998; Felson and Paré 2005; Kelly and Regan 2003) and it is likely a significant deterrent for disclosure to other state agencies. Additionally, we also know that when women perceive that they are disbelieved when they do engage with authorities, this can be particularly difficult for them (McMillan and Thomas 2009).

It is of vital importance when women do disclose experiences of sexual violence that any support or intervention that is offered is sensitive and does not contribute to this secondary victimisation. This research project revealed that in particular when sexual violence occurs within an ongoing intimate or familial relationship, survivors are likely to be concerned that on disclosing, pressure will be put on them to leave the relationship or family, as noted by the respondent below when discussing their concern about having gone to the police:

> How can you say that? How can you say, because anyone outside of it you'd go well...bloody hell if someone said that to me I'd be like you've got to go, you've got to leave, so I knew in my head that I'd get... I knew I had to go but then it's people sort of saying to you you've got to go, and then already you're feeling... I mean just the lowest of low aren't you.

Additionally, when becoming involved with statutory agencies, women may begin to feel like 'victims' as this is the status accorded to those who experience sexual violence when they engage with the justice process in particular. Whilst some women may resonate with the meaning of 'victim' in relation to their experience of rape – in that they have been harmed, wronged and violated – it is a status that many women are reluctant to take on in that it differentiates them from others and does not recognise their capacity to heal and survive:

> Yeah. I am *so* worried that I am now just a victim, and that makes me a different kind of person as well…it's not something you talk about in polite society, I even worry about telling my parents [half laughs], which is weird 'cause I've technically done nothing wrong, but there is still a huge taboo around it.

During the research interview survivors were asked what concerns they had about engaging in the justice process. Interestingly this revealed concerns about their lives being 'taken over' by the incident and the aftermath of it. In particular, survivors were concerned with people 'crawling all over' their lives, and a big 'drama' being created. For example:

> If I tell, people will be crawling all over my life.

> I didn't want a massive drama and I didn't want our mutual friends to be involved in a massive drama either, so that was definitely a concern.

> Mainly because everyone would know, everyone would find out and my life wouldn't be my own anymore.

What this draws attention to is that survivors have a real concern about losing their autonomy and agency and highlights that any involvement with criminal justice agencies, and indeed other statutory agencies like social work, must allow for women's agency and must not disempower them further. Survivors are also often aware of the protracted and difficult process ahead of them when they do engage with criminal justice, as this survivor notes:

> Would I deal with it or actually go through the process because (pause) to be battered and bruised even further with a process that is absolutely relentless I don't know if I would have the strength, I think I am a pretty strong person but, but would I not turn the other cheek, but would I just try and deal with it and get on with it.

Given this, it is not surprising that many women withdraw from the criminal justice process sometime after reporting the incident (Stanko and Williams 2009; McMillan 2010). Indeed, analysis of data in the case review for this research shows a withdrawal rate of 34 per cent (n = 140). It is also therefore important not to assume that withdrawal from the justice process, or withdrawal from engagement with other statutory agencies, means that rape and sexual assault did not happen. Rather, it means women are exercising their agency and capacity for choice to say they do not want to be subjected to the challenges inherent in engagement.

The research also revealed that the challenges that all women (and men) survivors of sexual violence face when engaging with the police may be particularly marked or experienced particularly acutely by those with additional vulnerabilities. For example, the following excerpt from a survivor who has mental health issues shows her concern at how she would be perceived:

> Well because mental health questions how you perceive reality, how on earth can that be tried and tested in a court of law? ... And... I don't know, women can be seen as drama queens and attention seeking and that goes with mental health issues. You think about society's perceptions of somebody who says 'I am depressed', a lot of people think they are whinging over nothing, so you'd get a double whammy of judgement, first of all saying that you'd been raped and secondly saying that you'd got mental health issues, you can't get past that.

This quote aptly illustrates the concern women feel about how they will be received by authorities and whether other aspects of themselves or their lives will be used to question their experiences of rape and sexual assault. Given the capacity of state agencies to revictimize survivors, often through seemingly 'innocent' practices and questioning (McMillan and Thomas 2009), it is of vital importance to approach all intervention and interaction with survivors with the utmost sensitivity, and to seek to challenge myths and stereotypes when they are exhibited by ourselves or our colleagues.

Conclusion

It is clear from this recent research that women's decision to disclose sexual violence to anyone, and to engage in criminal justice processes, is quite a complex one and there are clear and understandable reasons why women may be reluctant to do so. It is also evident when women do disclose to criminal justice authorities that there are aspects of the process that are likely to be particularly challenging. What is also notable is that following any disclosure it is of particular importance that women are met with sensitive interventions and not ones that further traumatise or contribute to the 'second rape' (Madigan and Gamble 1991). Given that women may disclose to any number of statutory agencies and may seek help from many different sources (Campbell 1998), including social work, it is vitally important that practitioners are equipped with the knowledge and understanding to support women, to provide sensitive interventions and to increase women's agency rather than to further disempower them.

Further, where social workers are involved with individual women – and potentially their families when sexual violence takes place in intimate relationships and/or among family members – who decide to use the criminal justice process it is likely that support will be required for what is often a difficult and protracted process (particularly when the women involved have additional vulnerabilities). The overwhelming majority of rape and sexual violence is not reported to the police and for those that are, very few will end in conviction (see McMillan 2010), and therefore the dominant form of 'justice' that women experience is unlikely to be from criminal justice. As such, other state agencies, such as social work, have the capacity to provide alternative forms of 'justice' through caring and compassionate engagement and intervention, and to support women in their journey from 'victim' to survivor.

References

Bachar, K. and Koss, M.P. (2001) 'From Prevalence to Prevention: Closing the Gap Between What We Know About Rape and What We Do.' In C.M. Renzetti, J.L. Edleson and R.K. Bergen (eds) *Sourcebook on Violence Against Women*. Thousand Oaks, CA: SAGE.

Bachman, R. (1998) 'Factors related to rape reporting and arrest: New evidence from the NCVS.' *Criminal Justice and Behaviour 25*, 1, 8–29.

Bryman, A. (2008) *Social Research Methods*, Third Edition. Oxford: Oxford University Press.

Byrne, C.A. and Kilpatrick, D.G. (1999) 'Female victims of partner versus non-partner violence: experience with the criminal justice system.' *Criminal Justice and Behaviour 26*, 3, 275–292.

Campbell, R. (1998) 'The community response to rape: victims' experiences with the legal, medical and mental health systems.' *American Journal of Community Psychology 26*, 3, 355–379.

Campbell, R. (2008) 'The psychological impact of rape victims' experiences with the legal, medical, and mental health systems.' *American Psychologist 63*, 8, 702–717.

Campbell, R. and Bybee, D. (1997) 'Emergency medical services for rape victims: detecting the cracks in service delivery.' *Women's Health Research on Gender, Behaviour and Policy 3*, 2, 75–101.

Campbell, R., Sefl, T., Barnes, H.E., Ahrens, C.E., Wasco, S.M. and Zaragoza-Diesfeld, Y. (1999) 'Community services for rape survivors: Enhancing psychological well-being or increasing trauma?' *Journal of Consulting and Clinical Psychology 67*, 6, 847–858.

Chesney-Lind, M. (1999) 'Challenging girls' invisibility in juvenile court.' *Annals of the American Academy of Political and Social Science 564*, 1, 185–202.

Cohen, S. (2001) *States of Denial.* Cambridge: Polity Press.

Felson, R. and Paré, P. (2005) 'The reporting of domestic violence and sexual assault by non-strangers to the police.' *Journal of Marriage and Family 67*, 3, 597–610.

Frohmann, L. (1991) 'Discrediting victims' allegations of sexual assault: Prosecutorial accounts of case rejection.' *Social Problems 38*, 2, 213–226.

Frohmann, L. (1997) 'Convictability and discordant locales: Reproducing race, class and gender ideologies in prosecutorial decision making.' *Law and Society Review 31*, 3, 531–555.

Frohmann, L. (1998) 'Constituting power in sexual assault cases: Prosecutorial strategies for victim management.' *Social Problems 45*, 3, 393–407.

Greenfield, L. (1997) *Sex Offences and Sex Offenders: An Analysis of Date Rape and Sexual Assault.* US Department of Justice Bureau of Justice Statistics, NCJ-163392.

Harris, J. and Grace, S. (1999) *A Question of Evidence? Investigating and Prosecuting Rape in the 1990s.* Research Study Number 196. London: Home Office.

Hudson, B. (1998) 'Restorative justice: The challenge of sexual and racial violence.' *The Journal of Law and Society 25*, 2, 237–256.

Kelly, L. (1988) *Surviving Sexual Violence.* Cambridge: Polity Press.

Kelly, L. and Regan, L. (2003) *Rape: Still a Forgotten Issue.* London: Child and Women Abuse Studies Unit.

Kelly, L., Lovett, J. and Regan, L. (2005) *A Gap or a Chasm: Attrition in Reported Rape Cases.* London: Home Office Research Study.

Kerstetter, W.A. (1990) 'Gateway to justice: Police and prosecutorial response to sexual assaults against women.' *Journal of Criminal Law and Criminology 81*, 2, 267–313.

Kessler, R.C., Sonnega, A., Bromet, E., Hughes, H. and Nelson, C.B. (1995) 'Post-traumatic Stress Disorder in the National Co-morbidity Survey.' *Archives of General Psychiatry 52*, 12, 1048–60.

Koss, M.P. (1993) 'Rape: Scope, impact, interventions and public policy reponses.' *American Psychologist 48*, 10, 1062–1069.

Koss, M.P. and Harvey M.R. (1991) *The Rape Victim: Clinical and Community Interventions.* Newbury Park, CA: Sage.

Koss, M.P. and Heslet, L. (1992) 'Somatic consequences of violence against women.' *Archives of Family Medicine 1*, 1, 53–59.

Koss, M.P., Koss, P.G. and Woodruff, J. (1991) 'Deleterious effects of criminal victimization on women's health and medical utilization.' *Archives of Internal Medicine 151*, 342–347.

LaFree, G. (1989) *Rape and Criminal Justice: The Social Construction of Sexual Assault,* Belmont, CA: Wadsworth.

Madigan, L. and Gamble, N. (1991) *The Second Rape: Society's Continued Betrayal of the Victim.* New York: Lexington.

Martin, P.Y. and Powell, M.R. (1994) 'Accounting for the "second assault".' *Law and Social Inquiry 19*, 4, 853–890.

Matoesian, G.M. (1993) *Reproducing Rape: Domination Through Talk in the Courtroom.* Chicago: Chicago University Press.

McKie, L. (2005) *Families, Violence and Social Change.* Buckingham: Open University Press.

McMahon, S. and Schwartz, R. (2011) 'A review of rape in the social work literature: A call to action.' *Affilia: Journal of Women and Social Work 26*, 3, 250–263.

McMillan, L. (2007) *Feminists Organizing Against Gendered Violence.* London: Palgrave.

McMillan, L. (2010) *Understanding Attrition in Rape Cases ESRC End of Award Report.* RES-061-23-0138-A. Swindon: ESRC.

McMillan, L. (2011) 'Sexual Violence Policy in Europe: Human Rights, Policies and Outcomes.' In M. Koch, L. McMillan and B. Peper (eds) *Diversity, Standardization and Social Transformation: Gender, Ethnicity and Inequality in Europe.* Farnham: Ashgate.

McMillan, L. and Thomas, M. (2009) 'Police Interviews of Rape Victims: Tensions and Contradictions.' In M. Horvath and J. Brown (eds) *Rape: Challenging Contemporary Thinking.* Cullompton: Willan Publishing.

Myhill, A. and Allen, J. (2002) *Rape and Sexual Assault of Women: The Extent and Nature of the Problem – Findings from the British Crime Survey.* London: Home Office Research Study.

New, M. and Berliner, L. (2000) 'Mental Health Service Utilization by Victims of Crime.' *Journal of Traumatic Stress 13,* 4, 693–707.

Painter, K. (1991) *Wife Rape, Marriage and the Law: Survey Report Key Findings and Recommendations.* Manchester: Manchester University, Department of Social Policy and Social Work.

Plichta, S.B. and Falik, M. (2001) 'Prevalence of violence and its implications for women's health.' *Women's Health Issues 11,* 3, 234–247.

Russell, D. (1982) *Rape in Marriage.* New York: Macmillan.

Russell, D. (1984) *Sexual Exploitation.* Beverley Hills: Sage.

Spohn, C. and Trellis, K. (2012) 'The Criminal Justice System's Response to Sexual Violence.' *Violence Against Women 18,* 2, 169–192.

Spohn, C., Beichner, D. and Davis-Frenzel, E. (2001) 'Prosecutorial explanations for sexual assault case rejection: Guarding the gateway to justice.' *Social Problems 48,* 2, 206–235.

Stanko, E. (1984) 'Fear of Crime and the Myth of the Safe Home.' In K. Yllo, and M. Bograd (eds) *Feminist Perspectives on Wife Abuse.* Newbury Park, CA: Sage.

Stanko, E. and Williams, E. (2009) 'Reviewing Rape and Rape Allegations in London: What are the Vulnerabilities of the Victims who Report to the Police?' In M. Horvath and J. Brown (eds) *Rape: Challenging Contemporary Thinking.* Cullompton: Willan Publishing.

Ullman, S.E. (2007) 'Mental health services seeking in sexual assault victims.' *Women and Therapy 30,* 1-2, 61–84.

UNICEF (1997) *The Progress of Nations.* New York: UNICEF.

Waigandt, A., Wallace, D.L., Phelps, L. and Miller, D.A. (1990) 'The impact of sexual assault on physical health status.' *Journal of Traumatic Stress 3,* 1, 93–102.

Walby, S. and Allen, J. (2004) *Domestic Violence, Sexual Assault and Stalking: Findings from the British Crime Survey.* London: Home Office Research Study.

Williams, J.E. (1984) 'Secondary victimisation: confronting public attitudes about rape.' *Victimology 9,* 1, 66–81.

World Health Organisation (2005) *The Solid Facts on Unintentional Injuries and Violence in the WHO European Region.* Geneva: World Health Organisation.

CHAPTER 5

Violence Against Sex Workers in the UK

Alison Phipps

In 2008, truck driver Steve Wright was found guilty of the murders of five street sex workers: Gemma Adams, Anneli Alderton, Paula Clennell, Tania Nicol and Annette Nicholls. All were drug users between the ages of 19 and 29. Wright dumped their remains in isolated spots around the town of Ipswich during a six-and-a-half-week period in 2006 (Malkin 2008). In 2010, PhD student Stephen Griffiths, who termed himself the 'crossbow cannibal', was convicted of the murders of street sex workers Shelley Armitage, Suzanne Blamires and Susan Rushworth, after body parts were found floating in the river Aire. The women, all drug users aged between 31 and 43, had disappeared over a period of just under a year (Carter 2010; Press Association 2010). The £300-an-hour call girl blogger Belle du Jour, revealed in 2009 to be Bristol research scientist Dr Brooke Magnanti, may appear to be working in a different industry to these women. However, in an interview with the *Times* in 2009, Magnanti described herself as 'very lucky' because she had not experienced violence as she had known many others who had. 'You need to be aware of your surroundings: if it goes wrong, how can I get out of this room; how can I get into a taxi; how can I brush someone off if I need to?' (Knight 2009).

Although sex work is a multi-faceted industry with a diverse workforce, a central feature is the risk, or experience, of violence. Sex workers are a resourceful group, who as individuals and communities have developed a complex set of coping and safety strategies. These do not often bring them into contact with statutory services: but social workers in these and third sector organisations who are aware of the issues and can operate without judgement may be able to offer support.

Introduction

In the last 30 years demand for commercial sex has soared in Western countries. Sex is now a multi-billion dollar industry, thriving alongside efforts by governments and police forces to regulate or obliterate it (Bernstein 2001). This explosion of demand sits within the social and economic context of late capitalism, with its merging of public and private, extension of the service sector and commodification of experiences, including sexual ones (Bernstein 2001; Brents and Hausbeck 2007). It also reflects a general trend for commercial specialisation, encompassing text, image and video pornography, live sex shows, strip and lap-dancing clubs, telephone and cyber-sex companies, escort agencies, independent sex workers and organised sex tourism. Parts of this industry, such as soft pornography, lap-dancing clubs and high-class escorts are becoming more mainstream, with the ITV drama *Secret Diary of a Call Girl*, based on Belle du Jour's blog, averaging 1,242,125 viewers per episode for its first series and currently in planning for its fourth (Broadcasters' Audience Research Board 2007). However, other sectors such as street prostitution remain marginal and stigmatised, with workers suffering from low wages and poor conditions (Brents and Hausbeck 2007, pp.427–428).

This chapter looks at violence against sex workers participating in prostitution, who engage in sexual acts with another person or persons as part of a commercial transaction.[1] This industry is divided into indoor and outdoor markets, outdoor workers soliciting on the street while indoor workers provide services in brothels/massage parlours/saunas, hotels or private homes. There is no reliable data on the number of sex workers or their clients in the UK, since these populations remain largely underground. However, researchers working for the UK Network of Sex Work Projects estimate that there may be over 100,000 prostituted people (mostly women) in the UK (Cusick *et al.* 2009). Seventy per cent

---

1   The term 'sex worker', as used in this chapter, will therefore refer to these workers and does not include strippers, lap dancers, phone and cyber sex workers or actors and models involved in pornography. This chapter also looks solely at women involved in sex work, in keeping with the focus of this book on violence against women. However, this is not to imply that male sex workers are not also at risk of violence.

of sex work is carried out indoors, a sector which is growing rapidly via the internet (Kinnell 2008, p.110; Sanders 2006, pp.92–94). Sex workers are concentrated in towns and cities, and tend to reflect the ethnic composition of these areas.

Women working in the sex industry normally enter it before they are 21 years of age, and many report childhood abuse or periods spent in care (Home Office 2004). However, there are differences between street and indoor workers: women who work in indoor markets are less likely to be from socially excluded backgrounds, and it is common for them to have been involved in mainstream work and to have professional credentials. Indoor workers are also less likely to report chronic/acute illnesses and more likely to be registered with a GP, and have limited levels of drug use compared with the high levels of street workers (Sanders 2007).

The average user of sexual services in the UK is male, around 30 years old, employed full time, married, and with no criminal convictions (Home Office 2004). Studies internationally have highlighted the similarities between users of sex workers and so-called 'ordinary' men (Monto 2004, p.168), and paying for sexual services is rapidly becoming normalised. The National Survey of Sexual Attitudes conducted in 2001 found that 4.3 per cent of British men admitted having paid for sex in the past five years (Home Office 2004, p.17).

Throughout the UK, the exchange of sexual services for money is not illegal. However, associated activities including street soliciting, advertising in telephone boxes, kerb crawling, pimping and brothel-keeping are criminal offences.[2] In the 2000s, there was widespread debate about whether England and Wales should follow the example set by countries such as the Netherlands and New Zealand and institute more permissive laws. However, ideas for initiatives such as tolerance zones for street prostitution (previously implemented in Scotland) and legalising small brothels were eventually abandoned by the New Labour government in favour of a tighter legal framework criminalising demand and attempting to deal with exploitation. In 2009, provisions in the Policing and Crime Act (applying to England, Wales and Northern Ireland) made it illegal for a client to pay for services from a sex worker who had been subject to force, even if the client thought they were

---

2 A brothel is constituted by more than one sex worker working from an indoor premises: plans to review this definition in light of threats to the safety of lone sex workers were abandoned in 2006.

freely consenting. The act also introduced tougher police powers in relation to kerb-crawling (making it illegal for the first time in Northern Ireland) and solicitation, and new powers to close brothels (UK Parliament 2009). In Scotland, kerb-crawling was outlawed in 2007, by the Prostitution (Public Places) (Scotland) Act (McMillan 2010; Scottish Parliament 2007): similarly, this Act was passed after a failed debate around introducing a more liberal legislative structure. Following the 2010 'crossbow cannibal' case, British Prime Minister David Cameron promised a review of prostitution legislation (Edwards and Whitehead 2010). However, at the time of writing this review was not under way and it was unclear what direction any discussion might take.

Prevalence of violence against sex workers

In general, it is highly likely that sex workers will experience violence. This can take a variety of forms ranging from harassment to robbery, physical assault, rape and murder. These acts may be perpetrated in both public and private spheres, by clients, pimps, other sex workers, intimate partners, police, or members of local communities (Benson 1998 cited in Sanders 2004; Campbell, Coleman and Torkington 1996 cited in Sanders 2004; Hubbard 1998; May, Harocopos and Hough 2000; Sanders 2004). Street sex workers are thought to be at very high risk, particularly of more extreme forms of violence (Busch et al. 2002; Jeal and Salisbury 2004b; Penfold et al. 2004; Sanders 2008a). In a 2001 study of three British cities, it was found that 81 per cent of street workers had experienced violence (Church et al. 2001). A 1999 study of 193 street workers found that 68 per cent had experienced physical assault (Ward, Day and Weber 1999), and in 2004, a study of 125 street workers in five cities found that three-quarters had experienced physical violence (Hester and Westmarland 2004). A 2004 study of 71 street workers in Bristol (Jeal and Salisbury 2004a) found that rape and physical violence using weapons such as guns, machetes and chainsaws had been experienced by 73 per cent. Between the early 1990s and early 2000s, at least 60 sex workers were known to have been murdered in the UK, most working on the street (Penfold et al. 2004, p.366), and it has been estimated that street sex workers are 12 times more likely to die from violence at work than other women (Sanders and Campbell 2007, p.2).[3]

The high risk of violence faced by street sex workers is often attributed to the drug-saturated nature of these markets and the general levels of violence this creates, as well as the need for 'survival sex' with clients who may not have been adequately vetted (Sanders 2004, 2007). It can also be linked to the criminalisation of the sex worker, which creates the possibility of conflicts with police officers, encourages reprisals from members of the public, and means that sex work is undertaken at particular hours of the day and night (often the most dangerous ones) and clients are accepted in a hurry (Hubbard 2001; Penfold et al. 2004; Sanders 2004, 2007; Sanders and Campbell 2007). Crackdowns on street sex work have been blamed for a cycle of arrests, convictions and fines (paid off through further sex work), and geographical displacement of sex workers as they avoid ASBOs and raids (Penfold et al. 2004; Hubbard 2006; Kinnell 2008; Sanders 2004, 2008b).

There is also a gender politics at work in the issue of sex workers and violence. The belief that sex workers can be treated differently from other women (Monto and Hotaling 2001) is partly due to the impression (and reality) that there will be few reprisals when they are attacked (Penfold et al. 2004). In addition, research with clients indicates that although rape-supportive attitudes are not particularly prevalent, they may feel that the exchange of money discharges them from the consideration and respect associated with relationships (Plumridge, Chetwynd and Reed 1997; Monto 2004). However, this 'discourse of disposability' around sex workers (Sanders 2007, p.793) observed among both clients and law enforcement is linked at a deeper level to their social marginalisation and position at the bottom of the hierarchy of femininity between Madonna and whore (Phipps 2009).

Due to the matrix of push/pull factors which can structure the entry of sex workers into the industry, as well as evidence around the prevalence of childhood sexual abuse experiences and dissociation strategies, some feminists see the buying and selling of sex as an intrinsic

---

3   Sex workers who have been subjected to coerced migration or trafficking are also thought to be at high risk of violence (Sullivan 2003), and migrant sex workers in general (who may work on the street or indoors and are thought to constitute around 37% of female sex workers in the UK) are highly unlikely to report crimes or seek support (UK Network of Sex Work Projects 2008a). However, trafficking is a complex phenomenon which could easily be the topic of a book chapter in itself, so it will not be covered here.

harm and sex work itself as a form of violence against women (see e.g. Dworkin 1981; Jeffreys 2008). Within this formulation, the sex industry is an ideal environment for aggressive misogyny because it is built upon men's rights to purchase and use women's bodies. However, this view is challenged by those who see sex work as a choice (Agustín 2007), and violence against sex workers as the product of a repressive society in which neuroses about sex are violently displaced on to the body of the liberated sex worker (Johnson 2006).

In contrast to the environment of the street, indoor sex work is often portrayed as consensual and non-violent (McElroy 1998; Weitzer 2000). Sanders (2006) argues that indoor workers operate in a professional and entrepreneurial occupational culture which helps protect them from harm. It is true that the location of indoor workers in the private sphere lessens street-based harassment and can lighten police regulation, although from 2000 onwards indoor markets became more of a focal point for law enforcement due to concerns about immigration and trafficking (Kinnell 2008). Indoor workers also tend to form stronger bonds with clients and to provide emotional input alongside sexual services, which may lessen some risks (Plumridge et al. 1997; Monto 2004; Sanders 2008a) but which may also create new ones, for instance the possibility of stalking. There is certainly evidence of indoor workers managing their own businesses and having more control over their working environments and activities. However, the unregulated nature of indoor markets means that workers can still be exposed to exploitative management and unsafe working conditions (Sanders 2007). Additionally, the law against two or more indoor workers working together creates isolation and risk of robbery and violence (Sanders 2006, 2007).

Furthermore, the statistics tell us that indoor sex work is not non-violent. In the study of three British cities mentioned above (Church et al. 2001), 48 per cent of indoor workers reported violence: this high level of victimisation is often overshadowed by the even higher figures on street workers. Kinnell's (2008, pp.116–136) study conducted in London between 2000 and 2005 found an average of 97 attacks on indoor workers per year. Indoor workers are also vulnerable to robbery by clients and harassment from local communities (Sanders 2005; Sanders and Campbell 2007). For the purpose of this chapter, I conducted research on an online message board hosted by the organisation Support and Advice for Escorts and found 118 incidents of violence reported by indoor workers in the UK between 2007 and 2009, many involving more than one type of offence. Twenty-five per cent of these involved physical and sexual violence, 25 per cent robbery, and 30 per cent physical and sexual harassment (including stalking). Almost half the incidents involved more than one sex worker, and a fifth involved five or more sex workers. Only 15 of these incidents had been reported to the police.

Research conducted internationally also shows risks to indoor workers: a Chicago study found that the types of violence perpetrated against them, namely sexual violence and being threatened with weapons, were often more serious than the physical violence which was a fact of life for street workers (Raphael and Shapiro 2004). It has been argued that a relatively small number of clients are responsible for this violence and that they may offend more than once (Penfold *et al.* 2004, p.366), which is supported by some of the empirical data. However, less extreme forms of violence such as harassment may be more widely perpetrated and yet normalised and therefore invisible.

Experiencing violence and seeking support

There is little information on sex workers' experiences of violence and general emotional wellbeing (Jackson, Bennett and Sowinski 2007). However, available evidence suggests that they feel the same psychological effects as other women. A high percentage of sex workers suffer from post-traumatic stress disorder (PTSD), symptoms of which are acute anxiety, depression, insomnia, irritability, flashbacks, emotional numbing, and a state of emotional and physical hyperalertness (Farley and Barkan 1998). In a study conducted in the late 1990s, 67 per cent of sex workers surveyed in five countries (South Africa, Thailand, Turkey, USA, Zambia) met the criteria for a diagnosis of PTSD, a rate similar to that of battered women, rape survivors, and state-sponsored torture survivors (Farley *et al.* 1998). There are also more general emotional stresses around managing unsavoury and potentially violent clients, witnessing violence, and knowing other workers who have been attacked and even killed (Romero-Daza, Weeks and Singer 2003; Jackson *et al.* 2007).

In addition to these emotional issues, there are physical injuries to be dealt with (Fick 2005), which can have a long-term effect. An extreme example is that of a street worker quoted in Giobbe (1992, p.126):

> I've had three broken arms, nose broken twice, [and] I'm partially deaf in one ear… I have a small fragment of a bone floating in my head that gives me migraines. I've had a fractured skull. My legs ain't worth shit no more; my toes

have been broken. My feet, bottom of my feet, have been burned; they've been whopped with a hot iron and clothes hanger...the hair on my pussy had been burned off at one time...I have scars. I've been cut with a knife, beat with guns, two by fours. There hasn't been a place on my body that hasn't been bruised somehow.

A variety of health problems are related to physical and sexual violence. High rates of the sexually transmitted infections chlamydia, gonorrhoea, pelvic inflammatory disease and Hepatitis C have been identified amongst sex workers, as well as frequent terminations of pregnancies and a high likelihood of infertility (Home Office 2004, p.42). HIV levels are indirectly linked to violence through intravenous drug use, a common coping mechanism (Surratt *et al.* 2004). Sex workers often suffer chronic ill-health: an interview survey of 71 street workers in Bristol, of whom 73 per cent had experienced extreme forms of violence, found that all reported long-term health issues and drug or alcohol dependency, and that STIs were up to 60 times more common than in the general population (Jeal and Salisbury 2004a). Women involved in sex work have an 80 per cent chance of suffering depression (Bagley 1999), and links have also been made to low self-esteem and eating disorders (Fick 2005; Sanders 2005). These problems can all lead to an inability to work and loss of earnings, and sex workers who have been robbed can find themselves in debt and poverty (Phoenix 2000). Those who flee from violent clients, the police or community retribution may become homeless, and for those who stay put, the threat of community or police violence can confine them to their homes (Fick 2005).

Long-term effects of violence can also include its normalisation as an aspect of the job, which can lead to further victimisation due to a lack of vigilance in accepting clients or acceptance of aggressive behaviour (Fick 2005; Sanders 2005; Surratt *et al.* 2004). Conversely, the stress of having to remain watchful can cause fearfulness, anxiety and isolation and means that like other women, sex workers are highly likely to blame themselves when they are attacked (Fick 2005). Drug use connected to violence may create a cycle in which women become lax about vetting clients due to their need for a hit (Jackson *et al.* 2007; Romero-Daza *et al.* 2003). This all contributes to the repeat victimisation, often beginning in childhood, which has been identified among many sex workers (Surratt *et al.* 2004). Sex workers' coping strategies, which have been likened to those of sexual abuse survivors, include blanking out, maintaining strict boundaries, avoiding intimate relationships, constructing rationalisation narratives and using clothing and beauty rituals to act in and out of the sex worker role (Sanders 2005). They often rely on these in the absence of other forms of support, since stigmatisation and social marginalisation mean that either help is not readily available or they are unlikely to seek it (Fick 2005; Romero-Daza *et al.* 2003). Sex workers rarely approach statutory services, and although they may be registered with a health care provider do not often disclose their line of work, usually due to fear of judgement or prosecution (Jeal and Salisbury 2004b). They also have little contact with non-governmental services such as Rape Crisis (Surratt *et al.* 2004).

The main source of support available to outdoor sex workers comes from sex work projects, which operate largely in cities and provide drop-in and outreach in the areas of sexual and mental health, and support and advocacy for women who have experienced violence. These projects operate within a non-judgemental framework, which makes sex workers more likely to seek them out than to avail themselves of statutory assistance (Jackson *et al.* 2007). Indoor workers may also access these projects, and these workers may have additional provision from (sympathetic) employers and online communities. As a result of their higher levels of education (Sanders 2007) and better access to information technology, many indoor sex workers are active on the internet (Holt and Blevins 2007). A large number of internet communities have formed around the sale and purchase of commercial sex, operating via websites or message boards on which sex workers post advertisements, clients post reviews, and sex workers post warnings about violent clients. This offers a platform for the establishment of norms and rules (Sanders 2006), as well as support and a form of community policing.

Tackling and preventing violence

Official policing of sex work can often be driven by morals rather than concerns for workers' health and safety (Kinnell 2008; Sanders and Campbell 2007), and recently in the UK there has been an emphasis on criminalising the purchase of commercial sex, which has been blamed for putting sex workers at risk by making them reluctant to report crimes (Campbell and Kinnell 2001; Penfold *et al.* 2004; Pitcher 2006). However, it should be remembered that targeting clients does not necessarily involve criminalising the sex worker, and that since the early 2000s onwards law enforcement has become more sensitive to sex workers' safety (Hubbard 2006), with examples from this time and earlier of the winding down of specialist vice squads and strategies of targeting trafficking and exploitation and tolerating other forms of sex work believed to be more consensual (Matthews 2005). 'Tolerance zones' for street sex work introduced in cities such as Bolton, Manchester, Aberdeen, Glasgow and Edinburgh were thought to reduce the incidence of violence (ACPO 2004; Penfold *et al.* 2004; Sanders and Campbell 2007), although this was not conclusively proven and the introduction of such initiatives at national level in England and Wales was rejected by the New Labour government, with attempts at liberalising legislation in Scotland also abandoned (Home Office 2004, 2006).

A more likely deterrent to tackling violence is the fact that sex workers are generally regarded as implausible complainants by police and judiciary alike, particularly because of the assumption that a rape victim should be 'respectable' and sexually chaste (Phipps 2009). This is often at the root of the reluctance to report crime, which means that prevention and policing of violence is undertaken by sex workers themselves, either through safety strategies adopted by individuals or in parlours and brothels, or informal monitoring of dangerous clients by sex work outreach projects and online commercial sex communities.

Sanders and Campbell (2007) argue that a community-based understanding of crime prevention is evident amongst sex workers, receptionists, brothel and parlour owners and managers, outreach projects and male clients. In their study, safety strategies fell into three categories: managing the environment (installing security cameras and locks/bolts, employing reception/security staff, using rooms without windows); individual protection mechanisms (not wearing jewellery, keeping footwear on, limiting sexual contact/positions, using humour in tense/nervous moments); and collective control (working in groups, employing different methods of vetting clients prior to the transaction). However, indoor workers, particularly those who operate out of parlours or brothels with other staff or sex workers present, more easily put such strategies in place: and they only superficially address the hazards of sex work as a profession.

Informal policing of dangerous clients is achieved through gathering and distributing intelligence, historically a function performed by sex work projects, which receive and disseminate reports of violent incidents (Penfold *et al.* 2004; Kinnell 2008). Such 'ugly mugs' schemes define violence from the sex workers' perspective, focusing on acts such as condom removal and 'timewasting' (not keeping appointments) as well as more serious forms of physical and sexual violence. Web-based commercial sex communities operate similar systems on messageboards where sex workers place warnings about violent clients: these are particularly useful due to the fact that sex work projects face difficulties maintaining contact with service users (Kinnell 2008) and acquiring funding. This policing function is not currently fulfilled elsewhere, recognised in the government's 2009 Violence Against Women Strategy which backed the establishment of a nationwide 'ugly mugs' initiative (ACPO 2009; HM Government 2009). However, there is a limit to what such schemes can achieve in terms of criminal justice, as reports are often not passed on to police forces. This community policing also reflects the fact that, like all women, sex workers are expected to manage their own exposure to violence, in the absence of state initiatives to deal with their dangerous working conditions (Sanders and Campbell 2007).

Social workers may come into contact with sex workers through substance abuse services, health clinics and hospitals, housing, homeless shelters, child protection and prisons (Williamson and Folaron 2003; Williamson and Baker 2009), and there are a number of ways in which they can assist those who have suffered violence. However, sex workers can be suspicious of social care professionals, due to issues around anonymity and judgement (Carter and Dalla 2006; Sanders 2005; Sharpe 1998). Social workers must ensure that they deliver care without morality and with appropriate confidentiality, in order to create trust (Williamson and Folaron 2003; Sanders 2007). They also need to be sensitive to the emotional and physical issues sex workers face (Ward and Roe-Sepowitz 2009), while being aware that experiences and needs may radically differ depending on the type of sex work performed, geographical location, nationality and social positions such as class, 'race' and sexual orientation (Williamson and Baker 2009). It is important to avoid defining sex workers as victims, to respect their coping strategies and to work with, as well as broadening, their existing resources and networks.

Social workers may be able to provide support to sex workers who wish to report violence to the police. However, bearing in mind the troubled history of sex work and law enforcement, it is advisable not to insist that a sex worker does so. Alternatively, they can be encouraged to contact a local 'ugly mugs' scheme or to post a warning on a website, although the limitations of this in terms of achieving justice should be recognised. It is important not to pressure a sex worker to leave the industry as a response to violence, as this may create the impression that they are being judged, and in order to be sustainable this desire to leave must come from the client (Williamson and Folaron 2003). However, if a sex worker is considering exiting, there are a number of practical needs which must be met, such as for housing and alternative employment or education, access to benefits and financial advice, and help with physical and mental health, relationships, and any substance abuse or immigration issues. The 'cycle of change', originally developed by Prochaska *et al.* in the context of drug treatment services, has been used successfully by those engaged in supporting exiting sex workers (UK Network of Sex Work Projects 2008b).

Other social work tools which may be useful include motivational interviewing, solution-focused therapy, task-centred casework and crisis intervention. Outreach can be used as a tool to build trust and relationships with sex workers, and it is essential to engage in partnership working with other agencies which can provide specialist services, information and support. There is little mainstream professional guidance on therapeutic options for sex workers (Carter and Dalla 2006), especially those who work indoors. Social workers are strongly advised to consult the good practice guidance developed by the UK Network of Sex Work Projects (UKNSWP), available on its website at www.uknswp.org. Local sex work projects can also be a valuable resource, and the UKNSWP maintains an up-to-date list of these online. It is not ideal that the main source of professional support comes from independent agencies which face increasing difficulties obtaining funding. Nevertheless, social workers must operate within these constraints and attempt to achieve the best possible outcome for their clients. Above all, operating without judgement and engaging in reflective practice will help them to do this.

Acknowledgements

Thanks are due to social workers Jo Rooke and Jan Phipps for their help with the final section of this chapter.

References

Agustín, L. (2007) *Sex at the Margins: Migration, Labour Markets and the Rescue Industry*. London: Zed Books.

Association of Chief Police Officers (ACPO) (2004) *Policing Prostitution: ACPO's Policy, Strategy and Operational Guidelines for Dealing with Exploitation and Abuse through Prostitution*. London: ACPO.

Association of Chief Police Officers (ACPO) (2009) *Tackling Perpetrators of Violence Against Women and Girls: ACPO Review for the Home Secretary*. London: ACPO.

Bagley, C. (1999) 'Adolescent prostitution in Canada and the Philippines.' *International Social Work* 42, 4, 445–454.

Benson, C. (1998) *Violence Against Female Prostitutes.* Loughborough: Department of Social Sciences, Loughborough University.

Bernstein, E. (2001) 'The meaning of the purchase: Desire, demand and the commerce of sex.' *Ethnography 2,* 3, 389–420.

Brents, B.G. and Hausbeck, K. (2007) 'Marketing sex: US legal brothels and late capitalist consumption.' *Sexualities 10,* 4, 425–439.

Broadcasters' Audience Research Board (2007) *Weekly Viewing Figures: Secret Diary of a Call Girl.* Available at www.barb.co.uk, accessed on 19 July 2012.

Busch, N.B., Bell, H., Hotaling, N. and Monto, M.A. (2002) 'Male customers of prostituted women: Exploring perceptions of entitlement to power and control and implications for violent behavior toward women.' *Violence Against Women 8,* 9, 1093–1112.

Campbell, R. and Kinnell, H. (2001) 'We shouldn't have to put up with this: Street sex work and violence.' *Criminal Justice Matters 42* (Winter), 12.

Campbell, R., Coleman, S. and Torkington, P. (1996) *Street Prostitution in Inner-City Liverpool.* Liverpool: Hope University College.

Carter, D.J. and Dalla, R.L. (2006) 'Transactional analysis case report: Street-level prostituted women as mental health care clients.' *Sexual Addiction and Compulsivity 13,* 1, 95–119.

Carter, H. (2010) 'The Bradford sex workers Stephen Griffiths is accused of killing.' *The Guardian,* 27 May 2010.

Church, S., Henderson, M., Barnard, M. and Hart, G. (2001) 'Violence by clients towards female prostitutes in different work settings: Questionnaire survey.' *British Medical Journal 322,* 524–525.

Cusick, L., Kinnell, H., Brooks-Gordon, B. and Campbell, R. (2009) 'Wild guesses and conflated meanings? Estimating the size of the sex worker population in Britain.' *Critical Social Policy 29,* 4, 703–719.

Dworkin, A. (1981) *Pornography: Men Possessing Women.* London: The Women's Press.

Edwards, R. and Whitehead, T. (2010) 'David Cameron calls for laws on legalising prostitution to be "looked at".' *The Daily Telegraph,* 29 May 2010.

Farley, M. and Barkan, H. (1998) 'Prostitution, violence, and posttraumatic stress disorder.' *Women and Health 27,* 3, 37–49.

Farley, M., Baral, I., Kiremire, M. and Sezgin U. (1998) 'Prostitution in five countries: violence and posttraumatic stress disorder.' *Feminism and Psychology 8,* 4, 405–426.

Fick, N. (2005) *Coping with Stigma, Discrimination and Violence: Sex Workers Talk about their Experiences.* Cape Town: Sex Worker Education and Advocacy Taskforce.

Giobbe, E. (1992) 'Juvenile Prostitution: Profile of Recruitment.' In A. Burgess (ed.) *Child Trauma: Issues and Research.* New York: Garland Publishing.

Hester, M. and Westmarland, N. (2004) *Tackling Street Prostitution: Towards an Holistic Approach* (Home Office Research Study 279). London: HMSO.

HM Government (2009) *Together We Can End Violence Against Women and Girls: A Strategy.* London: HMSO.

Holt, T.J. and Blevins, K.R. (2007) 'Examining sex work from the client's perspective: Assessing johns using online data.' *Deviant Behaviour 28,* 4, 333–354.

Home Office (2004) *Paying the Price: A Consultation Paper on Prostitution.* London: HMSO.

Home Office (2006) *A Coordinated Prostitution Strategy and a Summary of Responses to 'Paying the Price'.* London: HMSO.

Hubbard, P. (1998) 'Community action and the displacement of street prostitution: evidence from British cities.' *Geoforum 29,* 3, 269–286.

Hubbard, P. (2001) 'Sex zones: Intimacy, citizenship and public space.' *Sexualities 4*, 1, 51–71.

Hubbard, P. (2006) 'Out of Touch and Out of Time? The Contemporary Policing of Sex Work.' In R. Campbell and M. O'Neill (eds) *Sex Work Now*. Cullompton, Devon: Willan Publishing.

Jackson, L.A., Bennett, C.G. and Sowinski, B.A. (2007) 'Stress in the sex trade and beyond: Women working in the sex trade talk about the emotional stressors in their working and home lives.' *Critical Public Health 17*, 3, 257–271.

Jeal, N. and Salisbury, C. (2004a) 'A health needs assessment of street-based prostitutes: Cross-sectional survey.' *Journal of Public Health 26*, 2, 147–151.

Jeal, N. and Salisbury, C. (2004b) 'Self-reported experiences of health services among female street-based prostitutes: A cross-sectional survey.' *British Journal of General Practice 54*, 504, 515–519.

Jeffreys, S. (2008) *The Industrial Vagina: The Political Economy of the Global Sex Trade*. London: Routledge.

Johnson, M.L. (2006) 'Stripper Bashing: An Autovideography of Violence Against Strippers.' In R.D. Egan, K. Frank and M.L. Johnson (eds) *Flesh for Fantasy: Producing and Consuming Exotic Dance*. New York: Thunder's Mouth Press.

Kinnell, H. (2008) *Violence and Sex Work in Britain*. Cullompton, Devon: Willan Publishing.

Knight, I. (2009) 'I'm Belle du Jour.' *The Sunday Times*, 15 November 2009.

Malkin, B. (2008) 'Steve Wright guilty of Ipswich prostitutes murders.' *The Daily Telegraph*, 21 February 2008.

Matthews, R. (2005) 'Policing prostitution: Ten years on.' *British Journal of Criminology 45*, 6, 877–895.

May, T., Harocopos, A. and Hough, M. (2000) *For Love or Money: Pimps and the Management of Sex Work* (Police Research Series Paper 134). London: HMSO.

McElroy, W. (1998) 'Prostitutes, Anti Pro Feminists and the Economic Associates of Whores.' In J. Elias, V. Bullough, V. Elias and G. Brewer (eds) *Prostitution: On Whores, Hustlers and Johns*. Amherst, NY: Prometheus Books.

McMillan, L. (2010) 'Gender, Crime and Criminal Justice in Scotland.' In H. Croall, G. Mooney and M. Munro (eds) *Criminal Justice in Contemporary Scotland*. Cullompton, Devon: Willan Publishing.

Monto, M.A. (2004) 'Female prostitution, customers and violence.' *Violence Against Women 10*, 2, 160–188.

Monto, M.A. and Hotaling, N. (2001) 'Predictors of rape myth acceptance among male clients of female street prostitutes.' *Violence Against Women 7*, 3, 275–293.

Penfold, C., Hunter, G., Campbell, R. and Barham, L. (2004) 'Tackling client violence in female street prostitution: Inter-agency working between outreach agencies and the police.' *Policing and Society 14*, 4, 365–379.

Phipps, A. (2009) 'Rape and respectability: Ideas about sexual violence and social class.' *Sociology 43*, 4, 667–683.

Phoenix, J. (2000) 'Prostitute identities: Men, money and violence.' *British Journal of Criminology 40*, 1, 37–55.

Pitcher, J. (2006) 'Support Services for Women Working in the Sex Industry.' In R. Campbell and M. O'Neill (eds) *Sex Work Now*. Cullompton, Devon: Willan Publishing.

Plumridge, E.W., Chetwynd, S.J. and Reed, A. (1997) 'Control and condoms in commercial sex: Client perspectives.' *Sociology of Health and Illness 19*, 2, 228–243.

Press Association (2010) 'Man charged over prostitute murders.' *The Guardian*, 27 May 2010.

Raphael, J. and Shapiro, D.L. (2004) 'Violence in indoor and outdoor prostitution venues.' *Violence Against Women 10*, 2, 126–139.

Romero-Daza, N., Weeks, M. and Singer, M. (2003) 'Nobody gives a damn if I live or die: Violence, drugs, and street-level prostitution in inner-city Hartford, Connecticut.' *Medical Anthropology 22*, 3, 233–259.

Sanders, T. (2004) 'The risks of street prostitution: Punters, police and protesters.' *Urban Studies 41*, 9, 1703–1717.

Sanders, T. (2005) *Sex Work: A Risky Business.* Cullompton, Devon: Willan Publishing.

Sanders, T. (2006) 'Behind the Personal Ads: The Indoor Sex Markets in Britain.' In R. Campbell and M. O'Neill (eds) *Sex Work Now.* Cullompton, Devon: Willan Publishing.

Sanders, T. (2007) 'Protecting the health and safety of female sex workers: the responsibility of all.' *British Journal of Obstetrics and Gynaecology 114*, 7, 791–793.

Sanders, T. (2008a) 'Male sexual scripts: Intimacy, sexuality and pleasure in the purchase of commercial sex.' *Sociology 42*, 3, 400–417.

Sanders, T. (2008b) *Paying for Pleasure: Men Who Buy Sex.* Cullompton, Devon: Willan Publishing.

Sanders, T. and Campbell, R. (2007) 'Designing out vulnerability, building in respect: violence, safety and sex work policy.' *British Journal of Sociology 58*, 1, 1–19.

Scottish Parliament (2007) *Prostitution (Public Places) (Scotland) Act 2007.* Holyrood: Scottish Parliament.

Sharpe, K. (1998) *Red Light, Blue Light: Prostitutes, Punters and Police.* Aldershot: Ashgate.

Sullivan, B. (2003) 'Trafficking in women: Feminism and new international law.' *International Feminist Journal of Politics 5*, 1, 67–91.

Surratt, H.L., Inciardi, J.A., Kurtz, S.P. and Kiley, M.C. (2004) 'Sex work and drug use in a subculture of violence.' *Crime and Delinquency 50*, 1, 43–59.

UK Network of Sex Work Projects (2008a) *Working with Migrant Sex Workers* (Good Practice Guidance No. 3). Manchester: UK Network of Sex Work Projects. Available at www.uknswp. org, accessed on 19 July 2012.

UK Network of Sex Work Projects (2008b) *Working with Sex Workers: Exiting* (Good Practice Guidance No. 5). Manchester: UK Network of Sex Work Projects. Available at www.uknswp. org, accessed on 19 July 2012.

UK Parliament (2009) *Policing and Crime Act 2009.* London: HMSO.

Ward, A. and Roe-Sepowitz, D. (2009) 'Assessing the effectiveness of a trauma-oriented approach to treating prostituted women in a prison and community exiting program.' *Journal of Aggression, Maltreatment and Trauma 18*, 3, 293–312.

Ward, H., Day, S. and Weber, J. (1999) 'Risky business: Health and safety in the sex industry over a nine-year period.' *Sexually Transmitted Infections 75*, 5, 340–343.

Weitzer, R. (2000) 'Why We Need More Research on Sex Work.' In R. Weitzer (ed.) *Sex for Sale: Prostitution, Pornography and the Sex Industry.* New York: Routledge.

Williamson, C. and Baker, L.M (2009) 'Women in street-based prostitution: A typology of their work styles.' *Qualitative Social Work 8*, 1, 27–44.

Williamson, C. and Folaron, G. (2003) 'Understanding the experiences of street-level prostitutes.' *Qualitative Social Work 2*, 3, 271–287.

CHAPTER 6

Love, Power and Control
Girls' Experiences of Relationship Exploitation and Violence

Christine Barter and Melanie McCarry

Introduction

Teenage experiences of partner violence have received little attention in the UK, either within social welfare research, policy or practice. This is despite the fact that young people themselves have repeatedly identified peer relationships, and especially those involving abuse and violence, to be among the main areas of anxiety and unhappiness in their lives (Barter *et al.* 2004; Utting 1997). In addition, given the critical nature of adolescence as a developmental period, it is even more surprising that so little attention has been given to this social problem (Barter 2006; O'Keefe, Brockopp and Chew 1986; Williams and Martinez 1999). The UK studies which do exist confirm its impact and seriousness for young people's welfare (see Barter 2009; Hird 2000). To address this gap in the UK literature, the current authors with others undertook a three-year research project exploring violence and exploitation in teenage relationships (Barter *et al.* 2009).

In this chapter the research findings, with a specific focus on the experiences of girls, are presented. We firstly explain the terminology used and outline the research methodology. The victimisation experiences of girls (and boys) in relation to physical, sexual and emotional forms of violence are explored including the impact of these on their welfare. The risk and protective factors associated with this form of intimate violence are then addressed. Lastly we explore the implications our findings hold for social work policy and practice.

The use of appropriate terminology presents an issue for both academics and practitioners. Much of the wider international literature has adopted the term 'dating violence' to describe this area of work. However, this does not transfer well in the UK context. It is important that the terminology used is viewed as appropriate and accessible by young people. In collaboration with the group of young people who advised the project (see McCarry 2012) we agreed on using the term 'partner violence', as young people felt this was applicable to a range of intimate relationships from long-term relationships to one-off encounters.

Research methodology and aims

The overall aim of the research was to examine in depth young people's experiences of partner violence and how best to respond to this problem. The study utilised a wide definition of violence which incorporated emotional, verbal, physical and sexual forms of violence. These were looked at both discretely and as they co-exist within young people's relationships.

The research used a multi-method framework combining both quantitative and qualitative approaches (Plano Clark and Creswell 2008). Two data collection techniques were used: a self-completion survey; and face to face semi-structured, in-depth interviews with vignettes. The surveys were conducted in eight secondary schools in England (4), Scotland (2) and Wales (2), in both rural (3) and urban (5) areas and in locations categorised as experiencing low (1), average (3), high (2) or very high (2) levels of deprivation as indicated by free school meal allocation. All eight schools were in the public sector and one was a faith-based (Catholic) school.

Overall, 1377 young people completed the survey; 24 (2%) surveys were spoiled, thus 1353 questionnaire responses were analysed. All the young people were aged between 13 and 17 years old. A total of 91 interviews were undertaken with a subsample of 62 girls and 29 boys. Young people were given the option of having a joint interview with a friend and three interviews were conducted in this way.

The main aims of the survey were to document: demographic characteristics of respondents; incidence rates for different types of violence in partner relationships; identification of the broad dynamics involved; impact on young people's welfare; help-seeking behaviour and support; past experiences of child abuse/inter-parental violence and wider peer violence. The questionnaire was divided into two sections. The first section asked about violence that the young people had experienced from a partner and the second section asked about their own use of violence against a partner. Whilst the main research report focused on the experiences of girls and boys, in this chapter the authors take the opportunity to look more specifically at girls' experiences, reflecting the title of this edited collection.

The vast majority, 88 per cent, of young people reported at least one relationship experience and the majority reported partners only of the opposite sex (96%). Fifty respondents, 21 females and 29 males, reported a same-sex partner.

The majority of female respondents had an older partner (58%), with 11 per cent of partners being 'much older'. In the interviews the young people indicated that a 'much older' partner referred to someone about two years older. Just under half of 13-year-old girls had an older partner, increasing to 66 per cent of 15-year-olds and 60 per cent of 16-year-olds. Only a minority of each age group reported a younger partner. For girls, ethnic group was not significantly associated with age of partner, although Asian girls were less likely than any other groups to have an older partner.

In contrast, most male respondents (59%) stated that their partners had either been the same age as them or younger. For boys, age of partner was unrelated to respondent's age or ethnicity.

Sample-interview participants

Interviews were conducted in six schools with 91 young people who had completed the questionnaire. Twice as many girls were interviewed (62 girls and 29 boys). To compensate, in a linked study on disadvantaged young people and intimate violence we interviewed more boys than girls (Wood, Barter and Berridge 2011). The findings from this second study broadly reflected the school-based results regarding gender and violence presented in this chapter.

The majority of interviewees were aged between 15 and 17 years old (n = 81), although ten young people were aged 13 to 14 years old. Over half were ethnic white, 12 were Asian, 12 black and 11 mixed ethnicity. The majority stated they had no religion (n = 54), 23 said they were Christian, 7 Sikh and 5 Muslim. The vast majority lived with both biological parents, 22 with a single parent, 12 in a reconstituted family and 5 stated other.

Experiences of teenage partner violence

Physical violence

Respondents were asked if any of their partners had ever used physical force such as 'pushing, slapping, hitting or holding you down'. A quarter of girls reported some form of physical violence from a partner in comparison to 18 per cent of boys, which represented a statistically significant difference ($\chi^2(1) = 9.381$, $p < .005$). Girls were also much more likely to report that physical violence had occurred more than once, indicating that girls may be experiencing more repeated patterns of victimisation than boys. Respondents were then asked if their partners had ever used any *more severe* physical force such as 'punching, strangling, beating you up, hitting you with an object'. Overall, fewer young people reported this level of physical violence: 11 per cent of girls and 4 per cent of boys. Girls were, however, three times more likely than boys to have experienced *repeated* severe violence.

Our findings reflect previous research which demonstrates that girls generally suffer more severe forms of physical violence than boys (Arriaga and Foshee 2004; Foshee 1996; Gamache 1991; Jackson, Cram and Seymour 2000).

Although it is obviously important to know how frequently young people experience relationship violence, unless we also understand the impact that violence has on their wellbeing we will only ever be able to present a limited understanding of the issue. Additionally we will be unable to develop appropriate responses which reflect young people's own understandings and experiences. Much of the US literature on 'dating' violence fails to adequately represent both incidence and impact and presents incidence rates with little consideration of the gendered nature of impact (Barter 2009).

TABLE 6.1 EVER EXPERIENCED PHYSICAL VIOLENCE FROM PARTNER

Have any partners	Used physical force such as pushing, slapping, hitting or holding you down?		Used any more severe physical force such as punching, strangling, beating you up, hitting you with an object?	
	Female	Male	Female	Male
Once	47 (8%)	36 (6%)	38 (6%)	14 (2%)
A few times	84 (14%)	54 (9%)	24 (4%)	7 (1%)
Often	15 (2%)	5 (1%)	3 (0.5%)	1 –
All the time	4 (0.5%)	5 (1%)	1 –	2 –

Consequently, in addition to incidence we wanted to understand more about the impact of violence on young people and asked whether the violence had a negative impact (i.e. made them feel scared/frightened, upset/unhappy, angry/annoyed or humiliated) or no impact (i.e. made them feel loved/protected, thought it was funny or had no impact). We did recognise that feeling loved and protected as a result of experiencing violence or control may represent a negative outcome; however, unfortunately we were unable to ascertain from the survey responses the reasoning behind this response. Due to this uncertainty we decided to include the response in the no-impact category. However, in the interviews, especially those with young women, it became clear that feeling loved and protected was often associated with normative views regarding violence and relationships. This issue is explored later in this chapter under emotional violence.

For presentation purposes we have aggregated all the impact responses and no-impact responses into two categories. Over 75 per cent of girls reported that the physical violence had a negative impact on them, compared with 14 per cent of boys. Furthermore, *all* the girls who reported severe physical violence reported a negative impact. Additionally, most girls identified more than one negative impact on their wellbeing. Overall, the most commonly reported effect was to feel scared/frightened and upset/unhappy.

In the interviews many of the young women recounted experiences of physical violence instigated by their male partners; in some of these instances the violence was severe, as illustrated by Amy (aged 15):

Interviewer: Did you think that Joel loved you?

Amy: At one point.

Interviewer: At one point, did it stop feeling like love at some point?

Amy: Yeah.

Interviewer: Yeah, what point did it stop feeling like love do you think?

Amy: When he started hitting me and beating me up.

Interviewer: Did he hurt you?

Amy: Yeah.

Interviewer: Did you have to go and see the doctor?

Amy: Yeah...

Interviewer: So what did you tell them?

Amy: I just said that...I'd had a fight at school, I'd come in with cuts all over my face and up my arms as well...and he [the doctor] was asking if I was sure and stuff and 'cos I was like 'yeah, I'm sure' because I had handprints all up my arms, I just got really defensive about it so I think he knew what was going on but he didn't want to say anything. He just gave me painkillers...

Worryingly, in some of the narratives the young women blamed themselves for their partner's violence, as further discussed by Amy:

Amy: ...and he raised his fist to hit me and I was stood there and I was thinking, I, and at one point I know it sounds stupid but I wanted him to, because I felt, I felt as if I deserved it, but I was, I was scared.

A minority of male interviewees discussed their girlfriends' violence towards them. However, on closer examination of each incident it appeared that the female partner's violence was almost exclusively used in retaliation or self-protection in response to their own initial use of violence, as indicated by Rebecca (aged 15):

Rebecca: … You're scared as well, and like, it's like all a flash like really, and he's coming at you and like the first thing you do is defend yourself […] I pushed [name of boyfriend] as well, pushed him over and I pushed him into a fence.

In other instances male participants viewed their female partner's use of violence as amusing. In one interview, Callum (aged 16) explained that whilst his girlfriend did try to 'batter' [hit] him it was 'just for fun' and did not have any impact on him.

Sexual violence

Previous work on young people's experiences of sexual violence has recognised the role that both physical force and sexual coercion or pressure play in young women's sexual victimisation (Cawson *et al.* 2000). The survey questions, reflecting this, asked if respondents had ever been *pressured* or *physically forced* 'to do something sexual, such as kissing, touching or something else' and if they had been *pressured* or *physically forced* into 'sexual intercourse'. Our findings clearly show that sexual violence represents a major problem for many teenage girls. The data also showed that girls were significantly more likely than boys to experience sexual violence. When responses to all four questions were combined, we find that, disconcertingly, one in three girls (31%), and 16 per cent of boys, reported at least one experience of sexual violence from their partners, a statistically significant gender difference ($\chi^2(1) = 34.026$, $p < .001$). Our analysis identified that both girls and boys were more likely to have been pressured into sexual activity rather than physically forced.

Table 6.2 illustrates that just over a quarter of girls have been pressured into doing something sexual and for the majority this had happened either once or a few times. However, for a small minority this had been a regular occurrence. A further 16 per cent of girls had been pressured into sexual intercourse. Moving on to look at physical force, 13 per cent of girls reported that they had been physically forced into doing something sexual and 6 per cent into sexual intercourse.

TABLE 6.2 EVER EXPERIENCED SEXUAL VIOLENCE FROM PARTNER

Have any partners…	Pressured you into kissing, touching or something else?		Physically forced you into kissing, touching or something else?		Pressured you into sexual intercourse?		Physically forced you into having sexual intercourse?	
	Female	Male	Female	Male	Female	Male	Female	Male
Once	78 (13%)	33 (6%)	49 (8%)	12 (2%)	57 (10%)	13 (2%)	30 (5%)	9 (2%)
A few times	75 (12%)	35 (6%)	27 (5%)	15 (3%)	34 (6%)	14 (2%)	4 (1%)	8 (1%)
Often	7 (1%)	7 (1%)	3 —	7 (1%)	1 —	2 —	0 —	1 —
All the time	2 —	9 (2%)	1 —	1 —	1 —	6 1%	1 —	1 —

The research team held some concerns regarding the validity of the boys' data on sexual violence: we subsequently found that a group of male participants in one school accounted for a high proportion of all sexual violence reported by boys, and especially repeated forced sexual violence. The researchers noted a great deal of chatting and laughing within this group when they were reading the sexual violence questions. We agreed to include their responses but urge caution when interpreting this aspect of the data (see Barter *et al.* 2009 for more discussion of the methodology).

As with the physical violence we asked questions about the impact of sexual violence. The results show that the vast majority of girls, 70 per cent, reported that the sexual violence did have a negative impact on their wellbeing. In direct contrast, the vast majority of boys, 87 per cent, reported no adverse effect.

Whilst statutory agencies such as the police or social services may believe that being physically forced into sexual activity is especially damaging, the young women in our interview sample explained that being pressured into sexual activity was as traumatising. The interviews revealed that where young women were pressured they often felt responsible for 'going along with' what happened, whereas if they were physically forced it was clearer to them that they had been made to do something against their wishes. The young women discussed the various coercive tactics employed by boyfriends to 'persuade' them to have sexual contact, such as being threatened with the termination of the relationship as described by Rebecca (aged 15) who discussed an incident with an ex-boyfriend which occurred when she was 12 years old and he was 15 years:

> **Rebecca:** He tried making me, he like, he was like oh, he kept trying to make me have sex with him and I was like, and first of all I was like 'no, no, no' and then he was like trying kissing my neck and stuff like that to try and make me do it… I was like 'no, no, no' because I hadn't done it before he was like 'go on, go on, go on' and I was like 'no' and then I finally like give in to him and we went off to go and do it. But obviously like I was like 'I don't want to do it', it was the most stupid place he took me.

> **Interviewer:** Did he keep trying?

> **Rebecca:** Yeah and I was like 'no I can't I can't' and he, oh my god, and he made me suck his dick and it was horrible, and then he

never made me but he kept telling me to do it and I was like 'no', because I'd never done anything like that before and I was like 'no, no, no' and then I done it and it was proper horrible and I'm never doing it again but it was horrible and I can't believe I done it. Then like afterwards where I'd been seeing him for so long I thought we'd go out with each other…but then afterwards, once he done that he didn't really speak to me again. And I was so young as well, I didn't know what I was doing.

Many of the young women had similar experiences to Rebecca. These accounts illustrate the difficulty they experienced in articulating what had happened to them, especially if they stayed in the relationships. The following excerpt is from a group interview with Tasminder (aged 16) and Jasleen (aged 16) who discussed the impact of their experiences and their reasons for remaining in a violent relationship:

> **Tasminder:** See with my relationship it wasn't up to me [when to have sex].
>
> **Jasleen:** And same here.
>
> **Interviewer:** That's not alright is it really?
>
> **Jasleen:** But when it happens it just kind of happens and then afterwards you think 'oh my god'.
>
> **Interviewer:** How did you feel afterwards?
>
> **Tasminder:** I just couldn't, I couldn't even look at myself in the mirror.
>
> **Jasleen:** Yeah, same here…but the weirdest thing is you still go back, we still go back to them, we still see them again because we have feelings for them obviously, but we shouldn't have went back to them.

Some of the young women also had difficulty in identifying their experiences as abusive and conceptualised it as normative behaviour in their relationships (see Chung 2007). Some of the female participants stated that being in a relationship, especially with an older male partner, meant that they had implicitly agreed to certain sexual expectations. Consequently, for some, the sexual pressure and force they experienced was viewed as a normative aspect of their relationship.

Emotional violence

Prevalence and incidence of emotional forms of violence are possibly the most difficult to ascertain. Stark (2007) argues that what he terms 'coercive control' is the most common form of domestic violence, as it underpins both physical and sexual forms of intimate violence, but is often the most hidden. He continues that this is due to the individualised form this abuse takes, with perpetrators targeting specific behaviour at their victims, which becomes meaningful only when placed within the wider context of an abusive history. As argued above, young women often do not identify some forms of violence, and especially non-physical forms, as constituting abuse and instead perceive such behaviour as a normative, although often unwelcome, aspect of relationships.

Consequently, the complexity of emotional violence, and the wide range of behaviours which can constitute this form of abuse, makes it especially difficult to adequately determine in a survey. Nevertheless, other research in this area reports high incidence rates for emotional violence in teenage relationships (Bergman 1992; Collin-Vézina *et al.* 2006; Hird 2000; Halpern *et al.* 2001; Jezl, Molidor and Wihte 1996; Sears *et al.* 2006; Sears, Byers and Price 2007) with some studies identifying rates as high as 90 per cent (Jezl *et al.* 1996). We used eight questions in the survey to gauge the incidence of emotional violence in the lives of participants (see Table 6.3).

For each of the eight questions, a higher proportion of girls reported victimisation. The most commonly experienced form of emotional violence was 'being made fun of', with nearly half of girls and a third of boys reporting this. The second most frequently reported form of emotional abuse was 'constantly being checked-up on by partners' (42% of girls and 29% of boys). Analysis of overt forms of controlling behaviour produced a more distinct gender divide; a third of girls compared with 13 per cent of boys reported being told whom they could see and where they could go. Similarly, over a third of girls reported their partners had shouted at them, screamed in their face or called them hurtful names and 35 per cent stated that their partners had said negative things about their appearance, body, friends or family. Emotional violence also included the use of threats to intimidate partners, with girls being more often the recipients of such tactics. Nearly one in ten girls (9%), compared with 6 per cent of boys, stated that their partners had threatened to use personal information to make them do things against their wishes. The gender divide widened in relation to threats of direct physical violence, with 11 per cent of girls and 4 per cent of boys reporting this.

TABLE 6.3 EVER EXPERIENCED EMOTIONAL VIOLENCE FROM PARTNER

Have any partners…	Made fun of you?		Shouted at you/screamed in your face/called you hurtful names?		Said negative things about your appearance/body/friends/family?		Threatened to hurt you physically unless you did what they wanted?	
	Female	Male	Female	Male	Female	Male	Female	Male
Once	90 (15%)	60 (11%)	83 (14%)	54 (9.5%)	87 (15%)	44 (8%)	38 (6%)	14 (3%)
A few times	159 (27%)	87 (15%)	109 (18%)	54 (9.5%)	103 (17%)	31 (5%)	22 (4%)	6 (1%)
Often	21 (4%)	16 (3%)	19 (3%)	7 (1%)	19 (3%)	6 (1%)	5 (1%)	1 –
All the time	12 (2%)	7 (1%)	5 (1%)	5 (1%)	3 (1%)	5 (1%)	2 –	2 –

Have any partners…	Told you who you could see and where you could go?		Constantly checked up on what you were doing e.g. by phone or texts?		Used private information to make you do something?		Used mobile phones or the internet to humiliate or threaten you?	
	Female	Male	Female	Male	Female	Male	Female	Male
Once	59 (10%)	30 (5%)	67 (11%)	45 (8%)	37 (6%)	17 (3%)	42 (7%)	14 (2%)
A few times	77 (13%)	26 (5%)	116 (19%)	73 (13%)	17 (3%)	12 (2%)	28 (5%)	5 (1%)
Often	29 (5%)	7 (1%)	49 (8%)	30 (5%)	1 –	2 –	1 –	1 –
All the time	15 (3%)	11 (2%)	22 (4%)	19 (3%)	0 –	1 –	0 –	3 –

There clearly exists a wide gender differential in relation to emotional violence: girls are more likely to experience emotional violence; more frequently experience more than one form of emotional violence; and are more likely to experience direct intimidation and control. This gender distinction continues when we observe repeat victimisation. A third of girls stated they had been made fun of at least a few times, and a similar proportion report that their partners frequently checked up on what they were doing. Around one in five girls reported that partners often: shouted at them; said negative things about them or their families; and/or told them whom they could see or where they could go. In all these categories boys reported much lower repeated victimisation.

By combining all responses to these questions we find that three-quarters of girls and half of boys experienced some kind of emotional violence from their partner, which again represents a statistically significant gender divide ($\chi^2(1) = 50.662$, $p < .001$). When asked about impact, one-third of girls claimed they were negatively affected by emotional violence compared with 6 per cent of boys.

Interview data confirms the high levels of controlling behaviour that young women commonly experience from their boyfriend. The control ranged from wanting to know what their girlfriends were doing at all times of the day and night to forbidding them from seeing their other friends. Both Emma (aged 15) and Amy (aged 15) give examples of their boyfriends restricting their socialising and using physical control to implement this:

Emma: Like when I'd be out with my friends and he'd drag me off and say he didn't want me out any longer and I'd got to go in and it could be like half past six.

Amy: Yeah like saying 'I don't like her' or 'I don't like him', 'you're not allowed to speak to them anymore'.

Interviewer: And what would you say?

Amy: I'd say at the end of the day they're my friends I'll speak to whoever I want to and then he'd get really mad.

Interviewer: So if you did see the people he didn't want you to see what would happen?

Amy: He'd drag me away from them.

Interviewer: Physically drag you away?

Amy: Yeah. Just drag me away and then say that I'm not allowed out
kind of thing unless it's with him, I'm with him, or I've got some
lads to keep an eye on me. He didn't trust me...I'd go out with
my friends and then he'd turn up or I'd have to go down with
his friends and I weren't...I'd just have to sit there and I wasn't
allowed to move or anything...and then he'd get funny with his
friends if they tried to talk to me.

The control was often exerted through the use of new technologies
such as mobile phone calling and texting or through social networking
internet sites such as Bebo and instant messaging through MSN. Natalie
(aged 15) and Keira (aged 16) describe examples of the surveillance their
boyfriends used:

Natalie: He reckoned that he didn't phone me all the time, he said
'I don't phone all the time' but he didn't stop phoning me or
texting me. And if I didn't text him back he'd go mad. And he
wouldn't like it, and then he'd keep texting me and trying to text.

Interviewer: How many times a day?

Natalie: Oh he'd phone...I'd go in about half ten in the night and
he'd stay on the phone to me until like one in the morning and
he wouldn't get off the phone. ... Yeah, I'd been out with him
like...I'd go in like about...as soon as I went it like, he'd phone
me and then I'd say 'Oh I'm having my food' or whatever and
talking to my mother, phone me after. And then he'd just like
phone me half an hour later and stay on the phone to me like for
ages. And when I didn't go out with him on the weekends when
he was out with his friends and I was out with mine, he'd text me
and text me and text me, asking me what I was doing and that
and who was I with.

Keira: Like even on the computer if I took too long to reply he
would be like 'why, what are you doing, what are you doing,
do you not want to talk to me, do you not have time for me or
anything?' I would be like 'no that's not why, it's just because I
am doing something else'. Stuff like that all the time.

One of the worrying aspects of new technologies is that they can be
used to control another person irrespective of where they are, 24 hours
a day, as illustrated in the above quotes. Although in interviews boys
did report their girlfriend's attempts at control they were generally less

tolerant of this and reported that they ended the relationship when the control became too intrusive, as illustrated by Ryan (aged 15):

> **Ryan:** Yeah, I wanted to go out with my mates, she wanted like, every time I went out with my mates she'd be like 'oh I'm coming', and I'm like, 'no, you're not'.
>
> **Interviewer:** And you couldn't explain that to her?
>
> **Ryan:** No, I'd just be like 'well why do you have to come out, don't you trust me?' And she'd be like 'well yeah I trust you I just like, can't be bothered to stay in' and I'm like 'well go out with your mates then' and she was like 'I can't be bothered'. So we just ended.

In contrast to many of the girls' accounts, none of the boys' reported any fears or worries of possible repercussions due to ending a relationship.

Having considered the different forms of violence experienced we now move on to consider some of the associated risk factors and young people's help-seeking.

Family and peer violence

Overall, 29 per cent of girls and 16 per cent of boys reported that an adult in their home had been violent towards them, another young person or another adult. When we compared experiences of family violence to young people's own experiences on intimate violence a clear association for each form of partner violence became apparent. In each case, young people who reported family violence reported a significant increase in their experiences of partner victimisation, across each form of violence. For example, looking only at sexual violence, 18 per cent of the participants who did not experience family violence reported sexual victimisation from their partner. In contrast, 40 per cent of participants who reported family violence also reported sexual victimisation. This increased when we look only at girls. A quarter of girls who did not experience family violence reported sexual violence from a partner, rising to 45 per cent of girls who experienced family violence.

Our findings indicate that young people who have experiences of violence in the home are nearly four times as likely to have a violent relationship than those who have not. Additionally, those with a history of family violence are more likely to enter a relationship at a younger age than those without these experiences. Furthermore, girls with a history of family violence were also more likely to have an older partner, the significance of which will be seen later.

> **Interviewer:** ... Do you think that [father domestic violence perpetrator against mother] affected how you dealt with Joel?

> **Amy:** I put up with more because I thought I know what's going on and like...I knew how to deal with it because like I'd seen my mum and I'd be stuck, like some of their arguments, I'd be stuck in the middle and I just had to sit there and watch it. And I just didn't know what to do and then when it started to happen to me I thought 'I've been here before'.

Regarding their peers' use of violence, 7 per cent of girls and boys reported that their friends used aggression with their partners and 16 per cent stated that their friends used aggression with their peers. Furthermore, as young people got older they were more likely to report incidences of peer violence. Interestingly, when we compared the data we found that young people who experienced violence in the family were also more likely to report that their peers used violence. We also identified a significant association between having friends who used intimidation and increased reporting of violence from a partner.

Our data indicated that when reports of family violence and peer violence are compared, experiencing violence in one area is associated with an increased risk of aggression in another. Research from the United States has found a correlation between young people experiencing and using violence in their relationships and having friends who routinely use intimidation and aggression against peers (Arriaga and Foshee 2004; Bookwala et al. 1992; O'Keefe and Treister 1998; Roscoe and Callahan 1985). Consequently professionals working with young people who use violence in their general interactions need to also reconsider if they are using violence in their intimate relationships.

It should be emphasised that we are not suggesting that there is a simplistic or causal relationship between family violence and young people's own relationship experiences but that the survey data indicates an association between family and peer violence and violence in their own relationships. One possible explanation is that young people with prior exposure to violence in relationships may be more sensitised to it and therefore be more equipped to identify violence if it is perpetrated in their own relationships. Or it may be that the impact of family violence, for example low self-esteem, or uncertainty around issues of intimacy and trust, may make young people more vulnerable to controlling partners.

Age

Another concerning outcome of our research was the finding that girls were as likely to experience physical violence at age 13 as they were at the age of 16, although older teenage girls were more likely to report severe physical violence. Similarly, younger girls are as likely to report sexual violence as older girls, although girls in the 16 and over age range are more likely to be physically forced into sexual intercourse than the younger age groups. However, as girls get older they are more likely to experience emotional violence from their partners, an interesting contrast to the pattern found for the other forms of violence.

Age of partner

Girls were much more likely than boys to have an older partner and this represents a key risk factor in girls' victimisation experiences. Looking at physical violence first, 14 per cent of girls with a same-age partner, 23 per cent with a slightly older partner and, disconcertingly, 70 per cent with a much older partner experienced physical violence. Similarly, a significant association existed between age of partner and experiences of sexual violence: 76 per cent of *all* incidents of sexual violence for girls occurred with an older partner and three-quarters of girls with a much older partner reported sexual violence. Again, this pattern is evident in relation to emotional violence as four-fifths of girls with an older partner experienced emotional violence. Additionally, girls with an older partner were more likely to experience multiple forms of emotional abuse, and to experience them more often. Previous research also highlights how children and young people routinely separate childhood into specific age-related segments where older children are seen as being controlling over younger ones (Lombard 2011).

How professionals or interventions respond to this area is problematic. In our interviews the girls emphasised their preference for older boyfriends, viewing them as more mature and holding a higher status in some peer groups than boys of their own age. Many of the girls discussed how they felt flattered by the attentions of older boys which made them feel good about themselves, as illustrated by Louise (aged 14):

Louise: He was, like at the start he did kind of pamper me, and I was 12, I hadn't been used to that. I was like 'Oh oh, that's quite good'…can you imagine – 12 years old, starting to be a teenager, getting into, you know starting secondary, there's this guy you know older, pampering you, yeah that's cool… So it's easy to kind of get into that.

However, at the same time the girls acknowledged that older boyfriends held different expectations of relationships which included sexual relations (there is also the fact that older boys and men may target younger girls precisely because they are seen as easier to manipulate).

Help-seeking

The findings from our research are extremely worrying; however, this concern is further heightened when we consider that most of the young people in this research did not tell anyone about their experiences. Young people who experienced violence rarely approached adults, including their parents, and if they did tell someone it was most likely to be a friend. However, what also emerged was that some of the young women regarded their experiences of violence and control as normative, viewing the violence as an unwelcome although routine part of being in a relationship. This view was, at times, reinforced when friends dismissed and minimised their experiences: 'I thought he was weird and then I talked to my friends and all their boyfriends are the same' (Moira, aged 13). The response Moira received from her friends also illuminates a previous point regarding girls' and young women's reluctance to name their experiences as violence.

However, as the quote below from Emma (aged 15) illustrates, it may be that young people would like to talk about their experiences but do not have an appropriate adult to approach:

Emma: It's harder talking to no one… When you're older you might know how to handle it more but when you're like our age you don't know what to do. And if you haven't got people to talk to it makes it harder again.

However, in the interviews some girls did report positive experiences of help-seeking from school Learning Mentors. In some schools, Learning Mentors offer additional learning and pastoral support to students who have educational difficulties. Learning Mentors, a strand of the Excellence in Cities (EiC) initiative, are members of the local community whose role is to bridge academic and pastoral support through the development of effective and supportive mentoring relationships with young people and their families. For example, in one joint interview three South Asian young women, all of whom had experienced partner violence, explained that they could talk to the Learning Mentor because she was from the same community and culture as they were and understood the religious and 'cultural' practices followed by their families and the problem this caused in relation to their own intimate relationships (see Gangoli *et al.* 2006, 2009).

Conclusion

When incidence rates for teenage partner violence are looked at in relation to impact, it is clear that for girls, violence from a partner represents a significant social problem. Girls do not passively accept the violence they experience. Young women were active agents in their lives and responded to partner violence in a variety of ways. Some, for example, ended the relationships when their boyfriends acted in a controlling or violent way.

However, our findings showed that most girls remained in a violent relationship. It may be that they were scared of the possible repercussions which leaving may incur; a worry which was sadly borne out for some of the girls and young women in our study. Or it may be that these girls wanted the relationship but did not want the violence. It is important to remember that partners were not constantly violent and many stated that their partners could be caring and loving. Other commentators have argued that an essential aspect of domestic violence, love and emotion, has been largely ignored in the literature (Donovan and Hester 2010). Love for their partner and hope that their behaviour will change are key reasons why adult women remain in or return to violent relationships (Donovan *et al.* 2006). Donovan and Hester (2010) continue that many domestic violent relationships, irrespective of sexuality or gender, share similar practices of love from perpetrators which ensures that their partners remain emotionally invested in the relationship. According to Donovan and Hester (2010), strategies of love/emotion used by perpetrators include declarations of love by the perpetrator, especially at the point at which their partner threatens or attempts to leave. They conclude that practices of love constitute emotional violence in domestically violent relationships. For the young women in our study experiences of love, power and control were often intricately linked.

We also found clear protective factors in some girls' lives. What became evident through the interview data was that for some of the young women, having clear career or educational aspirations acted as a deterrent. These girls explained that their education and future careers were far more important to them than their intimate relationships, and that if their partner's behaviour in any way distracted them from their studies they would end the relationships. Some girls had decided not to have a relationship at this stage in their life for this very reason.

The need for professionals to recognise and respond to partner violence within young people's relationships is indisputable. However, these responses and interventions need to reflect the differential experiences of girls and boys, especially in relation to instigation of violence and its impacts (Barter *et al.* 2009). Our research showed that boys were victimised, and we do not wish to minimise their experiences; however, our analysis clearly demonstrates that, in relation to impact, boys' victimisation does not affect their welfare in the same way as it does for girls. Interventions need to reflect this gender divide.

Our findings clearly indicate that social work policy and practice needs to recognise that violence in teenage relationships is as damaging as violence in adult ones. Child welfare professionals should include assessments of violence in young people's own relationships as a routine aspect of all work with young people. The link between family violence and teenage partner violence is clearly evident. Professionals working with children and young people who have experienced domestic violence or child abuse need to recognise that these young people, and especially girls and young women, are especially vulnerable to violence in their own relationships. It is futile to address one form of childhood violence whilst leaving young people unprotected in another area of their lives. Our research, alongside others (see Barter 2009 for a research review), shows that young people rarely divulge their experiences of relationship violence to adults. Unless social welfare professions directly ask young people about any concerns they may have regarding their relationships, in a sensitive and open manner, and respond appropriately, young people will fail to be safeguarded from this form of abuse.

References

Arriaga, X.B. and Foshee, V.A. (2004) 'Adolescent dating violence: Do adolescents follow in their friend's or their parents' footsteps?' *Journal on Interpersonal Violence 19*, 2, 162–184.

Barter, C. (2006) 'Teenage dating violence: New DfES guidance for sexually active children – an evidence based response?' *ChildRight*, July, 22–25.

Barter, C. (2009) 'In the Name of Love; Exploitation and violence in teenage dating relationships.' *British Journal of Social Work 39*, 2, 211–232.

Barter, C., McCarry, M., Berridge, D. and Evans, K. (2009) *Exploitation and Violence in Young People's Intimate Relationships.* London: NSPCC and University of Bristol.

Barter, C., Renold, E., Cawson, P. and Berridge, D. (2004) *Peer Violence in Children's Residential Care.* London: Palgrave Macmillan.

Bergman, L. (1992) 'Dating violence among high school students.' *Social Work 31*, 1, 21–27.

Bookwala, J., Frieze, I.H., Smith, C. and Ryan, K. (1992) 'Predictors of dating violence: A multivariate analysis.' *Violence and Victims 7*, 4, 297–311.

Cawson, P., Wattam, C., Brooker, S. and Kelly, G. (2000) *Child Maltreatment in the United Kingdom: A Study of the Prevalence of Child Abuse and Neglect.* London: NSPCC.

Chung, D. (2007) 'Making meaning of relationships: Young women's experiences and understandings of dating violence.' *Violence Against Women 13*, 12, 1274–1295.

Collin-Vézina, D., Hébert, M., Manseau, H., Blais, M. and Fernet, M. (2006) 'Self-concept and dating violence in 220 adolescent girls in the child protection system.' *Child Youth Care Forum 35*, 4, 319–326.

Donovan, C. and Hester, M. (2010) 'I hate the word "victim": An exploration of recognition of domestic violence in same sex relationships.' *Social Policy and Society 9*, 2, 279–289.

Donovan, C., Hester, M., Holmes, J. and McCarry, M. (2006) *Comparing Domestic Abuse in Same Sex and Heterosexual Relationships.* Initial report to ESRC, Award No RES-000-23-0650.

Foshee, V.A. (1996) 'Gender differences in adolescent dating abuse: prevalence, types and injuries.' *Health Education Research 11*, 3, 275–286.

Gamache, D. (1991) 'Domination and Control: The Social Context of Dating Violence.' In B. Levy (ed.) *Dating Violence: Young Women in Danger.* Seattle, WA: Seal Press.

Gangoli, G., McCarry, M. and Razak, A. (2009) 'Child marriage or forced marriage?: South Asian communities in North East England.' *Children and Society 23*, 6, 418–429.

Gangoli, G., Razak, A. and McCarry, M. (2006) *Forced Marriage and Domestic Violence Among South Asian Communities in North East England.* Bristol: UoB and NRF.

Halpern, T.C., Oslak, S.G., Young, M.L., Martin, S.L. and Kupper, L.L. (2001) 'Partner violence among adolescents in opposite-sex romantic relationships: Findings from the national longitudinal study of adolescent health.' *American Journal of Public Health 91*, 10, 1679–1686.

Hird, M.J. (2000) 'An empirical study of adolescent dating aggression.' *Journal of Adolescence 23*, 1, 69–78.

Jackson, S.M., Cram, F. and Seymour, F.W. (2000) 'Violence and sexual coercion in high school students' dating relationships.' *Journal of Family Violence 15*, 1, 23–36.

Jezl, D., Molidor, C. and White, T. (1996) 'Physical, sexual and psychological abuse in high school dating relationships: Prevalence rates and self-esteem issues.' *Child and Adolescent Social Work Journal 13*, 1, 69–88.

Lombard, N. (2011) 'Young People's Attitudes about Violence.' *Centre for Families and Relationships.* Briefing 54. Edinburgh: University of Edinburgh.

McCarry, M. (2012) 'Who benefits? A critical reflection of children and young people's participation in sensitive research.' *International Journal for Social Research Methodology 15*, 1, 55–68.

O'Keefe, M. and Treister, L. (1998) 'Victims of dating violence among high school students: Are the predictors different for males and females?' *Violence Against Women 4*, 2, 195–223.

O'Keefe, M.K., Brockopp, K. and Chew, E. (1986) 'Teen dating violence.' *Social Work 31*, 6, 465–468.

Plano Clark, V.L. and Creswell J.W. (eds) (2008) *The Mixed Methods Reader.* Thousand Oaks, CA: Sage.

Roscoe, B. and Callahan, J.E. (1985) 'Adolescents' self-reporting of violence in families and dating relations.' *Adolescence 20*, 79, 546–553.

Sears, H., Byers, S. and Price, L. (2007) 'The co-occurrence of adolescent boys' and girls' use of psychologically, physically and sexually abusive behaviours in their dating relationships.' *Journal of Adolescence 30*, 3, 487–504.

Sears, H., Byers, S., Whelan, J., Saint-Pierre, G. and The Dating Violence Research Team (2006) '"If it hurts you, then it is not a joke." Adolescents' ideas and experiences of abusive behaviour in dating relationships.' *Journal of Interpersonal Violence 21*, 9, 1191–1207.

Stark, E. (2007) *Coercive Control: How Men Entrap Women in Personal Life.* Oxford: Oxford University Press.

Utting, W. (1997) *People Like Us: The Report on the Review of Safeguards for Children Living Away from Home.* London: The Stationery Office.

Williams, S.E. and Martinez, E. (1999) 'Psychiatric assessment of victims of adolescent dating violence in a primary care clinic.' *Clinical Child Psychology and Psychiatry 4*, 3, 427–439.

Wood, M., Barter, C. and Berridge, D. (2011) *Standing on My Own Two Feet: Disadvantaged Teenagers, Intimate Partner Violence and Coercive Control.* London: NSPCC.

CHAPTER 7

Older Women and Domestic Abuse
Where Ageism and Sexism Intersect

Nancy Lombard and Marsha Scott

Introduction

Research conducted for Help the Aged maintains that older women experience 'less' abuse than younger women (Blood 2004, p.2). Goergen (2011, p.1) confirms that existing data shows 'less' victimisation among older women and he maintains that:

> their [older women] neglect in research as well as in practice has been a silent and mainly unconscious one. Domestic violence institutions as well as research on domestic violence often maintain a focus upon young and middle aged women.

The experiences of older women are often ignored as many surveys (e.g. the British Crime Survey and the Scottish Crime Survey) exclude those over the age of 59. Therefore it is not that older women are not victimised but that their numbers are hidden. Older women, like younger women, experience domestic abuse in large numbers and suffer significant physical, emotional and social harm (see Mears 2003; Scott 2008; Scott *et al.* 2004; Straka and Montminy 2006; Zink *et al.* 2004).

This chapter will argue that older women's experiences of domestic abuse sit at the intersection of sexism and ageism for a number of reasons. Firstly a significant problem when exploring older women's experiences of domestic abuse is defining what constitutes an 'older woman'. How women are categorised impacts upon how their experiences are defined. Secondly there is a tendency within policy to conflate domestic abuse with elder abuse. Problems around how the issue is represented are discussed initially and then the gender-neutral term of 'elder abuse' is critiqued. The experiences of older women are then explored drawing upon qualitative studies to illustrate what is distinct about their experiences of domestic abuse. Such studies have identified particular differences in older women's experiences and, subsequently, their needs. The implications of these and recommendations for social work practice conclude the chapter.

Who are 'older' women?

There are difficulties in both defining and theorising the 'older woman'. Industrial societies focus policy and services upon children as 'the future' to the detriment of older citizens (McKie 2005). Attempts to define 'old' or 'older' often rely upon chronological age. The problem with this is that each study has a differing definition of what constitutes 'old' or 'older', with some drawing a line at over 40, some over 50 and some over 60 (McKie 2005; Morgan Disney and Associates 2000; Scott *et al.* 2004). Scott's (2004, p.38) qualitative study highlighted that 'chronological age *alone* is not a useful marker' for categorising this population, which echoes the recommendations of Morgan Disney and Associates:

> Consideration must be given to the consequences of defining the type of abuse by age as the only criterion. The literature points to the need for assessment of violence directed towards older women, in particular assessing for past history of violence in the relationship, differentiating between age related dependency and fragility and helplessness resulting from issues to do with life stages (less employment opportunities) and the impact of domestic violence on women's capacity to take charge of their lives. (Morgan Disney and Associates 2000, pp.1–2)

Society's constructions of old and elderly are often based upon an understanding of a homogenous group representing decline, fragility, inactivity and dependency (Tulle 2008). These narratives of decline (Gullette 1997) can inform how older women's experiences of abuse are understood rather than attempting to address their multifarious needs. With increases in medical discoveries and greater health care, people are living longer (European Parliament 2010) and the social construction of 'old age' is further emphasised. There has been an increase in academic focus upon the social construction of age and ageing (Gullette 1997) often as a challenge to the negative conations that are linked to it. Fennell, Phillipson and Evers (1988, p.113) claim that 'dependency in old age, and particularly for old women, is socially created and sustained'. Kelly and Johnson (2008) also argue that it is not the age of the person but rather 'ageism' that further compounds their experience of domestic abuse.

Older women are not a homogenous group, in the same way that 'black', 'disabled' and 'younger' women are not (Dicker and Piepmeier 2003, p.14) and they experience domestic abuse in various ways and circumstances which are not always linked to their age. While some older women are frail and dependent on carers, others are active, healthy and are carers themselves. There are some factors, however, that are specific to this particular life stage that other women may not encounter. Given this, other indicators to identify 'older women' are based upon life stage, such as women who are no longer of childbearing age, or women who have stopped work and can draw their 'old age' pensions, those with an increase in caring responsibilities and more health related concerns, such as dementia (McGarry 2008; McGarry, Simpson and Hinchliff-Smith 2011; McKie 2005; Ogg and Bennett 1992; Scott et al. 2004). Thus there is a tension between needing an age range to assess how many 'older' women experience domestic abuse to aid the implementation of strategies to support them, but at the same time recognising the limitations of categorising women purely upon their chronological age and responding to them only on that basis.

Weeks and LeBlanc (2011) suggest it is necessary to differentiate between the varying ages and stages of older women. They argue, for example, that the needs of a woman in her fifties are likely to be different from those of an 80-year-old. Zink, Fisher and Regan (2005) responded to this by analysing research data from women over 55 in three distinct chronological age groups, arguing that there were certain similarities between the life stages and circumstances experienced by their three cohorts. For example, those aged 50 were often at a different life stage than those aged 80, in terms of health needs, capabilities and support. Therefore when looking specifically at older women's needs we can learn from the literature which draws upon the social construction of the ageing process – the 'periodization of the life course' (Lombard 2010) – and the differing life stages or shared social experiences that women may have. It is suggested here that chronological age can be used as an indicator of 'older' women but should be juxtaposed with the heterogeneous model of 'life stages'. Using a life course perspective means a move away from chronology and looking instead at how key experiences and roles structure individuals' lives (Elder 2000).

Degendering the problem: domestic abuse or elder abuse?

In Scotland (where the authors are based) both governmental and voluntary organisations work within the national definition of domestic abuse, which frames it as gender-based violence (Scottish Executive 2000; Scottish Executive 2001). Domestic abuse is part of a continuum of violence that women disproportionately experience because of their gender (Dobash and Dobash 1979; Kelly 1988). Feminist research argues that men who perpetrate such violence are doing so within wider structures of gendered inequality. As is the case with their younger counterparts, older women are more likely to be victims of violence than older men, and experience such violence from a partner or ex-partner (McKie 2005, p.111).

However, as McKie points out, while the *National Strategy on Violence Against Women* (2001) illustrates the prevalence of women as victims, the same report also goes on to refer to older 'people' and not older 'women' when discussing abuse among the elderly:

> …while it is not gender specific, there is a gender dimension in that there are many more women than men in the age groups over 75. (Scottish Executive 2001, Section 3.7 cited in McKie 2005, p.113)

Therefore although the Scottish government highlights domestic abuse as gender based it only does so within certain age-related parameters. This inadvertently reframes older women's experiences of violence from their partners as 'elder abuse' constructing them as a gender-less group. Elder abuse is:

> A single or repeated act, or lack of appropriate action, occurring within any relationship where there is an expectation of trust, which causes harm or distress to an older person. (WHO 2002, p.3)

Scott *et al.* (2004) have argued that the particular experiences of older women are labelled as a 'subset' of abuse against older people. This perpetuates a narrow definition of abuse as it fails to incorporate gender in its construction and perpetration. By incorporating a single act it also takes away the significance of 'impact' which measures the effect of the event or, more usually, an ongoing pattern of feeling fearful and controlled (Hester 2009).

Other research confirms that when older women are the affected group, domestic abuse is often sidelined and problematically reframed as elder abuse (Aronson, Thornewell and Williams 1995; Harris 1996; Hightower 2002; Mears and Sargent 2002; Scott *et al.* 2004; Seaver 1996; Sedger 2001; Whittaker 1995). Aronson *et al.* (1995) illustrate the gender-neutral phrases used in much of the gerontological literature such as *spouse abuse* and *elder abuse*:

> This neutrality is at odds with the weight of theorizing, observation and day-to-day evidence that, in the vast majority of cases, the perpetration of violence in heterosexual partnerships is not evenly distributed between the sexes but is the abuse of women by men. (Dobash, Dobash, Wilson and Daly 1992 cited in Aronson *et al.* 1995, pp.74–75)

Hightower (2002, p.1) maintains that using elder abuse as the frame for older women experiencing domestic abuse reflects 'a view of the elderly as sexless, in which male and female victims of elder abuse are indistinguishable'. This gender neutrality ignores systemic explanations that look at structural power differences between women and men. The abuse they experience from their partners is gender-based abuse which is perpetrated against them because they are women. Indeed, research into elder abuse has confirmed that victimisation differs according to gender (Donder *et al.* 2011). Therefore a gendered perspective is necessary, not only because women dominate the older age groups as a result of living longer than men (Barford *et al.* 2006) but also because as a result of this greater longevity and 'a lifetime of inequities, they are more likely to be vulnerable in health, social and economic terms' (McKie 2005, p.111).

When advocates and service providers fail to view the abuse of older women through the same lenses of gender and power they would use for younger women, they often fail to see that older women have the same needs for safety, decent housing, stable income, connection to family and friends, and quality of life as do younger women (Hightower 2002; Scott *et al.* 2004).

The invisible older woman: the problematic framing of older women's experiences

Reliable incidence data documenting domestic abuse are notoriously difficult to produce (McMillan 2011; Walby 2005) and Band-Winterstein and Eisikovits (2009) maintain that older women are missing from much of the research and prevalence data on domestic abuse. There is widespread recognition that domestic abuse incidents are infrequently reported to police and research shows that this is particularly true for older women (Acierno *et al.* 2001). In fact, Morgan Disney and Associates (2000, p.5) state that the 'lack of data available about older women may be evidence in itself of the difficulty older women experience in speaking about their situation' and many of these women will have fallen through the definitional gap of elder and domestic abuse discussed earlier (Straka and Montminy 2006).

Differentiating older women's and younger women's experiences

Older and younger women will share many similar experiences of domestic abuse and of help-seeking behaviour. However, there will also be differences because of the multiple forms of identities that women have (as a heterogeneous group) and the intersections of oppressions that they experience (see Heywood and Drake 1997). Philips (2000) identified categories of domestic abuse that may be experienced differentially by older women because of their age: long-standing abuse that started earlier in life and continues into old age; new relationships beginning later in life and abuse starting then; and domestic abuse as occurring or worsening in old age. A report by Women's Aid (2007) identified that when abuse began in old age, it is likely to be linked to retirement, disability, changing roles of family members or sexual changes.

These categorisations of older women's abuse focus upon what differentiates their experiences from other women. It highlights how the abuse may impact upon them in differing ways alongside the historical dimensions of their experiences; how their age intersects with their gender. The first example illustrates the longevity of the relationship and the effects of long-term physical and emotional abuse. The long-standing nature of the abuse was a theme echoed in research by Scott *et al.* (2004, p.28):

> I was married at sixteen but I met him at fifteen. And from the beginning really but you don't see it when you're in it. From the beginning, the violence and the power – you're just ruled by fear. Or I was, just by fear. And what he would do to you if you ever left. And I always believed that and you do believe that… [T]hree children before I were twenty and then I had a daughter. So three sons quick and then a daughter. But all the way through you ask for help but you don't actually stand there and say will you help me, my husband beats me up. For many years I'd looked for help through the doctors, the Health Board, various numbers that were here to ring. But when you rang they wouldn't be there or they would say ring back later. And um, there wasn't the help in them days, you just got on with it. And for 39 years I got on with it.

Four themes emerged in the Scott *et al.* (2004) study that brought the particulars of older women's experiences into better focus, and these themes are echoed in the update to the literature review (Scott 2008) and in other qualitative research looking at older women's experiences. They were: shame; barriers to seeking help; dependence; and long-term exposure to trauma.

Shame

McKie (2005, p.68) defines shame as an acknowledgement that one has 'violated what might be considered appropriate behaviour for our gender, age and social situation'. The shame is often twofold: for not having 'fixed' the relationship and then for having lived with abuse for so long. New relationships starting later in life (and failing because of abuse) reiterate the feelings of shame that other studies on older women's victimisation have highlighted (Women's Aid 2007).

The gendering of such an emotion is confirmed by McKie (2005, pp.104–105) who argues that shame, 'is an emotion that women experience in a profound and gendered manner and such feelings maybe pronounced for older women'. The linking of shame to age is also made by Zink *et al.* (2003, p.1434) who maintain that 'years of criticism and hostility seemed to intensify the shame and embarrassment'. The theme was also prominent in research by MacDonald (2000) who interviewed 25 women who had experienced abuse, most of whom were in their fifties and sixties. She comments that:

> [T]he underlying factor which conspired to sustain and conceal the abuse was their deep sense of shame...this inner reality is intrinsically connected with an enduring social sanction of shame, imposed culturally on those who fail (by their own or others' perceptions) to conform to the norms and expectations of their role and gender... It seems that social shaming is more effectively (even if not always deliberately) imposed on victims than on perpetrators. (p.19)

The intersection of gender and age impacts upon older women in terms of shame and also reduces the likelihood that they will identify their situation as abuse (Scott *et al.* 2004). This has implications for their help-seeking behaviour. McGarry and Simpson (2011) maintain that older women who feel this pervasive sense of shame find that it severely impedes their ability to accept support and to access services. A service provider interviewed in Scotland concurred:

> ...all women access our service with great difficulty, but many older women have an even harder time because of issues around shame and embarrassment. (Scott *et al.* 2004, p.39)

Barriers to seeking help

The main issue for older women not seeking help was non-disclosure (Acierno *et al.* 2001). Older women may not report their abuse for the same reasons other women may not (Hague 1999). However, their tendency to under-report may be exacerbated by a complex range of issues. According to Straka and Montminy (2006, pp.252–253) these include: traditional attitudes towards the family; divorce and notions of privacy; financial constraints; and diminishing social networks. Older women may also have been living with domestic abuse for a very long time, be more skilled at protecting their privacy, and be less likely to report incidents or seek help (Scott *et al.* 2004; Scott 2008).

Hightower *et al.* (2001) maintain that a lack of knowledge about resources is a significant barrier to obtaining help or reporting the abuse. Studies have highlighted that older women often do not know where to go for help, or know what support is available (Beaulaurier *et al.* 2007). McGarry and Simpson (2011) found that even when older women knew of services they did not think their needs would be addressed. However, as those working in the field of domestic abuse will know, these issues are not always unique to older women.

Another factor that prevents older women from accessing help was the belief that younger women with children and with 'their lives in front of them' (Scott *et al.* 2004, p.40) were more deserving. Whilst not enshrined in policy, several studies have highlighted that due to funding constraints refuges often offer spaces to women with children first (Blood 2004; McGarry and Simpson 2011; Scott *et al.* 2004). Also refuges often lack facilities for those with reduced mobility or needing disability access which may be more of a necessity among older populations (Blood 2004).

Examples were provided in the research where older women did actively seek help, but there were either no services for them to be referred on to or no action was taken at the point of their disclosure. One woman in Scott's study made repeated pleas for help over the years:

> You don't actually ask for help like that but I think the doctors miss it, when you go constantly to the doctors. And you know they just don't ask the questions 'why are you always in here? Is there something wrong at home?' And you would tell that, you know, in a safe, private room where you know it won't go any further. But they never did – they never did. And once...[her daughter] called the doctor and he called an ambulance right away. But I could see him now standing there going, 'when are you gonna get out of this?' Them were right his words. And I said 'well, will you take me wi' you? Can I come wi' you and you'll look after me?' Then, the times I were in hospital, they would ask you why again, they would ask you what happened and you were like this because you'd been flung down the stairs. But you say you fell down. Because he's sitting with you. You can't tell them. They need to get him out of the room and then ask you. And every time I were in hospital I used to beg to stay. Nobody ever asked why

does she want to stay in hospital? ... And on the report they'll put 'an attentive husband.' He's not attentive. He knows if you're away from him for 2 seconds you might tell somebody. (Scott *et al.* 2004, pp.32–33)

Strümpel and Hackl (2011, p.324) have developed training courses within the EU for those working with older women experiencing domestic abuse based upon findings that suggested 'staff members are not always aware of what constitutes violence against older women and are not adequately prepared to deal with such cases.' Indeed, even when they are, a reluctance to cause friction with family members may prevent them from acting (Strümpel and Hackl 2011, p.327).

Dependence

The notion of 'older' women as vulnerable to abuse because of their frailty and reliance on carers perpetuated in the elder abuse findings was not supported by research into older women's experiences of domestic abuse (Scott *et al.* 2004). Instead it was found that women's dependence was a product of limited economic assets, constricted access to income and housing and progressively fewer avenues for obtaining financial independence as they aged. Younger women experience the same economic barriers, but older women suffer additional barriers to income equality. Older women experiencing domestic abuse and needing support are even less likely than younger women to have access to independent incomes, to pensions (state and private) and to paid work (Scott *et al.* 2004). Mears (2003, p.1486), citing data collected in interviews with over 250 women in Australia, comments:

> Foremost among their concerns was being unable to survive financially and being plunged into poverty or being inappropriately placed in residential care and losing their homes, families, and social networks.

Zink *et al.* (2006) found that older women experiencing abuse were more likely than younger women to be still living with their abusive partner. They also found that *all* women stayed or returned for similar reasons yet these motives were often magnified for older women. Zink *et al.* maintained that older women had more time invested in their families and communities and thus found it harder to leave as well as having fewer supports to enable them to do so (such as education and employment). McKie (2005, p.104) also makes references to the 'complex array of economic and social barriers to "starting again"'.

Dependence *on* others and dependence *of* others come together in sometimes surprising ways for older women. Dependency *on* others stemmed from economic disadvantage arising from women's historical lack of access to economic resources. For example: lack of saleable skills and access to paid work (especially well-paid work); lack of independent income; and lack of access to appropriate housing are all problems for older women (Aitken and Griffin 1996; Penhale 1999; Pillemer 1985; Seaver 1996; Whittaker 1995). Alongside this, research suggests that the dependency *of* a woman's partner can increase an older woman's risk of abuse (Penhale 1999; Pillemer 1985). Penhale (1999, p.3) goes as far as to argue:

> ...it is the dependency of the abuser rather than that of the victim of abuse that appears to be of most significance... Physical and financial abuse are linked with the dependency of the abuser on the abused.

This dependency of abusers on their women partners, when combined with the traditional attitudes towards marriage and gender roles that seem to be more common in older women, puts older women in a very difficult situation. That is, they may feel they need to stay in an abusive relationship as it is her duty to take care of her partner (who may face institutionalisation without her as carer) (Mears 2003; Scott *et al.* 2004). The obligation to care, however, is not always a personal one. Several survivors interviewed in Scotland also recounted stories of being pressured to 'take back' ex-partners by hospital or social work staff working on discharges planning (Scott *et al.* 2004).

Responsibilities for care and support of their older partners or ex-partners are a crucial element of many older women's experiences. Support workers doing assessments who identify a woman's status as a carer need to be aware of this element and be able to explore with older women the possibility that they are living with domestic abuse. Taking proactive steps to ask and encourage disclosure can be identified as a necessity here.

Long-term exposure to trauma: health effects

The kinds of impact of abuse on women are broadly similar across age groups, but some abuse affects older women more adversely or has different ramifications for them, particularly long-term exposure to trauma (Morgan Disney and Associates 2000; Wilke and Vinton 2005).

Research by Morgan Disney and Associates (2000) found that older women reported that the effect of abuse on their health was one of the factors that prompted them to leave. Further health consequences most frequently reported were anxiety (75%), depression (77%), eating issues (40%), fears and phobias (51%) and panic attacks (40%) (Morgan Disney and Associates 2000). The same study also noted the 'long-term debilitating effect on the ability of women to cope with either staying or planning and successfully leaving' (2000, pp.31–32). Wilke and Vinton (2005, pp.322–323) found that women over 45 years old were more likely to report having a chronic disease or health condition, having a chronic mental health condition, and having used tranquilisers or sedatives and antidepressants in the last month.

Fisher and Regan (2006) reported that older women experiencing domestic abuse were 'significantly more likely to report more health conditions than those who were not abused.' They go on to state that older women reporting psychological/emotional abuse:

> ...alone, repeatedly, or with other types of abuse – had significantly increased odds of reporting bone or joint problems, digestive problems, depression or anxiety, chronic pain, and high blood pressure or heart problems. (Fisher and Regan 2006, p.200)

Therefore, older women experiencing domestic abuse are likely to report particular health problems more often than either younger women or older women not experiencing domestic abuse (Fisher and Regan 2006). The implication here for practitioners is that older women might show up in a number of different contexts, presenting more frequently to health services, thereby reiterating the need to ask directly about domestic abuse whilst also targeting resources to where they are visible to older women, such as GP surgeries (McGarry and Simpson 2011).

Conclusions and implications for practice

A consequence of the lack of data available on older women's experiences of domestic abuse is the dearth of evidence on how to inform practice (Weeks and LeBlanc 2011). This concluding section aims to go a short way towards rectifying this and to providing those working within the field of social work and care with guidance on how to support older women experiencing domestic abuse. As discussed above, the barriers to disclosure for older women are similar to those for younger ones, including fear of increased abuse, fear that they will not be believed and isolation. In addition, older women may be reluctant to disclose because they feel too ashamed or they are afraid that they or their partners will be institutionalised (Morgan Disney and Associates 2000; Penhale 1999; Schaffer 1999; Seaver 1996). Supporting disclosure by integrating systematic screening for domestic abuse in routine assessments is likely to improve identification and subsequent service access. Research tells us that the 'most important support for an older woman wanting to escape abuse, was to be believed' (Morgan Disney and Associates 2000), therefore asking older women and believing their answers may be the most powerful intervention that can be offered.

The impact of dependence for older women, including that of an abuser on his partner, is a key practice finding. Carer assessments and other social work instruments should take account of this aspect of older women's experience of domestic abuse. Social workers engaging with older women who have roles as carers might usefully screen for abuse, especially when women present with some of the health concerns mentioned above.

Practitioners can also identify markers that should trigger concerns about the presence of domestic abuse in older women's lives. Zink *et al.* (2005, p.887) confirmed data from other studies showing depression and chronic pain to be common among women experiencing domestic abuse. They also suggested adding digestive problems to a list of 'red flag' conditions that should trigger enquiry about domestic abuse with older women.

Once women are identified, social workers can help by listening to them and finding out what their needs are (Women's Aid 2007). This will enable social workers to find appropriate social supports and link women with appropriate services in their area. To identify what these services and resources are, more training and information sessions need to be accessed by social work departments. Multi-agency networks and local women's groups can also help to identify services as well as highlight gaps in provision. Safety planning in support groups may be especially important given that older women are more likely than their younger counterparts to be still living with their abuser (Scott *et al.* 2004; Scott 2008). Women's Aid also promote the use of women of all ages in awareness-raising material as well as including older women within powerful and prominent positions in workplaces (Brandl 2003) to demonstrate their inclusion and importance.

This chapter has highlighted that older women and domestic abuse is a problem, but one which is neglected in existing research and wider policy and provision. For older women these issues may be compounded by expectations of the services they come into contact with. Domestic abuse is seen as a problem for younger women, so older women presenting to services may be more invisible than their younger counterparts. This includes incidents of domestic abuse being viewed as elder abuse. Furthermore, older women may have been living with domestic abuse for a very long time, be more skilled at protecting their privacy, and be less likely to report incidents or seek help (Scott *et al.* 2004; Scott 2008). The advice to practitioners and social workers highlighted above demonstrates the importance, as for all survivors, of listening to their needs and experiences before beginning to facilitate ways women can move on from their abusive relationships or helping them to remain safe within them should they make the choice to stay.

References

Acierno, R. *et al.* (2001) 'Rape and physical violence: Comparison of assault characteristics in older and younger adults in the national women's study.' *Journal of Traumatic Stress 14*, 685–695.

Aitken, L. and Griffin, G. (1996) 'Thinking in Numbers – the Feminization of Old Age and its Conditions.' In L. Aitken and G. Griffin (eds) *Gender Issues in Elder Abuse.* London: Sage.

Aronson J., Thornewell, C. and Williams, K. (1995) 'Wife assault in old age – coming out of obscurity.' *Canadian Journal on Aging – Revue Canadienne du Vieillissement 14*, 72–88.

Band-Winterstein, T. and Eisikovits, Z. (2009) '"Aging out" of violence: Multiple faces of intimate violence over the life span.' *Journal of Qualitative Health Research 19*, 2, 164–180.

Barford, A., Dorling, D., Davey Smith, G. *et al.* (2006) 'Life expectancy: women now on top everywhere.' *British Medical Journal 332*, 808.

Beaulaurier, R.L., Seff, L.R., Newman, F.L and Dunlop, B.D. (2007) 'External barriers to help seeking for older women who experience intimate partner violence.' *Journal of Family Violence 22*, 4, 747–755.

Blood, I. (2004) *Older Women and Domestic Violence: A Report for Help the Aged/hact.* Available at www.olderhomelessness.co.uk/documents/id2382_older_women_summary.pdf, accessed on 20 July 2012.

Dicker, R. and Piepmeier. A. (eds) (2003) *Catching a Wave: Reclaiming Feminism for the 21st Century.* Boston: Northeastern University Press.

Dobash, R.E. and Dobash, R.P. (1979) *Women, Violence and Social Change.* London: Routledge.

Dobash, R. P., Dobash, R. E., Wilson, M. and Daly, M. (1992) 'The myth of sexual symmetry in marital violence.' *Social Problems 39*, 1, 71–91.

Donder, L. De, Lang, G., Luoma, M.-L., Penhale, B., Ferreira-Alves, J., Tamutiene, I., Santos, A.J., Koivusilta, M., Enzenhofer, E., Perttu, S., Savola, T. and Verté, D. (2011) 'Perpetrators of abuse against older women: a multi-national study in Europe.' *The Journal of Adult Protection 13*, 6, 302–314.

European Parliament (2010) *Report on the Role of Women in an Ageing Society.* Brussels: Committee on Women's Rights and gender Equality.

Fennell, G., Phillipson, C. and Evers, H. (1988) *The Sociology of Old Age*. Milton Keynes: Open University Press.

Fisher, B. and Regan, S. (2006) 'The extent and frequency of abuse in the lives of older women and their relationship with health outcomes.' *The Gerontologist 46*, 2, 200–209.

Goergen, T. (2011) 'Older women and domestic violence.' *Journal of Adult Protection 13*, 6. Available at www.emeraldinsight.com/journals.htm?issn=1466-8203&volume=13&issue=6&article id=17005109&show=html&PHPSESSID=l5vkdd5oggra4n14tpjp8bb5i7, accessed on 10 October 2012.

Gullette, M.M. (1997) *Declining to Decline: Cultural Combat and the Politics of the Midlife*. Charlottesville: University press of Virginia.

Hague, G. (1999) 'Domestic Violence Policy in the 1990s.' In S. Watson and L. Doyal (eds) *Engendering Social Policy*. Buckingham: Open University Press.

Harris, S. (1996) 'For better or for worse: Spouse abuse grown old.' *Journal of Elder Abuse and Neglect 8*, 1, 1–33.

Hester, M. (2009) *Who Does What to Whom? Gender and Domestic Violence Perpetrators*. Bristol: University of Bristol in association with the Northern Rock Foundation.

Heywood, L. and Drake, J. (1997) *Third Wave Agenda: Being feminist, doing feminism*. Minnesota: University of Minnesota Press.

Hightower, J. (2002) *Violence and Abuse in the Lives of Older Women: Is it Elder Abuse or Violence Against Women? Does it Make Any Difference?* Background paper for INSTRAW Electronic Discussion Forum – Gender Aspects of Violence and Abuse of Older Persons; April 2002. Available at http://www.un-instraw.org/data/media/documents/publications/sc-age-Jill_Hightower_discussion_paper.pdf, accessed on 10 October 2012.

Hightower, J., Smith, M. & Hightower, H. (2001) *Silent and Invisible - A Report on Abuse and Violence in the Lives of Older Women in British Columbia and Yukon*. Vancouver: Society of Transition Houses.

Kelly, J.B. and Johnson, M.P. (2008) 'Differentiation among types of intimate partner violence: Research update and implications for interventions.' *Family Court Review 46*, 3, 476–499.

Kelly, L. (1988) *Surviving Sexual Violence*. Cambridge: Polity Press in association with Basil Blackwell.

Lombard, N. (2010) 'It's wrong for a boy to hit a girl because the girl might cry: Investigating young people's understandings of male violence against women.' Unpublished PhD thesis. Glasgow Caledonian University.

Macdonald, L.O. (2000) *Out of the Shadows: Christianity and Violence against Women in Scotland*. Edinburgh: Centre for Theology and Public Issues, University of Edinburgh.

McGarry, J. (2008) 'Older women and domestic violence: Defining the concept and raising awareness in practice.' *Nursing Older People 20*, 6, 10–11.

McGarry, J. and Simpson, C. (2011) 'Domestic abuse and older women: Exploring the opportunities for service development and care delivery.' *The Journal of Adult Protection 13*, 6, 294–301.

McGarry, J., Simpson, C. and Hinchliff-Smith, K. (2011) 'The impact of domestic abuse for older women: A review of the literature.' *Health & Social Care in the Community 19*, 1, 3–14.

McKie, L. (2005) *Families, Violence and Social Change*. Buckingham: Open University Press.

McMillan, L. (2011) 'Sexual Violence Policy in Europe: Human Rights, Policies and Outcomes.' In M. Koch, L. McMillan and B. Peper (eds) *Diversity, Standardization and Social Transformation: Gender, Ethnicity and Inequality in Europe*. Farnham: Ashgate.

Mears, J. (2003) 'Survival is not enough: Violence against older women in Australia.' *Violence Against Women 9*, 12, 1478–1489.

Mears, J. and Sargent, M. (2002) *Survival Is Not Enough. Project Report Two: For Professionals*. New South Wales, Australia: Older Women Speak Up.

Morgan Disney and Associates (2000) *Two Lives – Two Worlds: Older People and Domestic Violence* (Vols 1 and 2). Canberra: Partnerships Against Domestic Violence.

Ogg, J. and Bennett, G. (1992) 'Elder abuse in Britain.' *British Medical Journal 305*, 998–9.

Penhale, B. (1999) 'Bruises on the soul: Older women, domestic violence, and elder abuse.' *Journal of Elder Abuse and Neglect 11*, 1, 1–22.

Phillips, L. (2000) 'Domestic violence and aging women.' *Geriatric Nursing 21*, 4, 188–195.

Pillemer, K. (1985) 'The dangers of dependency: New findings on domestic violence against the elderly.' *Social Problems 33*, 2, 146–157.

Schaffer, J. (1999) 'Older and isolated women and domestic violence project.' *Journal of Elder Abuse & Neglect 11*, 1, 59–77.

Scott, M. (2008) *"Ye just hae to dae it yoursel'": Older Women and Domestic Abuse in Scotland.* Update 2008. Edinburgh: Centre for Research on Families and Relationships.

Scott, M., McKie, L., Morton, S., Seddon, E. and Wosoff, F. (2004) *"And for 39 years I got on with it…" Older Women and Domestic Violence in Scotland.* Produced for Health in Scotland by the Centre for Research on Families and Relationships. Edinburgh: Health Scotland.

Scottish Executive (2000) *National Strategy to Address Domestic Abuse in Scotland.* Edinburgh: Stationery Office.

Scottish Executive (2001) *Preventing Violence Against Women: Action across the Scottish Executive.* Edinburgh: Stationery Office.

Seaver, C. (1996) 'Muted lives: Older battered women.' *Journal of Elder Abuse and Neglect 8*, 2, 3–21.

Sedger, R. (2001) 'Is it aged abuse or domestic violence?' *Australian Domestic Family Violence Clearinghouse Newsletter 9*, 3–4. Available at www.www.adfvc.unsw.edu.au/PDF%20files/Newsletter_9.pdf, accessed on 22 November 2012.

Straka, S. and Montminy, L. (2006) 'Responding to the needs of older women experiencing domestic violence.' *Violence against Women 12*, 3, 251–267.

Strümpel, C. and Hackl, C. (2011) 'The Breaking the Taboo projects – raising awareness of, and training staff in community health and care services on violence against older women within families.' *The Journal of Adult Protection 13*, 6 323–335.

Tulle, E. (2008) *Ageing, the Body and Social Change: Running in Later Life.* Basingstoke, Hampshire: Palgrave Macmillan.

Walby, S. (2005) 'Improving the statistics on violence against women.' *Statistical Journal of the United Nations Economic Commission for Europe 22*, 4, 193–216.

Weeks, L.E. and LeBlanc, K. (2011) 'An ecological synthesis of research on older women's experiences of intimate partner violence.' *Journal of Women and Aging 23*, 4, 283–304.

Whittaker, T. (1995) 'Violence, gender and elder abuse – towards a feminist analysis and practice.' *Journal of Gender Studies 4*, 1, 35–45.

Wilke, D. and Vinton, L. (2005) The nature and impact of domestic violence across age cohorts.' *Affilia 20*, 3, 316–328.

Women's Aid (2007) *Older Women and Domestic Violence: An Overview.* London: Women's Aid. Available at www.womensaid.org.uk/downloads/Olderwomenanddvreport.pdf, accessed on 20 July 2012.

World Health Organisation (2002) *World Report on Violence and Health.* Geneva: WHO.

Zink, T., Fisher, B. and Regan, S. (2005) 'The prevalence and incidence of intimate partner violence in older women in primary care practices.' *Journal of General Internal Medicine 20*, 10, 884–888.

Zink, T., Jacobson, C., Regan, S. and Pabst, S. (2004) 'Hidden victims: the healthcare needs and experiences of older women in abusive relationships.' *Journal of Women's Health 13*, 8, 898–908.

Zink, T., Jacobson, C., Regan, S., Fisher, B. and Pabst, S. (2006) 'Older women's descriptions and understandings of their abusers.' *Violence Against Women 12*, 9, 851–865.

Zink, T., Regan, S., Jacobson, C. and Pabst, S. (2003) 'Cohort, period and aging effects: A qualitative study of older women's reasons for remaining in abusive relationships.' *Violence Against Women 9*, 12, 1429–1441.

CHAPTER 8

Intersecting Inequalities
Implications for Addressing Violence Against Black and Minority Ethnic Women in the United Kingdom

Aisha K. Gill

Introduction

It is only recently that campaigning by non-governmental organisations (NGOs) and women's groups (e.g. the Iranian and Kurdish Women's Rights Organisation and Kurdish Women's Action Against Honour Killings) has brought the true incidence of 'honour'-based violence (HBV) to light and raised awareness of the connections and intersections between this and other forms of violence against women (VAW). Now, governments across Western Europe are striving to address the continuum of forms of VAW, as opposed to just the more visible, mainstream ones.

This chapter assesses the recent hyper-visibility in British media and policy discourses of certain forms of violence against black and minority ethnic (BME) women, particularly forced marriage (FM) and HBV. FM and HBV have proven potent issues in debates on multiculturalism, community cohesion, identity and citizenship. In many of these discourses, BME women are portrayed as passive objects of cultural control: victims of their inferior position in a matrix of intersecting power relations. As a result, the approach to violence against BME women taken by the state and its public services revolves around the perceived 'otherness' of minority communities. Analysing the government's response to FM, HBV and other forms of VAW demonstrates the insidious influence of beliefs about 'us' (mainstream liberal British society) and 'them' (illiberal BME communities in Britain).

The resulting piecemeal approach to addressing FM, HBV and other forms of VAW has meant that many women 'fall through the gaps' between policy and practice, rhetoric and understanding. At the heart of this problem is the fact that current policy and legislation employ simplistic understandings that ignore the sophisticated ways in which women exercise agency despite multiple, significant constraints. Moreover, undue emphasis is placed on the importance of 'exit' from abusive situations rather than the fact that exit often entails the loss of many (if not all) significant relationships and other key markers of identity. Legislative bodies, policy-makers and support services must employ a coordinated, multi-faceted approach based on a more nuanced understanding of agency if *all* women in abusive situations are to be afforded effective assistance.

The chapter concludes by discussing a number of practical measures and policy recommendations derived from intersectional analyses, which suggests that VAW forms a continuum of related abuses and violations of women's rights. Instead of only looking at the commonalities or differences between forms of VAW, it is important to examine how the many different forms of inequality that impact women's lives intersect to shape both the forms of violence they face and their responses. Intersectional analyses produce more nuanced understandings of why certain forms of VAW appear specific to certain communities, while still allowing the parallels between different forms of VAW to be mapped and explored.

Intersectionality

Despite the difficulty of defining many of the key terms in the field, in recent years feminists have pushed for more widespread adoption of the term 'violence against women' (Horvath and Kelly 2007) in place of 'domestic violence' in order to focus attention on (i) the gendered nature of the violence in question (Walby and Allen 2004), and (ii) the fact that it exists within a complex continuum of violence constituted by multiple forms of inequality, including gender, race and class.

Intersectional theorists reject both the notion that there is a single, key oppression from which all other types of oppression derive, and the additive model of oppression, which assumes that BME women are subject to racial and gendered 'double jeopardy' (Brah and Phoenix 2004; Mirza 1997). Instead, intersectionality (Crenshaw 1992) suggests that BME women experience racial, gendered, sexual and class oppression, and that these multiple forms of oppression do not merely occur simultaneously but are inter-related and mutually reinforcing (Collins 2000). Specific locations in the matrix of intersecting axes of oppression represent unique experiences that are more significant than the sum of their parts: this reflects the multiplicative nature of intersecting oppressions (Crenshaw 1992).

Intersectionality sheds light on the ways in which class, education, employment status, sexuality, generational differences in outlook, differences in migration routes into the UK, region of origin, position within community networks in the UK, experiences of racism, and access to appropriate support services intersect to create the constraints and opportunities within which women exercise agency. Sokoloff and Dupont argue that 'intersections colour the meaning and nature of domestic violence, how it is experienced by the self and responded to by others, how personal and social consequences are represented and how and whether escape and safety can be obtained' (2005, p.43). Intersectionality has much to offer in exploring women's experiences of FM, and their different needs in response to it, so that policy and service delivery may be better tailored to meet these needs. For instance, the criminal justice system could benefit from an enhanced understanding of how best to obtain effective testimony from victims: as discussed below, a range of complex factors – personal, social, cultural and institutional – influence an individual's decision to remain silent or to speak out about abuse and, indeed, an individual's ability to provide useful testimony.

Forced marriage

Reports concerning the prevalence of FM and HBV continue to be heavily contested (Khanum 2008) as it is only recently that statistics on these forms of VAW have been collated by police forces and other services. Previously, these crimes were recorded under generic categories concerning domestic violence. However, since 1999, there has been an explosion of media interest in FM and other forms of VAW (such as dowry violence) that are assumed to only affect BME women. Media reports (Slack 2008) and research commissioned by policy-makers (Kazimirski *et al.* 2009; Khanum 2008) have estimated that there are between 3000 and 10,000 cases of FM in the UK every year, while the media (citing police sources) has indicated that up to 17,000 women experience HBV every year (*The Independent* 2008). Headlines sensationalising the issue – 'Tenfold rise in forced marriages in four years' (*Daily Mail* 2009) – have created a *perception* that it is a growing problem. However, it is likely that the recent recording of FM and HBV as specific crimes, coupled with an increase in the number of women reporting such crimes to the authorities due to the recent upsurge in publicity, has merely revealed the true extent of a pre-existing problem.

Moreover, variations in how domestic violence is defined make it difficult to obtain accurate statistics about *all* forms of VAW. For instance, although FM is specifically recognised as an abuse of human rights in a number of United Nations (UN) treaties and other international instruments, many of these employ different definitions. The 2005 Council of Europe study *Forced Marriages in Council of Europe Member States* uses a broad definition: it considers FM an:

> umbrella term covering marriage as slavery, arranged marriage, traditional marriage, marriage for reasons of custom, expediency or perceived respectability, child marriage,[1] early marriage, fictitious, bogus or sham marriage, marriage of convenience, unconsummated marriage, putative marriage, marriage to acquire nationality and undesirable marriage – in all of which the concept of consent to marriage is at issue[.][2]

The core issue is that FM violates an individual's fundamental human right to freely consent to marriage. This right is enshrined in numerous international instruments, including those collectively known as the

---

1 'Child marriage' is usually considered to represent a form of FM as minors are deemed unable to give informed consent.

2 Directorate General of Human Rights, *Forced marriages in Council of Europe member states: A comparative study of legislation and political initiatives*, Council of Europe, 2005, p.7. Available at www.coe.int/t/dghl/standardsetting/violence/Documents/CDEG-2005-1_Forced%20marriages_correctPDF.pdf.

International Bill of Human Rights: the Universal Declaration of Human Rights (1948),[3] the International Covenant on Civil and Political Rights (1966),[4] and the International Covenant on Economic, Social, and Cultural Rights.[5] Article 16(2) of the Universal Declaration of Human Rights affirms that 'Marriage shall be entered into only with the free and full consent of the intending spouses', according to the Declaration's underlying principles of self-determination and human dignity. Article 23 of the International Convention on Civil and Political Rights and Article 10(1) of the International Convention on Economic, Social, and Cultural Rights use similar wording. However, the complexities of what comprises 'free and full consent' remain unclear. This has significant implications for the professionals who seek to employ these instruments to help individual victims obtain redress. Various other international treaties specifically condemn and prohibit both FM and specific subtypes of FM. For instance, the Committee on the Elimination of Discrimination against Women (CEDAW) (the treaty body established by CEDAW) has highlighted the fact that the persistence of discriminatory customs and traditions, as well as failures to enforce domestic legislation, constitute violations of the Convention.[6] The CEDAW's recognition of the role of social factors in FM, including cultural values that give rise to various forms of discrimination, is significant: it points to both the complexities of the causal factors behind FM and other forms of VAW, and the ways in which different types of discrimination intersect to influence women's ability to give their full and free consent to marry.

In the UK, numerous influences, including state policies (particularly immigration policies), country of origin, and individual diasporic experiences intersect to shape individual experiences of coercion in matters of marriage. For instance, some parents in the diasporic context

---

3 Universal Declaration of Human Rights, UN General Assembly Resolution 217A, UN Doc. A/810, 12 December 1948. Available at www.un.org/en/documents/udhr.

4 International Covenant on Civil and Political Rights, UN General Assembly Resolution 2200A (XXI), UN Doc. A/6316, 16 December 1966. Available at www2.ohchr.org/english/law/ccpr.htm.

5 International Covenant on Economic, Social, and Cultural Rights, UN General Assembly Resolution 2200A (XXI), 16 December 1966. Available at www2.ohchr.org/english/law/cescr.htm.

6 Committee on the Elimination of Discrimination against Women, General Recommendation No 21: Equality in marriage and family relations, 13th session, 1994, UN Doc. A/49/38. Available at www.un.org/womenwatch/daw/cedaw/recommendations/recomm.htm#recom21.

seek to impose an unwanted marriage in order to stem the influence of Western culture over their daughters or to end their daughters' association with 'unsuitable' partners (Gangoli and Chantler 2009; Samad and Eade 2003, p.67). Similarly, consanguineous marriage (i.e. 'cousin marriage') may be re-asserted as a traditional cultural practice in order to facilitate the migration to kin out of a sense of obligation and/or the need to maintain links with the community's country of origin (Anitha and Gill 2011; Shaw 2001). With successive legislation restricting immigration routes into the UK, marriage is becoming an increasingly important means of migration to Britain for those outside the EU.

'Honour'-based violence

Attempts to attribute FM specifically and HBV more generally to particular geographical regions (primarily the Middle East), cultural factors (primarily South Asian or Kurdish traditions), faiths (primarily Islam) or types of society (primarily tribal societies) have failed because VAW transcends single-dimension causal explanations (Mojab and Abdo 2004; Ortner 1978). FM and HBV are part of a larger phenomenon of VAW that derives from a wide range of socio-cultural values and norms – many common to both mainstream British society and minority communities – that intersect to legitimise the control of women by men. Indeed, the fact that no class or ethnic group is exempt from gendered forms of violence has long served to emphasise the continuities between different forms of VAW.

The word 'honour' is placed within quotation marks here to draw attention to the problems inherent in using a word with so many positive socio-cultural connotations when discussing violence and murder. As Welchman and Hossain (2005, p.4) observe, the use of the term 'honour crime' is by no means straightforward: its application to forms of violence that overwhelmingly afflict women rather than men lends support to the idea that 'honour' is intricately tied to women's behaviour. Moreover, the word 'honour' is susceptible to 'exoticisation' (ibid.) as there is a tendency in the West to see honour crimes as emerging from 'backward' cultural traditions. However, HBV is more effectively conceptualised (as in this chapter) as a specific category of VAW that operates through honour codes legitimised by patriarchal values (Piper 2004, p.101) and family, community or other social structures. The primary justification for HBV is the protection of a socially constructed value-system, with associated norms and traditions, centred on the notion of honour as symbolic capital (Bourdieu 1977).

Bourdieu (1977) argues that honour is not an aspect of cultural practice but rather that it emerges from a constellation of interpersonal exchanges. Honour is a multi-dimensional concept that encompasses familial respect, patriotism and social prestige. It is determined by the interaction between a person's feelings of self-worth and the worth that his/her peer-group (i.e. 'honour group') assigns to him/her. As honour is bestowed in social contexts, it is ephemeral and can be lost (Gill 2009; Maris and Saharso 2001). Losing honour invites ridicule and disgrace, and subjects the individual and his/her family to shame. A wide range of acts are considered shameful, but none more so than those that are seen as compromising female chastity. Romance and even flirting may shame the offender and her family as female chastity constitutes a core aspect of the family's symbolic 'honour' capital. A woman who is perceived to have offended against the prevailing notion of honour must be punished in order to restore honour and remove shame. Therefore, the families of many honour killing victims do not publicly express regret or grief over the murder. Instead, they frequently condemn the victim for betraying family loyalty for personal gratification. Thus, male aggressors become victims and female victims become culprits (Husseini 2010).

Honour killings (and other forms of HBV) often result from accusations of female adultery, which threatens both personal honour and the honour of the wider community. In honour-based societies, romance has no place in marriage, the purpose of which is to uphold social structures and the alliances between families and clans: romance is perceived as a form of personal gratification. For this reason, all forms of romance are considered illicit and immoral in honour-based societies and provoke condemnation, ostracism and even violence (Anitha and Gill 2011; Lindholm 1998).

While HBV revolves specifically around socio-cultural values stemming from notions of honour, it has much in common with other forms of VAW: the underlying social structures that discriminate against women, and, thus, create the conditions under which VAW occurs, are similar in societies with honour systems and those oriented towards other values. However, in policy terms HBV tends to be treated as distinct from non-honour-based forms of VAW. For instance, while many British NGOs prefer the term VAW because it encompasses violence experienced by women from both majority and minority communities (Phillips and Dustin 2004), until recently the main government initiative on HBV focused specifically on FM. For this reason, little attention has been paid to developing a better understanding of HBV and VAW more widely.

Following the 9/11 terrorist attacks, most states in Western Europe became concerned that the movements of migrants had 'concealed a potential for terror attacks, a threat to security' (Jordan *et al.* 2003, p.197). In this context, the racially motivated violence that occurred in Oldham, Burnley and Bradford in the UK was generally held to have been initiated by 'immigrants who held "backward" attitudes and perpetrated oppressive practices (like forced marriage) against women' (Fekete 2006, p.7). Unsurprisingly, HBV came to be ideologically (re-)conceptualised not as patriarchal but as an expression of the atavistic nature of minority cultures; these, in turn, were conceptualised as standing in sharp contrast to mainstream 'liberal' (white) British society.

Therefore, the 1997–2010 Labour government's numerous initiatives on FM and HBV were built on the notion that BME women find themselves 'trapped by familial expectations' (MP Ann Cryer quoted in Alexander and Goldsmith 2007). According to this rhetoric, HBV is seen as a problem primarily because the experiences of its victims ('othered' women) and its perpetrators ('othered' men from 'othered' cultures) temporarily threaten the moral and, by extension, liberal culture of the nation (Gill and Anitha 2009; Gill and Mitra-Kahn 2012). Indeed, media portrayals of HBV and FM often suggest BME women are victims simply as a result of being women in BME communities/societies (Anitha and Gill 2011): thus, Western intervention is conceptualised as necessary to free BME women from oppression and violence. Critically, in the media and policy documents causality is attributed almost universally to the supposedly immutable and intrinsic traditions, customs and religious beliefs of these othered cultures, with little or no attention directed towards individual perpetrators.

If FM and HBV are blamed on socialisation into particular religious and cultural systems of belief, it follows that it is right and proper for the state to exert control over cultural issues in order to prevent human rights abuses: this logic allowed the former government to neatly sidestep charges of prejudice in relation to policies, especially immigration policies, that it claimed were necessary to address FM and HBV. For instance, paragraph 277 of the Immigration Rules was amended in 2008 to raise the minimum age from 18 to 21 for (i) a person to be granted a visa for the purposes of settling in the UK as a spouse or civil partner and (ii) to sponsor a person for such a visa. Ostensibly, the amendment was intended to deter and prevent FM. However, in the linked appeals of *R (Quila and another) v Secretary of State for the Home Department* and *R (Bibi and another) v Secretary of State for the Home Department*[7] the Supreme Court, by a 4–1 majority, ruled that the refusal to grant spousal visas to the respondents was an infringement of their rights under Article 8 of the European Convention on Human Rights, which is interpreted as broadly guaranteeing the right to family life. Thus, the Supreme Court ruled that the amendment was not a lawful way to achieve the goal of deterring and preventing FM.

However, arguing that culture and/or religion are not the sole or even primary causes of HBV is not to suggest that there is no cultural dimension to HBV. As Purna Sen argues, just as it is flawed to posit a cultural specificity that fails to see the linkages between particular manifestations of VAW, 'to deny specificity if it exists is also problematic' (Sen 2005, p.50). However, responses to HBV must not exoticise the problem: rather, it must be viewed as part of the larger struggle against VAW (Gill 2009). Those who seek to defend HBV, and other practices that discriminate against women, have argued that it is only in relation to Western values and norms that these practices are rendered problematic; therefore, attempts to prevent VAW can be construed as reminders of colonial domination and the imposition of Western morals and values (Spivak 1988).

The practice of female genital mutilation is a particularly thorny case in point: while many societies (e.g. Sudan, Iraqi Kurdistan) claim that the practice is a key socio-cultural tradition, the partial or total excision of women's external genitalia (when not performed for therapeutic reasons) is a serious violation of women's and girls' rights. Many consider the practice a form of torture (Njambi 2004) and still more condemn it in terms of the right to bodily integrity, not to mention the right to found a family (since it often has significant implications for fertility). While those seeking to assist victims of HBV are right to be concerned about violating individuals' rights to cultural and religious freedom, especially when working in minority communities they do not possess a deep understanding of, these concerns must not result in failures to assist and protect victims of VAW, no matter what their background; cultural sensitivity must not come at the price of allowing further abuses to occur through granting individuals, communities and societies impunity.

---

7   R (Quila and Anor) v SSHD; R (Bibi and Anor) v SSHD [2011] UKSC 45.

What are the implications for social workers?

The key to promoting more effective social worker engagement both with victims and with preventive measures centres on enhancing their understanding of the major causes and consequences of VAW in BME communities. The first step is for the mainstream media, as well as individual politicians and professionals, to acknowledge that attributing HBV to particular geographical regions, cultural factors, faiths or societies involves a concurrent failure to address the complexities of the intersections between these and other causal factors. As Narayan (1998), *inter alios*, has argued, feminist initiatives and political agendas alike need to be responsive to the diversity of women's lives. They must simultaneously be wary of cultural essentialism. Attention must be focused on the fact that HBV is part of a broader phenomenon of VAW: its expression in minority communities must not be divorced from its expression in mainstream British society in measures aimed at addressing and preventing abuses. It will also be necessary to tackle stereotypes associated with BME women, not least in relation to the impact of these stereotypes on the credibility of individual victims.

Perceptions of a victim's credibility can fundamentally affect the level and quality of service she receives from social services, the police and the courts as professionals' grasp of individual cases often hinges on their understanding of victims' credibility. For instance, a victim's account of her experiences may collapse in court if she does not receive careful preparatory assistance from a qualified *and* experienced professional who can understand the complex, intersecting reasons for her to speak out about some events while remaining silent on other points that, from a criminal justice perspective, may be more salient (for a detailed discussion, see Ellison and Munro 2010; Gupta and Sapnara 2011; Sweeney 2009). It is vital to remember that victims are often young and/or vulnerable: some may even be under-age. Care must be taken to ensure that they understand not only what will happen as their case proceeds (both inside and outside the courtroom) but also what is expected of them and how they may best advance their own interests.

Furthermore, it is not uncommon for FM to occur in otherwise law-abiding families that have previously demonstrated love and appropriate care for the victim. Many victims present as being heavily conflicted: they often make reluctant witnesses as they are torn between their desire for personal safety and concerns about their parents' feelings. For this reason, and their own deeply held socio-cultural beliefs, while victims do wish to escape abuse and coercion, they may also want to find a way to protect their parents' (and their own) 'honour'. Thus, victims often attempt to limit confrontational measures. For example, although Dr Humayra Abedin's parents imprisoned and drugged her in order to coerce her into a marriage in Bangladesh, when she returned to the UK after a Bangladeshi court order was issued, she announced that she did not want to pursue any charges against her family. Indeed, she professed her continued love for them. Her decision was widely criticised in the tabloid press (Baig 2008). Such contradictory impulses may manifest themselves in victims failing to give a full account of the family's abusive conduct in order to minimise family members' culpability. For example, a victim may argue that her parents are acting in response to coercive community pressures. The fact that a victim must draw heavily upon internal reservoirs of courage and resilience in order to take her family to court exposes the fact that the stereotypical image of the weak and passive BME woman so frequently seen in media and policy discourses is inaccurate (Gupta and Sapnara 2011, pp.208–209; Razack 2004). Social workers and other professionals must be mindful of the need to challenge the stereotypes with which they are presented if they are to assist victims and work effectively with communities to bring about the socio-cultural changes needed to prevent HBV.

Despite increased interest in VAW in the media, political circles and British society as a whole, BME women have not been identified by policy-makers as needing specialised assistance (Phillips and Dustin 2004). One exception has been the provision of specialist domestic violence services, including refuges. These services were developed in the late 1970s and early 1980s in response to campaigning by BME women who argued that they were not receiving effective support from mainstream services. However, despite the stated efforts of the 1997–2010 Labour government to be sensitive in its dealings with minority communities, in striving to ameliorate the problems of HBV and FM, the government framed the issue in cultural terms rather than viewing it as a specific manifestation of the wider problem of VAW (Anitha and Gill 2011). As discussed above, viewing HBV as a culturally sanctioned act practised solely by minorities positions the host nation as a liberal and neutral force – a socially superior society within which legal remedies can be constructed – with the corollary that the othered, minority society is essentialised as atavistic and illiberal (Razack 2004). As a result, the legal remedies to FM that are available in Britain have little to do with the rights and needs of BME women. Instead, they are primarily concerned with the policing of minority communities and the patrolling of the nation's borders (Dustin and Phillips 2008). Thus, immigration law presents a key point of contradiction for the UK government, which is simultaneously concerned with restrictions motivated by racialised hostility and with protecting individual human rights. This has resulted in BME women being caught between these often mutually exclusive concerns (Southall Black Sisters 2012).

Other changes to the statutory framework on VAW have started to close gaps in both legislation and provision, providing some BME women fleeing domestic violence with sufficient support to allow them to leave abusive relationships. However, legislative, policy and practical frameworks need to be extended if all women are to receive effective assistance. Vitally, avenues via which BME women may be allowed to stay in the UK on the grounds of domestic violence (e.g. the 'domestic violence rule': paragraph 289A of the Immigration Rules) must be provided and safeguarded. Furthermore, the state must recognise that only policies and practical measures that address the economic realities facing BME women and, thus, help them to achieve financial independence will provide these women with a viable avenue for leaving abusive spouses. The need for an intersectional approach is especially clear here: while one piece of legislation may offer assistance to victims affected by VAW, other pieces prevent them from taking up this assistance since the law, as a whole, does not currently speak to the complexities of the problems facing these women (Gill 2011).

The provision of effective support and assistance depends on the implications of women's individual circumstances (especially in relation to race, culture, socio-economic status, immigration status and language) being understood by professionals working on the front-line. Acknowledging the effect of these factors on an abused woman's assessment of her options is a key part of any effective solution: this is especially significant in light of research that indicates that BME women are less likely to access statutory services in relation to domestic violence for many complex reasons, including fear of racism and the desire to avoid reinforcing stereotypes about their communities (Batsleer *et al.* 2002). For this reason, it is particularly worrying that the recent policy shift towards community cohesion has led to the closure of many of the domestic violence services that cater specifically to the needs of BME women and, thus, have the expertise to understand and address their complex, intersecting problems. These closures threaten the only routes via which many BME women are willing and/or able to seek support in resisting coercion and violence within their families and communities. Moreover, they threaten to destroy one of the most important sources of expertise about FM and HBV in minority communities: information critical not only to helping individual victims but to creating effective preventive initiatives.

Recommendations

Professionals working in front-line services have argued that addressing FM and HBV more effectively depends on:

1. the development of efficient information systems for collecting and recording both more detailed and more accurate data about FM, HBV and other forms of VAW

2. the development of better working relationships between police and specialist VAW services in BME communities

3. enhancing social worker training in order to help these professionals to develop a more nuanced understanding of FM, HBV and related issues

4. addressing inconsistencies in police responses through training aimed at counteracting 'postcode lottery' effects, and

5. the provision of suitably resourced specialist services, including safe shelters for victims.

However, the primary recommendation put forward by a wide range of bodies and professionals concerns the need for a more holistic, coordinated approach to addressing and preventing HBV that recognises the complexity of the issue. An associated concern centres on the need for more resources to be directed towards securing the financial stability of specialist women's services, many of which are currently under threat as a result of major cutbacks in government funding (Gill 2011). As criminal justice professionals, healthcare providers, teachers and policy-makers are facing ever more stringent restrictions on spending, community resources, including specialist BME refuges and outreach services, are facing cutbacks and, in some cases, closure. However, these organisations are best placed to offer expertise and insights into best practice that would allow for more nuanced understandings of HBV to be developed and shared among all professionals dealing with these issues.

154 Violence Against Women

Moreover, these organisations represent a key element in the fight against VAW: developing a more coordinated approach to HBV depends on their involvement, not least because many BME women initially seek help from these organisations rather than public services. Indeed, work is also needed to determine why South Asian victims of VAW often flee their marital home without seeking support from the relevant authorities, resulting in violence and abuse often going unreported in these communities.

Moving forward, social work policies and responses to FM and HBV need to be more grounded in the reality of victims' experiences. Social workers need to recognise that specific gendered harms occur *within* a general framework of inequality that supports VAW; therefore, attempts to address specific forms of VAW must be conceptualised as part of a broader campaign to end gender-based violence. A more victim-centred, intersectional approach would facilitate women's agency and help those working in front-line services to better understand the specificity of their clients' needs and experiences: this, in turn, would allow social workers and other relevant professionals to address the constraints BME women face more effectively, extending and enhancing the opportunities available to them in seeking to escape from violence. Intersectional analyses have identified a series of urgent needs in this regard, including the need for:

1. provisions to establish victim safety

2. measures to offer women and their children the opportunity to access specialist support (including therapeutic assistance) that provides opportunities to express the impact of their experiences in their own words, without fear of implicit or explicit censure

3. support structures that recognise women's agency and their desire to have choices, and

4. outreach services that are sufficiently developed and resourced to implement preventative measures.

However, there is also much to be done in developing better training programmes, and in developing and disseminating best practice guidelines. For instance, social workers often fail to address the reasons that they are sometimes unable to respond effectively to the experiences of South Asian women (Gill 2009). Social workers (and, indeed, all those working in sensitive areas) must be willing to explore their own beliefs about VAW in BME communities if they are to ensure that personal biases do not negatively influence responses to victims (Coy, Kelly and Foord 2009). This is a critical aspect of the intersectional, victim-centred approach advocated in this chapter.

Conclusion

Taking action to end VAW in BME communities is far from easy because the phenomenon cannot be extricated from the many socio-cultural forces that sustain it. Given the fact that this grave problem stands at the intersection of multiple social forces, it is important to reiterate that potential solutions must be viewed as only *part* of a mosaic of necessary responses. All relevant agencies and professionals must acknowledge the complexity of BME women's experiences of, and responses to, gendered forms of violence and abuse: poverty, health status (both mental health and physical wellbeing), class, language ability, sexual orientation, religious beliefs, disability, experiences of racism and place of residence (whether urban or rural) – and the intersections of these factors – have a profound effect on women's ability to access the services and resources they need (Crenshaw 1992). Victims of VAW may also be trafficked or fleeing war and other forms of armed conflict, often with their children. All of these circumstances contribute to an individual's unique, gender-based 'herstory': these complicating factors need to be taken into account when designing preventative, protective and interventionist responses to VAW at both the individual and general level.

Tackling FM and so-called HBV effectively in the UK therefore necessitates a shift in political thinking. Instead of simplistically conceptualising these forms of VAW as cultural traditions common to a range of 'backward' (and, thus, 'othered') societies, the issue needs to be (re-)considered in the context of the prevalence of both patriarchal value systems and VAW. Gender-based violence affects women in all societies, though it does so in different ways and for different reasons: turning a political or media spotlight on forms of VAW that primarily afflict women from BME communities often means that attention is directed away from broader gender inequalities and human rights issues in favour of political debates about 'Britishness' and the perceived 'dangers' of non-assimilated (im)migrant communities. Thus, the experiences of BME women are often dismissed as manifestations of cultural difference rather than expressions of the broader problem of VAW. In this way, multiculturalism, for all its good intentions, has become a force of repression as it fails to recognise that VAW is a pan-cultural, human rights problem that should be dealt with on a universal level. An intersectional approach is vital to transcending this narrow vision and, instead, embracing a nuanced understanding of the complexities of FM and HBV that allows their specificity to be addressed in order to help victims and, at the same time, deal with the links between these and other forms of VAW and gender inequality. Only then can the broader phenomenon of VAW be effectively tackled.

References

Alexander, C. and Goldsmith, C. (2007) 'U.K. "Honour Killings", Cloaked in Family Silence, Stymie Police.' Bloomberg, 16 January 2007. Available at www.bloomberg.com/apps/news?pid=ne wsarchive&sid=aQe8VVyUR.qk&refer=uk, accessed on 23 July 2012.

Anitha, S. and Gill, A. (2011) 'The Social Construction of Forced Marriage and its "Victim" in Media Coverage and Crime Policy Discourses.' In A. Gill and S. Anitha (eds) *Forced Marriage: Introducing A Social Justice and Human Rights Perspective.* London: Zed Books.

Baig, A. (2008) 'When having it all isn't asking a lot.' *The Sun*, 19 December 2008. Available at www.thesun.co.uk/sol/homepage/woman/article2040899.ece, accessed on 23 July 2012.

Batsleer, J., Burman, E., Chantler, K. and McIntosh, H.S. (2002) *Domestic Violence and Minoritisation: Supporting Women to Independence.* Manchester :Women's Studies Research Centre, Manchester Metropolitan University.

Bourdieu, P. (1977) *Outline of a Theory of Practice.* Cambridge: Cambridge University Press.

Brah, A. and Phoenix, A. (2004) 'Ain't I a woman? Revisiting intersectionality.' *Journal of International Women's Studies 5*, 3, 74–87.

Collins, P. (2000) *Black Feminist Thought: Knowledge, Consciousness, and the Politics of Empowerment.* New York: Routledge.

Coy, M., Kelly, L. and Foord, J. (2009) *Map of Gaps 2: The Postcode Lottery of Violence Against Women Support Services in Britain.* London: End Violence Against Women and Equality and Human Rights Commission.

Crenshaw, K. (1992) 'Mapping the margins: Intersectionality, identity politics, and violence against women of colour.' *Stanford Law Review 43*, 6, 1241–1242.

Daily Mail (2009) 'Ten-fold rise in forced marriages in just four years.' Available at www.dailymail. co.uk/news/article-1196955/Ten-fold-rise-forced-marriages-just-years.html, accessed on 23 July 2012.

Dustin, M. and Phillips, A. (2008) 'Whose agenda is it? Abuses of women and abuses of "culture" in Britain.' *Ethnicities 8*, 3, 405–424.

Ellison, L., and Munro, V. (2010) 'Jury Deliberation and Complainant Credibility in Rape Trials.' In C. McGlynn and V. Munro (eds) *Rethinking Rape Law: International and Comparative Perspectives.* London: Ashgate.

Fekete, L. (2006) 'Enlightened fundamentalism? Immigration, feminism, and the right.' *Race and Class 48*, 2, 1–22.

Gangoli, G. and Chantler, K. (2009) 'Protecting victims of forced marriage: Is age a protective factor?' *Feminist Legal Studies 17*, 3, 267–288.

Gill, A. (2009) '"Honour" killings and the quest for justice in Black and Minority Ethnic Communities in the UK.' *Criminal Justice Policy Review 20*, 4, 475–494.

Gill, A. (2011) *Human Rights and Civil Legal Aid: The Case for Providing Funding for Civil Cases Involving Victims of Domestic Violence.* London: National Federation of Women's Institutes.

Gill, A. and Anitha, S. (2009) 'The illusion of protection? An analysis of Forced Marriage legislation and policy in the UK.' *Journal of Social Welfare and Family Law 31*, 3. 257–269.

Gill, A. and Mitra-Kahn, T. (2012) 'Modernising the "other": Assessing the ideological underpinnings of the policy discourse on forced marriage in the UK.' *Journal of Policy and Politics 40*, 1, 107–122.

Gupta, T. and Sapnara, K. (2011) 'The Law, the Courts and their Effectiveness.' In A. Gill and S. Anitha (eds) *Forced Marriage: Introducing a Social Justice and Human Rights Perspective.* London: Zed Books.

Horvath, M. and Kelly, L. (2007) *From the Outset: Why Violence Should be a Core Cross-strand Priority Theme for the Commission for Equality and Human Rights.* London: Child and Woman Abuse Studies Unit: London Metropolitan University.

Husseini, R. (2010) *Murder in the Name of Honour.* Oxford: Oneworld Publications.

Jordan, A., Wurzel, R., Zito, A. and Bruckner, L. (2003) 'European governance and the transfer of "new" environmental policy instruments (NEPIs) in the European Union.' *Public Administration 81*, 3, 555–574.

Kazimirski, A., Keogh, P., Smith, R. and Gowland, S. (2009) *Forced Marriage: Prevalence and Service Response.* London: Natcen.

Khanum, N. (2008) *Forced Marriage, Family Cohesion and Community Engagement.* Luton: Equality in Diversity.

Lindholm, C. (1998) 'Love and structure.' *Theory, Culture and Society 15*, 3-4, 243–263.

Maris, C. and Saharso, S. (2001) 'Honour killing: A reflection on gender, culture and violence.' *The Netherlands' Journal of Social Sciences 37*, 1, 52–73.

Mirza, H. (ed.) (1997) *Black British Feminism.* London: Routledge.

Mojab, S. and Abdo, N. (2004) *Violence in the Name of Honour: Theoretical and Political Challenges.* Istanbul: Bilgi University Press.

Narayan, U. (1998) 'Essence of culture and a sense of history: A feminist critique of cultural essentialism.' *Hypatia 13*, 2, 87–106.

Njambi, W. (2004) 'Dualisms and female bodies in representations of African female circumcision.' Online, *Feminist Theory 5*, 294–299.

Ortner, S. (1978) 'The virgin and the state.' *Feminist Studies 4*, 19–35.

Piper, N. (2004) *Gender and Migration: A Paper Prepared for the Policy Analysis and Research Programme of the Global Commission on International Migration.* Geneva: Global Commission on International Migration.

Phillips, A. and Dustin, M. (2004) 'UK initiatives on Forced Marriage: Regulation, dialogue and exit.' *Political Studies 52*, 3, 531–551.

Razack, S. (2004) 'Imperilled Muslim women, dangerous Muslim men and civilised europeans: Legal and social responses to forced marriages.' *Feminist Legal Studies 12*, 2, 129–174.

Samad, Y. and Eade, J. (2003) *Community Perceptions of Forced Marriage.* London: Community Liaison Unit, Foreign and Commonwealth Office.

Sen, P. (2005) '"Crimes of Honour", Value and Meaning.' In L. Welchman and S. Hossain (eds) *'Honour': Crimes, Paradigms and Violence Against Women.* London: Zed Books.

Shaw, A. (2001) 'Kinship, cultural preference and immigration: Consanguineous marriage among British Pakistanis.' *Journal of the Royal Anthropological Institute 7*, 2, 315–334.

Slack, J. (2008) 'More Than 3,000 Asian Children Vanishing from School and "Forced into Arranged Marriages".' *Daily Mail*, 11 March 2008. Available at www.dailymail.co.uk/news/article-530295/More-3-000-Asian-children-vanishing-school-forced-arranged-marriages.html, accessed on 23 July 2012.

Sokoloff, N.J. and Dupont, I. (2005) 'Domestic violence at the intersections of race, class and gender.' *Violence Against Women 3*, 1, 38–64.

Southall Black Sisters (2012) 'Landmark Supreme Court Ruling: Immigration policy on forced marriage is unlawful.' Available at www.southallblacksisters.org.uk/immigration-policy-on-forced-marriage-is-unlawful, accessed on 23 July 2012.

Spivak, G. (1988) 'Can the Subaltern Speak?' In C. Nelson and L. Grossberg (eds) *Marxism and the Interpretation of Culture*. Chicago: University of Illinois Press.

Sweeney, J. (2009) 'Credibility, proof and refugee law.' *International Journal of Refugee Law 21*, 4, 700–726.

The Independent (2008) 'A question of honour: Police say 17,000 women are victims every year.' Available at www.independent.co.uk/news/uk/home-news/a-question-of-honour-police-say-17000-women-are-victims-every-year-780522.html, accessed on 23 July 2012.

Walby, S. and Allen, J. (2004) *Domestic Violence, Sexual Assault and Stalking: Findings from the British Crime Survey*. Home Office Research Study 276. London: Home Office.

Welchman, L. and S. Hossain (eds) (2005) *'Honour': Crimes, Paradigms and Violence against Women*. London: Zed Books.

CHAPTER 9

Domestic Abuse in the UK
Why We Need to Understand Perpetrators

Elizabeth Gilchrist

Introduction

> Rather than attempting to define masculinity as an object...we need to focus on the processes by which men and women conduct gendered lives.
>
> (Connell 1995, p.71 cited in Gadd 2002)

This chapter seeks to explain why it is important to understand what characteristics perpetrators share and why it is important to understand these. The chapter briefly reviews some limitations of traditional approaches which focused more strongly on providing appropriate responses for victims post-abuse, suggests a number of theories which have been identified as potentially adding to our understanding of aspects of men's abuse of women, and identifies current thinking about risk and intervention with perpetrators so the reader is informed about current practice in the UK.

Why focus on perpetrators?

There is now developing knowledge about characteristics of domestic abuse (DA) offenders and we can identify features correlating with risk. We still know too little about the relevance of typologies in understanding risk in male perpetrators; little about how to reconcile different subtypes of family violence (Johnson 2006; Kelly and Johnson 2008); and less about female offenders and those who offend within same-sex relationships. However, we do know that women's violence tends to be reactive rather than proactive (Walker 1983), sometimes termed 'violent resistance' (Muftic, Bouffard and Bouffard 2007), and still needs to be seen in the context of the woman as victim (Giles 2005; Dobash and Dobash 2004; Swan and Snow 2002; Miller and Meloy 2006).

To add complexity, there is no one offence of domestic abuse. DA offenders are likely to have been convicted of a range of offences. In a probation sample in the UK, 38 per cent of offenders referred to domestic abuse perpetrators' groups were convicted of assault occasioning actual bodily harm (ABH), 37 per cent of common assault, and 2 per cent of assault occasioning grievous bodily harm (GBH). The remaining offenders were convicted of a range of offences in which the intimate partner and abusive element of the offending was evident only through the individual circumstances of the offence (criminal damage 11%, harassment 6%, threats to kill 5%, affray 5%) (Gilchrist *et al.* 2003). Similarly data from victims (Pence and Paymar 1993a, b) identifies that physical violence is only one of a range of abusive strategies within an abusive relationship. The sensitivity of professionals to the possibility of a DA context for a range of offences is key to appropriate risk assessment and victim safety planning.

Figure 9.1 indicates the range of behaviours within an intimate partner violent relationship.

FIGURE 9.1: RANGE OF ABUSING BEHAVIOURS IN INTIMATE
PARTNER ABUSE: THE POWER AND CONTROL WHEEL
SOURCE: DEVELOPED BY DOMESTIC ABUSE INTERVENTION PROJECT 202 EAST
SUPERIOR STREET, DULUTH, MN 55802, 218.722.4134, WWW.THEDULUTH MODEL.ORG

Traditional approaches and limitations

Early theoretical work focused on single-factor explanations for this
complex range of behaviours and, unsurprisingly, empirical testing of
these models found equivocal support. Some of the key problems with
these early theories is that they over-predict numbers of male perpetrators
within broadly patriarchal cultures (Sugarman and Frankel 1996), they
do not explain female perpetrators nor abuse in same-sex relationships,
they ignore other factors which are relevant predictors of other violent
behaviours, and do not differentiate levels of risk. It is suggested that
there is a need to move to models which are more comprehensive, are
linked into forensic literature and which integrate the different levels
of explanation. The pathways into lower or higher levels of abusing
behaviour for all perpetrators should be addressed with a view to

focusing resources and challenging risky behaviours. Current theories of DA have also been criticised for failing to consider the crossover with other forms of family violence, for example child abuse, stalking and sexual abuse (Ehrensaft 2008). The crossover with general criminality is noted in the empirical literature, but not fully incorporated even into the multi-factorial explanations of DA. Similarly the high level of traits associated with personality disorders in perpetrators is noted but not addressed theoretically, or in terms of risk.

These individual factors do not have to be seen as causal factors to inform risk judgements. In the pathway towards abuse it may be that cultural values set the preconditions for abuse to occur, but many other factors at different levels will influence the nature and severity of abuses perpetrated, against whom, how often and under what conditions, if at all. Thus these cannot be ignored. Over the past ten to twenty years, work from North America and, more recently, research conducted in the United Kingdom has suggested that characteristics of those likely to be convicted of an offence related to domestic abuse can be identified. In addition, factors associated with an increased risk of further offending and risk of more serious offending can be described.

Range of explanations

There are a variety of levels of explanation which have been proposed to explain DA offending (Gilchrist and Kebbell 2004). They range from explanations at a societal/cultural level to those focusing on individuals and individual pathologies. Feminist ideology has also had a great impact in this area (e.g. Dobash et al. 2002). The broad theoretical approaches are outlined below.

Socio-cultural explanations at this level tend to argue that DA is a product of societal level features, often citing patriarchical society or aggressive society as key factors in the etiology of DA. These types of society are seen to allow, and even support, male use of violence to control women (Pence 1989), or the particular culture is seen as supporting the use of violence in general as a means of problem solving; there is a 'culture of violence' (Gelles and Straus 1979). Traditional feminist approaches would be a subset of this level of explanation but are considered separately due to the influence of feminist thinking in this area.

Feminist approaches identify DA as being a gendered issue, due to the predominance of male perpetrators and female victims, and propose that it is gender-based inequality across society that facilitates and perpetuates DA. The evidence supporting a feminist analysis tends to be predicated on the observed gender disparity in those seeking help in response to DA, for example women who have sought help from various agencies or who have reported their partners to the police, and on the high rates of DA in strongly patriarchal cultures (Archer 2006). The data from these types of studies identify men as the primary aggressors (Dobash and Dobash 2004). This work has greatly improved our understanding of the range of abuses perpetrated as DA, raised the issues of entitlement, control and sexual jealousy as important aspects of DA, and improved services for victims, but it has also to some extent stifled research on individual factors which interact and are linked to risk (Archer 2000).

Interpersonal explanations tend to situate the problem within family interactions, and cite factors such as stress and generally problematic family interactions as being linked to the incidence of domestic abuse and to other types of family violence. The major tenet is that it is the family interactions which are problematic, rather than the behaviour of any one individual within that family (Lane and Russell 1989).

With individual/intrapersonal theories, there are a variety of factors which are linked to domestic abuse. For example, social learning theory incorporates the notion of modelling and proposes that the use of violence against one's partner is learned through interaction with, and is modelled on, one's own family of origin, one's peers and wider society. The behaviour, once learned, is then reinforced through positive short-term gratification and the lack of negative sanctions following the behaviour in general (Hamberger and Hastings 1986). Other theories at this level have identified different types of psychopathology, for example jealousy, dependency, attachment (Dutton and Browning 1988), impulse control (Faulk 1974) and self-esteem models (Sonkin 1985), as being associated with domestic abuse offending. Finally, attitudinal or cognitive styles or deficits have been linked to the use of violence and similar arguments to the cultural acceptance of violence have been made; however, in this case the attitudinal differences lie at the individual level (Saunders 1992).

Many studies have focused on identifying characteristics that distinguish DA offenders from non-offenders, and in some cases non-DA offenders. However, these distinguishing characteristics may not necessarily be criminogenic (i.e. directly related to offending; see Tolman and Bennett 1990), and in the case of attitudinal variables may simply reflect post hoc justifications and rationalisations of behaviour (Holtzworth-Munroe *et al.* 1997). Factors identified as being linked to increased risk of DA are: violence in the family of origin (Simons *et al.* 1995; Lackey and Williams 1995; Kunitz *et al.* 1998; Jonhson-Reid 1998; Magdol *et al.* 1998; Capaldi and Clark 1998); poor attachment (Dutton 2006); anger (Stith *et al.* 2004); jealousy, rejection, abandonment, and attribution of negative intent to their partners (Moore, Eisler and Franchina 2000); alcohol (Gilchrist *et al.* 2003; McMurran and Gilchrist 2008), particularly chronic alcohol use and drug use (Tolman and Bennett 1990); and personality disorders including antisocial and narcissistic and borderline traits (Dutton and Holtzworth-Munroe 1997). Recent work has focused on social cognition (Eckhardt *et al.* 2008) and skills deficits in perpetrators of domestic abuse and suggests that poor social skills, poor conflict resolution skills, perhaps in conjunction with unhelpful interpretations of relationship interactions, contribute to abuse in intimate relationships (Eckhardt and Dye 2000; Holtzworth-Munroe *et al.* 1994a).

Integrated/multi-level models

One useful approach which integrates these different levels is the nested ecological approach (Dutton 1985). This proposes that a multi-factor and multi-level explanation is required to explain a social phenomenon of this complexity. Within this model multiple levels from the influence of broad societal structures (macrosystem), the impact of subcultural values, e.g. influence of peers, sibling beliefs (exosystem), the family system and the specific setting of the abuse (microsystem) and the individual abilities and responses (ontogenetic) must be considered. Whilst very appealing in its attempt to integrate approaches and move to a comprehensive theory, this approach has yet to be fully tested empirically and fails to be totally clear as to how these levels interact and mesh theoretically such that the relative weighting of various factors would still be difficult to specify.

Heterogeneity in male perpetrators

One final key issue to emerge from the research recently is that whilst there are many similarities within those defined as domestic abuse offenders, there are also significant differences (Wangmann 2011). It is now suggested that there may be two or three types of domestic abuse offender whose offending follows slightly different patterns, whose background characteristics differ, and for whom the risk of further violence, the level at which this might be predicted and the interventions required, differ (Holtzworth-Munroe and Stuart 1994a; Tweed and Dutton 1998; Hamberger *et al.* 1996). Three main groups have been identified in North America which vary on dimensions of severity of violence, generality of violence and psychopathology. These dimensions separate those who perpetrate lower levels of physical abuse and mostly abuse against intimate partners and evidence low levels of other pathologies (family only) from those who perpetrate higher levels of abuse against a wider range of victims alongside general antisocial behaviours (generally violent abuser) and a separate group who perpetrate a different pattern of serious abuse mostly focused on intimate partners and different pathology more focused on sexual jealousy and dependency and triggered by potential loss of relationship and attachment issues (borderline/dysphoric, emotionally volatile) (Holtzworth-Munroe and Stuart 1994a; Waltz *et al.* 2000). Data from England and Wales identified a very similar grouping with three groups varying by levels of narcissism and anti-sociality and one group standing out as being far more dependent and emotionally volatile (Gilchrist *et al.* 2003).

Risk factors

When comparing domestic abuse offenders with other types of violent offender some similar and some slightly different characteristics can be identified. Although domestic abuse crosses all social classes and groups, those who have been *convicted* of DA, in common with other convicted groups, are likely to be unemployed, have previous convictions, for both violent and non-violent offences, and many have witnessed domestic abuse or experienced abuse within their family of origin (Gilchrist *et al.* 2003).

In contrast to other offending groups the level of alcohol dependence appears higher within this group (56%) and the level of mental health difficulties reported also seems high (depression 22%, clinically elevated symptoms of anger 2% and anxiety 1%). The assaults tended to take place within the context of jealousy, separation and childcare issues. The level of minimising and victim blaming within this sample is higher than in other types of offender, and unstable attributions as to the cause of the violence is also high, for example blaming alcohol (Gilchrist *et al.* 2003).

In terms of risk of lethality, there are a number of factors that have been identified based on research comparing lethal and non-lethal DA.

Factors which should be considered as markers of potentially lethal risk include but are not limited to: recent escalation of the severity and/or frequency of assaults; credible threats to partner combined with access to a weapon (knife); stalking behaviours; recent separation; forced sex; and extreme jealousy (Campbell 2004; Dobash *et al.* 2002; Straus and Gelles 1990).

Risk assessment

Two of the most common risk assessment tools in this area are the Spousal Assault Risk Assessment (SARA) (Kropp *et al.* 1995) tool and the Danger Assessment instrument (Campbell 1995). The focus of the assessment differs for these tools with the SARA being primarily focused on predicting re-assault and the Danger Assessment focusing more on predicting lethality. Despite some limitations (focus on offending history and lack of discrimination among subgroups of domestic abuse offender) the SARA in particular is widely used across the UK and is quite helpful as a structured clinical tool. It has relatively good predictive ability (Williams and Grant 2006) and can be helpful in informing risk management as it prompts the assessor to consider a range of victims and allows for idiosyncratic factors to override a 'score' and informs future risk scenario planning.

Further shorter tools for use by police and other criminal justice professionals (e.g. Brief Spousal Assault Form for the Evaluation of Risk (B-Safer – Kropp, Hart, and Belfrage 2004; Domestic Violence Screening Instrument (DVSI) – Hisashima 2008; the Ontario Domestic Assault Risk Assessment (ODARA) – Hilton, Harris and Rice 2010; and the Domestic Violence Risk Appraisal Guide (DVRAG) – Hilton *et al.* 2010) have also been developed. Tools such as the Propensity for Abusiveness Scale (PAS) (Dutton 1995) have also been developed primarily for screening men in and out of specific interventions. As yet these are less common in the UK.

Some of the UK police forces have developed their own domestic violence screening tools identifying six high-risk factors forming the acronym SPECSS (Separation, Pregnancy, Escalation, Cultural Issues, Stalking and Sexual Assault) which, alongside a number of general risk factors, allow police to classify the risk in a domestic situation as being standard, medium or high (Richards 2003). Little academic work has been published exploring these tools as yet, but unpublished doctoral research suggests that the SPECSS model has some merit although it may fail to identify high-risk cases, and developments of concise tools for the police, such as the MeRIT tool being developed in Merseyside, are seen as being of great value in the field (Nixon 2008).

It should also be noted, though, that some of the general risk assessment tools, for example the Violence Risk Appraisal Guide (VRAG) and the Psychopathy Checklist Revised (PCL-R), have performed as well as the specific domestic abuse assessment tools in some studies (Hilton *et al.* 2008). These tools, however, do not inform risk management and thus can be limited in terms of application.

Limitations of risk tools

Many of the tools routinely used by criminal justice professionals (DVSI, DVRAG, SARA) focus more on static (i.e. unchanging) offending history factors (e.g. age at first conviction) which have been shown to have predictive utility, but at the expense of gathering appropriate victim information about the pattern and function of the violence and abuse, and many also fail to consider important chronic (ongoing issues which increase the chance of offending, e.g. chronic alcohol dependency or relationship conflict) and acute (specific situations which indicate the offending will happen now, e.g. intoxication or threat of separation) dynamic (changeable) factors. Some of this is linked to the lack of access to victim data for these professionals; however, it is important when at all possible to gather at least the victim statement as the high incidence of victim-blaming and minimising and denying within this specific type of offender means that any assessment based on self-report alone is likely to seriously underestimate risk.

The routine risk assessment tools tend to be focused on predicting re-occurrence of violence rather than severity. The Danger Assessment is set up to predict lethality but it is a victim-based assessment tool, thus it can be difficult to administer within criminal justice settings in the UK as access to victims or victim data can be severely restricted. Also the Danger Assessment does not assess general offending history or previous non-compliance, both of which are of use in predicting later re-assault. The SARA and B-Safer do not take heterogeneity into account and thus can mislead professionals as borderline offenders and some subgroups of lethal offenders may not evidence the accepted pattern of increasing control and abuse, and this lack of risk markers may lead to an underestimation of risk (Belfrage and Rying 2004). The PAS provides a detailed psychological profile but is more linked to emotional abuse than physical abuse.

At present there is no ideal tool for risk assessment in domestic abuse cases and none which have been rigorously tested across female or same-sex offenders. One study which did assess risk in both male and female offenders suggests that many women arrested for domestic abuse will later present as victims rather than offenders, and that there are serious limitations to the use of many tools (including the SARA, DVSI and ODARA) with women, as male validated scales are likely to over-predict dangerousness (women were found half as likely to recidivate) and there was a distinct set of features linked to female re-offending (women who were underemployed, had less education and less childhood adversity were more likely to recidivate) (Henning, Martinsson and Holdford 2009). Also, there is little information of 'crossover' of risk from domestic abuse to more generalised violence or sexual assault, and these are further areas which require development.

Spousal Assault Risk Assessment

The SARA identifies 20 items: 10 historic and 10 relating to current offending and presentation (see Table 9.1 on p.176). The practitioner is guided as to how to identify items as present, possibly present or absent and then helped to consider possible extraordinary features of a case which might be indicative of idiosyncratic risk. There is a possibility of 'scoring' the SARA and comparing the individual to group norms which can be of some value, particularly if there are different potential interventions available depending on initial assessment of risk (e.g. in UK prisons there are different levels of group programmes to address domestic abuse issues, one for 'moderate' risk offenders and another for 'high' risk offenders, which is longer and of greater intensity). Whilst the statistics behind our current actuarial risk assessment instruments (ARAIs) mean that there are limitations to the use of categories and cut-off scores both to classify people into groups and to inform risk assessment of individuals, structured information to focus resources is seen as being one of the areas where this information might be useful. Hart, Michie and Cooke (2007, p.63) state: 'An appropriate use of ARAIs may be for making administrative decisions regarding the frequency or intensity of risk management strategies recommended for a given individual (e.g. number of office visits, priority for admission into treatment groups).'

The SARA, unlike other structured professional judgement tools (e.g. Risk of Sexual Violence Protocol, RSVP) (Hart *et al.* 2003) does not specifically require the assessor to consider scenario planning to inform risk assessment and management but a scenario planning approach is generally of value, is specifically recommended in risk assessment guidance in Scotland (RMA 2006) and would be highly recommended when assessing risk of domestic abuse (Kropp *et al.* 1999). Scenario planning asks the assessor to speculate on the basis of credible and persuasive evidence what conditions would have to be in place for various scenarios: a 'repeat' scenario (repeat of previous behaviour, same offending happening again); 'twist' scenario (offender continues offending but possibly not in an identical manner, maybe location of offending); 'increase' scenario (offending escalates, e.g. moves from lower level violence to assault with a weapon); and 'reduce' scenario (reduction in type, severity or frequency of offending or offender may desist from offending often if there has been successful intervention or lifestyle has stabilised) (Hart *et al.* 2003).

Interventions for domestic abuse

The treatment of choice in the UK is often perpetrator groups with linked but separate support for women, and sometimes children (Bowen, Brown and Gilchrist 2002). Most often these groups are psycho-educational (Duluth) or CBT (Babcock *et al.* 2004; Saunders 2008; Bowen 2011) and focus on skills acquisition and gender re-socialisation, although psychodynamic groups are also used (Babcock *et al.* 2004). Alternative groups of couples together, individual work and conjoint couple therapy have also been used (O'Leary, Heyman and Neidig 1999; Stith, Rosen and McCollum 2003; Stith *et al.* 2004). It appears that the group process is an important factor in facilitating change, and there is data to suggest that group-based or 'multi-couple' may be more effective than individual couple therapy (Stith *et al.* 2004; Saunders and Hamill 2003).

Concern has also been raised about the possibility of a therapist colluding with an abuser and inadvertently supporting the abuse, particularly where there is unequal power within the relationship, and issues have been raised about how realistic it is for victims to disclose their experiences honestly in such settings. Whilst most therapists require both parties to sign up to a 'non-abuse pact' the impact of previous abuse on full disclosure also needs to be considered. However, despite these issues and political and ideological debates as to appropriate modes and foci of intervention, there is little evidence to support one intervention over another (Babcock *et al.* 2004; Saunders and Hamill 2003) and meta-analyses have concluded that overall DA treatment effectiveness is low (Babcock *et al.* 2004; Stover, Meadows and Kaufmann 2009).

Whilst overall treatment effects are low, there is data which shows that, for some, intervention can be of benefit. There are specific features which appear to increase effectiveness of interventions. As noted, group work seems to be more effective; treatment that is matched to the participants' 'readiness to change', and to the type of offender in the group is more effective (Smedslund *et al.* 2009). Pre-group motivational input has been found to be beneficial for increasing the impact of intervention (Levesque *et al.* 2008). Interestingly, criminal justice intervention which does not focus on individual change, but which does hold perpetrators accountable for their actions, can be effective in itself (Stith *et al.* 2004; Daly and Pelowski 2000; Rosenfeld 1992). Also co-ordinated interventions which have clear information-sharing across agencies are found to be more effective.

Drawing the literature together it appears that interventions with perpetrators will be enhanced it they include individual motivation sessions pre-group, possibly focusing on the costs of abuse and using 'enlightened self-focus' (rather than victim empathy which may be low at the start of intervention) to motivate. There should be some limited focus on anger and lack of control or skills deficits, and current evidence favours structured CBT programmes focusing on cognitive skills as well as challenging patriarchal thinking (Saunders and Hamill 2003).

It is strongly recommended that all domestic abuse interventions should be linked with support agencies for partners (Mullender 1996). The partner input should include telephone contact, information about the contents and aims of perpetrator groups and victim safety planning. It is suggested that individual and group support and counselling for adult and child victims in the family might also be offered (Bowen 2011; Murphy *et al.* 1998; Kistenmacher *et al.* 2008).

One influential programme in Scotland which demonstrates many of these characteristics and which uses a strengths-based approach linked to the Good Lives Model (Langlands, Ward and Gilchrist 2009a, b) and is being piloted across a number of local authorities in Scotland is the Caledonian System (Scottish Government 2010). Readers who have a particular interest in interventions for DA would benefit from looking at this, the earlier Change programme (Dobash *et al.* 2000; Morran and Wilson 1999), the original Duluth intervention (Pence and Paymar

1993a, b) and the London-based Domestic Violence Intervention Project (DVIP) work (Graham-Kevan 2007; Scourfield and Dobash 1999).

Conclusions

It is clear from this brief look at domestic abuse and risks that this is an area which requires attention; there are a number of markers which indicate heightened risk of recidivism and also of lethality, and there are two or three groups of domestic abuse offender whose offending may evidence different patterns and link with different proximal and distal triggers or precursors. At this stage there is still a great deal of work to be done. In terms of research we need to do further study on lethal violence, to explore precursors to lethal DA violence and identify more clearly the risk markers which could alert us to significant risk in cases where there is no pattern of DA. In terms of risk management, there is limited evidence of effective individual change (Babcock *et al.* 2004), thus a range of strategies including individual monitoring, supervision and victim safety measures, and more general strategies such as increasing public intolerance of DA, and increasing bystander input, have to be considered and evaluated.

References

Archer, J. (2000) 'Sex differences in aggression between heterosexual partners: A meta-analytic review.' *Psychological Bulletin 126*, 5, 651–680.

Archer, J. (2006) 'Cross-cultural differences in physical aggression between partners: A social-role analysis.' *Personality and Social Psychology Review 10*, 2, 133–153.

Archer, J. and Graham-Kevan, N. (2003) 'Intimate terrorism and common couple violence: A test of Johnsons predictions in four British samples.' *Journal of Interpersonal Violence 18*, 11, 1247–1270.

Babcock, J.C., Green, C.E. and Robie, C. (2004) 'Does "batterers" treatment work? A meta-analytic review of domestic violence treatment.' *Clinical Psychology Review 23*, 8, 1023–1053.

Babcock, J.C., Waltz J., Jacobson, N.S. and Gottman, J.M. (1993) 'Power and violence: The relation between communication patterns, power discrepancies, and domestic violence.' *Journal of Consulting and Clinical Psychology 61*, 1, 40–50.

Belfrage, H. and Rying, M. (2004) 'Characteristics of spousal homicide perpetrators.' *Criminal Behaviour and Mental Health 14*, 121–133.

Bowen, E. (2011) *The Rehabilitation of Partner Violent Men.* Chichester: Wiley.

Bowen, E., Brown, L. and Gilchrist, E. (2002) 'Evaluating probation based offender programmes for domestic violence perpetrators: A pro-feminist approach.' *The Howard Journal of Criminal Justice 41*, 3, 221–236.

Campbell, J.C. (1992) 'The Danger Assessment Instrument: Risk Factors of Homicide of and by Battered Women.' In C.R. Block and R.L. Block (eds) *Questions and Answers in Lethal and Non-Lethal Violence.* Washington, DC: National Institute of Justice.

Campbell, J. (1995) *Assessing Dangerousness: Violence by Sex Offenders, Batterers and Child Abusers.* Thousand Oaks, CA: Sage.

Capaldi, D. M. and Clark, S. (1998) 'Prospective family predictors of aggression toward female partners for young at-risk males.' *Developmental Psychology 34*, 6, 1175–1188.

Connell, R. (1995) *Masculinities.* Cambridge: Polity Press.

Daly, J. and Pelowski, S. (2000) 'Predictors of dropout among men who batter: A review of studies with implications for research and practice.' *Violence and Victims 15*, 2, 137–160.

Dobash, R.P. and Dobash, R.E. (2004) 'Women's violence to men in intimate relationships: Working on a puzzle.' *British Journal of Criminology 44*, 3, 324–349.

Dobash, R.E., Dobash, R.P., Cavanagh, K. and Lewis, R. (2000) *Changing Violent Men.* Thousand Oaks, CA: Sage.

Dobash, R.P., Dobash, R.E., Cavanagh, K. and Lewis, R. (2002) *Homicide in Britain: Risk Factors, Situational Contexts and Lethal Intentions (focus on male offender).* Research Bulletin, No. 1. Manchester: Dept. Applied Social Sciences, University of Manchester.

Dobash, R.P., Dobash, R.E., Cavanagh, K. and Medina-Ariza, J. (2007) 'Lethal and nonlethal violence against an intimate partner.' *Violence Against Women 13*, 4, 329–353.

Dutton, D.G. (1985) 'An ecologically nested theory of male violence toward intimates.' *International Journal of Women's Studies 8*, 4, 404–413.

Dutton, D.G. (1995) 'Male abusiveness in intimate relationships.' *Clinical Psychology Review 15*, 6, 567–581.

Dutton, D.G. (2006) *Rethinking Domestic Violence.* Vancouver, BC: UBC Press.

Dutton, D.G. and Browning, J.J. (1988) 'Concern for Power, Fear of Intimacy, and Wife Abuse.' In G.T. Hotaling, D. Finkelhor, J.T. Kirkpatrick, and M. Straus (eds) *New Directions in Family Violence Research.* Beverly Hills, CA: Sage.

Dutton, D.G. and Holtzworth-Munroe, A. (1997) 'The Role of Early Trauma in Males who Assault their Wives.' In D.C.S.L. Toth (ed.) *Rochester Symposium on Developmental Psychopathology: Developmental Perspectives on Trauma-theory, Research and Intervention.* Rochester, NY: University of Rochester Press.

Eckhardt, C. and Dye, M. (2000) 'The cognitive characteristics of maritally violent men: Theory and evidence.' *Cognitive Therapy and Research 24*, 2, 139–158.

Eckhardt, C., Holtzworth-Munroe, A., Norlander, B., Sibley, A. and Cahill, M. (2008) 'Readiness to change, partner violence subtypes and treatment outcomes among men in treatment for partner assault.' *Violence and Victims 23*, 4, 446–475.

Ehrensaft, M.K. (2008) 'Intimate partner violence: Persistence of myths and implications for intervention.' *Children and Youth Service Review 30*, 3, 276–286.

Faulk, M. (1974) 'Men who assault their wives.' *Medicine, Science and Law 14*, 80–183.

Gadd, D. 'Masculinities and violence against female partners.' *Social & Legal Studies 11*, 1, 61–80.

Gelles, R.J. and Straus, M.A. (1979) 'Determinants of Violence in the Family: Toward a Theoretical Integration.' In W.R. Burr, R. Hill, F.I. Nye and I.L. Reiss (eds) *Contemporary Theories about the Family* (volume 1). New York: Free Press.

Gilchrist, E. (2007) 'The Cognition of Domestic Abusers: Explanations, Evidence, and Treatment.' In T. Gannon (ed.), A. Ward (co-ed.), A. Beech (co-ed.) and D. Fisher (co-ed.) *Aggressive Offenders' Cognition: Theory, Research and Practice.* Chichester: Wiley.

Gilchrist, E. and Kebbell, M. (2004) 'Domestic Violence: Current Issues in Definitions and Intervention.' In J. Adler (ed.) *Forensic Psychology: debates, concepts, practice.* Cullompton, Devon: Willan Publishers.

Gilchrist, E., Johnson, R., Takriti, R., Beech, A., Kebbell, M. and Weston, S. (2003) *Domestic violence offenders: Characteristics and Offending Related Needs.* Findings No. 217. London: Home Office.

Giles, J. (2005) '"Woman bites dog" – making sense of media research reports that claim women and men are equally violent'. *New Zealand Madical Journal 118*, 1225, 1–8.

Graham-Kevan, N. (2007) 'Domestic violence: Research and implications for batterer programmes in Europe.' *European Journal on Criminal Policy and Research 13*, 3-4, 213–225.

Hamberger, L.K. and Hastings, J.E. (1986) 'Personality correlates of men who abuse their partners: A cross-validation study.' *Journal of Family Violence 1*, 4, 323–341.

Hamberger, L.K., Lohr, J.M., Bonge, D. and Tollin, D.F. (1996) 'A large sample empirical typology of male spouse abusers and its relationship to dimensions of abuse.' *Violence and Victims 11*, 4, 277–291.

Hart, S.D., Kropp, P.R., Laws, D.R., Klaver, J., Logan, C. and Watt, K.A. (2003) *The Risk for Sexual Violence Protocol (RSVP): Structured Professional Guidelines for Assessing Risk of Sexual Violence.* Burnaby, British Columbia: Mental Health, Law, and Policy Institute, Simon Fraser University.

Hart, S.D., Michie, C. and Cooke, D.J. (2007) 'Precision of Actuarial Risk Assessment Instruments: evaluating the "margins of error" of group v. individual predictions of violence.' *The British Journal of Psychiatry 190*, s60–s65.

Henning, K., Martinsson, R. and Holdford, R. (2009) 'Gender differences in risk factors for intimate partner violence recidivism.' *Journal of Aggression, Maltreatment & Trauma 18*, 6, 623–645.

Hilton, N.Z., Harris, G.T. and Rice, M.E. (2010) *Risk Assessment for Domestically Violent Men: Tools for Criminal Justice, Offender Intervention, and Victim Services.* Washington, DC: American Psychological Association.

Hilton, N.Z., Harris, G.T., Rice, M.E., Houghton, R.E. and Eke, A.W. (2008) 'An in-depth actuarial assessment for wife assault recidivism: The Domestic Violence Risk Appraisal Guide.' *Law and Human Behavior 32*, 2, 150–163.

Hisashima, J. (2008) *Validation Study of the Domestic Violence Screening Instrument (DVSI).* Hawaii: State Department of Health. Available at http://hawaii.gov/icis/documents/DVSI%20Validation%202003-2007%20(Jan%202008).pdf, accessed on 25 July 2012.

Holtzworth-Munroe, A. (2000) 'Cognitive factors in male intimate violence.' *Cognitive Therapy and Research 24*, 2, 135–139.

Holtzworth-Munroe, A. and Hutchinson, G. (1993) 'Attributing negative intent to wife behaviour: The attributions of maritally violent versus non-violent men.' *Journal of Abnormal Behaviour 102*, 2, 206–211.

Holtzworth-Munroe, A. and Stuart, G.L. (1994a) 'Typologies of male batterers: Three subtypes and the differences among them.' *Psychological Bulletin 116*, 3, 476–497.

Holtzworth-Munroe, A. and Stuart, G.L. (1994b) 'The relationship standards and assumptions of violent versus nonviolent husbands.' *Cognitive Therapy and Research 18*, 2, 87–103.

Holtzworth-Munroe, A., Bates, L., Smutzler, N. and Sandin, E. (1997) 'A brief review of the research on husband violence. Part I: Maritally violent versus nonviolent men.' *Aggression and Violent Behavior: A Review Journal 2*, 3, 65–99.

Jacobson, N.S., Gottman, J.M., Waltz, J., Rushe, R., Babcock, A. and Holtzworth-Munroe, A. (2000) 'Affect, verbal content, and psychophysiology in the arguments of couples with a violent husband.' *Prevention and Treatment 3*, Art. 19.

Johnson, M.P. (1995) 'Patriarchal terrorism and common couple violence: Two forms of violence against women.' *Journal of Marriage and Family 57*, 2, 283–294.

Johnson, M.P. (2006) 'Conflict and control: Gender symmetry and asymmetry in domestic violence.' *Violence Against Women 12*, 11, 1003–1018.

Johnson, R., Gilchrist, E., Beech, A.R., Weston, S., Takriti, R. and Freeman, R. (2006) 'A psychometric typology of U.K. domestic violence offenders.' *Journal of Interpersonal Violence 21*, 10, 1270–1285.

Johnson-Reid, M. (1998) 'Youth violence and exposure to violence in childhood: An ecological review.' *Aggression and Violent Behavior 13*, 3, 159–179.

Kelly, J. and Johnson, M. (2008) 'Differentiation among types of intimate partner violence: Research updates and implications for interventions.' *Family Court Review 46*, 3, 476–499.

Kistenmacher, B.R. and Weiss, R.L. (2008) 'Motivational interviewing as a mechanism for change in men who batter: A randomized control trial.' *Violence and Victim 23*, 5, 558–570.

Kropp, P.R., Hart, S.D. and Belfrage, H. (2004) *The Development of the Brief Spousal Assault Form for the Evaluation of Risk (B-SAFER): A Tool for Criminal Justice Professionals.* Available at www.justice. gc.ca/eng/pi/rs/rep-rap/2005/rr05_fv1-rr05_vf1/d1.html, accessed on 25 July 2012.

Kropp, P.R., Hart, S.D., Webster, C.D. and Eaves, D. (1999) *Spousal Assault Risk Assessment: User's Guide.* Toronto, ON: Multi-Health Systems.

Kunitz, S.J., Levy, J.E., McCloskey, J. and Gabriel, K.R. (1998) 'Alcohol dependence and domestic violence as sequelae of abuse and conduct disorder in childhood.' *Child Abuse and Neglect 22*, 11, 1079–1091.

Lackey, C. and Williams, K.R. (1995) 'Social bonding and the cessation of partner violence across generations.' *Journal of Marriage and Family 57*, 2, 295–305.

Lane, G. and Russell, T. (1989) 'Second-order Systematic Work with Violent Couples.' In P.L Caeser and K.L Hamberger (eds) *Treating Men Who Batter: Theory, Practice and Programs.* New York: Springer.

Langlands, R., Ward, T. and Gilchrist, E. (2009a) 'Applying the Good Lives Models to male perpetrators of domestic violence.' *Behaviour Change 26*, 2, 113–129.

Langlands, R., Ward, T. and Gilchrist, E. (2009b) 'Applying the Good Lives Models to male perpetrators of domestic violence.' In P. Lehmann and C.A. Simmons (eds) *Strengths Based Batterer Intervention: A New Paradigm in Ending Family Violence.* New York: Springer.

Levesque, F., Driskell, M., Prochaska, J. and Prochaska, J. (2008) 'Acceptability of a stage matched expert system intervention for domestic violence offenders.' *Violence and Victims 23*, 4, 432–445.

Magdol, L., Moffitt, T.E., Caspi, A. and Silva, P.A. (1998) 'Developmental antecedents of partner abuse: A prospective-longitudinal study.' *Journal of Abnormal Psychology 107*, 3, 375–389.

McCollum, E. and Stith, S. (2008) 'Couples treatment for interpersonal violence: A review of outcome research literature and current clinical practices.' *Violence and Victims 23*, 2, 187–201.

McMurran, M. and Gilchrist, E. (2008) 'Anger control and alcohol use: Appropriate interventions for perpetrators of domestic violence?' *Psychology, Crime and Law 14*, 2, 107–116.

Miller, S.L. and Meloy, M.L. (2006) 'Women's use of force: Voices of women arrested for domestic violence.' *Violence Against Women 12*, 1, 89–115.

Moore, T.M. and Stuart, G.L. (2001) 'A review of the literature on masculinity and partner violence.' *Psychology of Men and Masculinity 6*, 1, 46–61.

Moore, T.M., Eisler, R. and Franchina, J.J. (2000) 'Causal attributions and affective responses to provocative female partner behaviour by abusive and non abusive males.' *Journal of Family Violence 15*, 1, 69–80.

Morran, D. and Wilson, M. (1999) *The CHANGE Programme Manual: Men who are Violent to Women: A Group Work Practice Manual.* Grangemouth: CHANGE.

Muftic, L.R., Bouffard, J.A. and Bouffard, L.A. (2007) 'An exploratory study of women arrested for intimate partner violence: Violent women or violent resistance?' *Journal of Interpersonal Violence 22*, 6, 753–774.

Mullender, A. (1996) 'Groupwork with male domestic abusers: Models and dilemmas.' *Groupwork 9*, 1, 27–47.

Murphy, C.M., Musser, P.H. and Maton, K.I. (1998) 'Coordinated community intervention for domestic abusers: Intervention, system involvement, and criminal recidivism.' *Journal of Family Violence 13*, 3, 263–284.

Nixon K. (2008) [Unpublished report] *Evaluation of MeRIT (Merseyside Risk Identification Toolkit) for Merseyside Police.* University of Liverpool.

O'Leary, D., Heyman, R. and Neidig, P. (1999) 'Treatment of wife abuse: A comparison of gender specific and conjoint approaches.' *Behaviour Therapy 30*, 3, 475–505.

Pence, E. (1989) *The Justice System's Responses to Domestic Assault Cases: A Guide for Policy Development.* Minnesota: Duluth.

Pence, E. and Paymar, M. (1993a) *Domestic Violence Information Manual: The Duluth Domestic Abuse Intervention Project.* New York: Springer. Available at www.duluth-model.org, accessed on 25 July 2012.

Pence, E. and Paymar, M. (1993b) *Education Groups for Men who Batter: The Duluth Model.* New York: Springer.

Richards L. (2003) *Findings from the Multi-agency Domestic Violence Murder Reviews in London.* London: Metropolitan Police Service.

Risk Management Authority (2006) Standards and Guidelines for Risk Assessment. Paisely: Risk management authority.

Rosenfeld, B.D. (1992) 'Court ordered treatment of spouse abuse.' *Clinical Psychology Review 12,* 2, 205–226.

Saunders, D.G. (1992) 'A typology of men who batter: Three types derived from cluster analysis.' *American Journal of Orthopsychiatry 62,* 2, 264–275.

Saunders, D. (2008) 'Group interventions for men who batter: A summary of program descriptions and research.' *Violence and Victims 23,* 2, 156–172.

Saunders, D. and Hamill, R. (2003) *Violence Against Women: Synthesis of Research on Offender Interventions.* NCJ 201222. Washington, DC: National Institute of Justice.

Scottish Government (2010) *The Caledonian System.* Available at www.scotland.gov.uk/Topics/ People/Equality/violence-women/CaledonianSystem, accessed on 25 July 2012.

Scourfield, J.B. and Dobash, R.P. (1999) 'Programmes for violent men: recent developments in the UK.' *The Howard Journal of Criminal Justice 38,* 2, 128–143.

Simons, R.L., Wu, C.I., Johnson, C. and Conger, R.D. (1995) 'A test of various perspectives on the intergenerational transmission of domestic violence.' *Criminology 33,* 1, 141–172.

Smedslund, G., Dalsbo, T., Steiro, A., Winsvold, A. and Clench-Aas, J. (2009) *Cognitive Behavioural Therapy for Men who Psychically Abuse their Female Partner.* The Cochrane Collaboration. Available at www.thecochranelibrary.com, accessed on 25 July 2012.

Sonkin, D.J. (1985) 'The male batterer: An overview I.' *The Military Family 5,* 1, 3–5.

Sonkin, D.J., Martin, D. and Walker, L. (1985) *The Male Batterer: A Treatment Approach.* New York: Springer.

Stith, S., Rosen, K. and McCollum, E. (2003) 'Effectiveness of couples treatment for spouse abuse.' *Journal of Marital and Family Therapy 29,* 3, 407–426.

Stith, S., Rosen, K., McCollum, E. and Thomsen, C. (2004) 'Treating intimate partner violence within intact couple relationships: Outcomes of Multi-couple Therapy versus Individual Couple Therapy.' *Journal of Marital and Family Therapy 30,* 3, 305–318.

Stover, C.S., Meadows, A. and Kaufman, J. (2009) 'Interventions for intimate partner violence: Review and directions for evidence based practice.' *Professional Psychology: Research and Practice 40,* 3, 223–233.

Straus, M.A. and Gelles, R.J. (1990) *Physical Violence in American Families: Risk Factors and Adaptations to Violence in 8,145 Families.* New Brunswick, NJ: Transaction.

Sugarman, D.B. and Frankel, S.L. (1996) 'Patriarchal ideology and wife-assault: A meta-analytic review.' *Journal of Family Violence 11,* 1, 13–40.

Swan, S.C. and Snow, D.L. (2002) 'A typology of women's use of violence in intimate relationships.' *Violence Against Women 8,* 3, 286–319.

Tolman, R.M. and Bennett, L.W. (1990) 'A review of the quantitative research on men who batter.' *Journal of Interpersonal Violence 5,* 1, 87–118.

Tweed, R.G. and Dutton, D.G. (1998) 'A comparison of impulsive and instrumental subgroups of batterers.' *Violence and Victims 13,* 3, 215–230.

Walker, L. (1983) 'Victimology and the psychological perspectives of battered women.' *Victimology: An International Journal 8*, 82–104.

Waltz, J., Babcock, J.C., Jacobson, N.S. and Gottman, J.M. (2000) 'Testing a typology of batterers.' *Journal of Consulting and Clinical Psychology 68*, 4, 658–669.

Wangmann, J. (2011) *Different Types of Intimate Partner Violence – An Exploration of the Literature.* Issues Paper 22. Sydney: Australian Domestic and Family Violence Clearinghouse, The University of New South Wales.

Williams, K.R. and Grant, S.R. (2006) 'Empirically examining the risk of intimate partner violence: The Revised Domestic Violence Screening Instrument (DVSI-R).' *Public Health Reports 121*, 4, 400–408.

TABLE 9.1 SARA ITEMS

SARA (items 1–10) (general)	SARA (items 11–20) (DV)
Past assault of family members	Past physical assault of intimate partner
Past assault of strangers or acquaintances	Past sexual assault/sexual jealousy
Past violation of conditional release	Past use of weapons or credible threats of death
Recent relationship problems	Recent escalation or frequency or severity of assault
Recent employment problems	Past violations of no contact orders
Victim of/witness to family violence as child	Extreme minimisation or denial or spousal assault history
Recent substance abuse/dependence	Attitudes that support or condone spousal assault
Recent suicidal ideation/intent	Severe and/or sexual assault (index offence)
Recent psychotic or manic symptoms	Use of weapons and/or credible threats of death (index offence)
Personality disorder with anger, impulsivity or behavioural instability	Violation of no contact order (index offence)

CHAPTER 10

'What About the Men?'
Understanding Men's Experiences of Domestic Abuse Within a Gender-based Model of Violence

Nancy Lombard

Introduction

The explicit focus of this collection is violence against *women* and contributors in the volume are exclusively talking about the victimisation of women within domestically abusive relationships. Yet for those working and researching in the field of violence against women a question often heard is 'What about male victims?' It is the purpose of this chapter to provide a theoretical framework to explain and demonstrate why a gendered analysis is necessary for understanding domestic abuse. In doing so, the chapter will provide an overview of men's experiences of abuse. It is imperative to note that a gender-based definition of domestic abuse does not exclude men, rather it positions violence within a gendered model of understanding that illustrates why women are predominantly 'victims' and men perpetrators. This chapter will provide a context for social workers who may have questions about male victims so they can frame their daily practice with an understanding of the gendered nature of such violence.

The chapter begins by illustrating the specific case of Scotland and its working definition of domestic abuse as gender-based abuse. Then an overview of the concept of gender and what is meant by a gendered analysis is provided. From this the construction of violent masculine identities is explored drawing particularly on the work of Connell (1995, 2005). Research on men and women's use of familial violence is discussed and critiqued drawing upon the influential work of Johnson (1995, 2005) and Stark (2007). Then two case studies are presented (Gadd *et al.* 2002; Hester 2009), the findings from which support a gendered definition of domestic abuse. The evidence from both studies is that men and women use and experience violence differently and the impact of violence is different (because of their gendered position in society). They show that men who experience violence are less likely to live in fear and that women are more likely to be repeatedly victimised and subjected to abuse that can be described as coercive control (Stark 2007) or intimate terrorism (Johnson 1995, 2005). The need for a gendered analysis of violence and the implications this has for social work practice conclude the chapter.

The unique position of Scotland

Through the process of devolution and the creation of the Scottish Executive (in 1999) and the Scottish Government (in 2011) Scotland's policies now differ from those of the rest of the United Kingdom. In the United Kingdom, Scotland is the only country to recognise a gender-based definition of domestic abuse (see *National Strategy to Address Domestic Abuse in Scotland*, Scottish Executive 2000; *Preventing Violence Against Women: Action Across the Scottish Executive*, Scottish Executive 2001). This means that:

> Domestic abuse is associated with broader gender inequality and should be understood in its historical context, whereby societies have given greater status, wealth, influence, control and power to men. It is part of a range of behaviours constituting male abuse of power, and is linked to other forms of male violence. (Scottish Executive 2000, p.5)

In generating this definition the Scottish government acknowledges the 'broader gender inequalities which women face' (Scottish Executive 2000). These inequalities include, but are not limited to, economic, social, cultural and sexual inequities where women and girls are disadvantaged because of their gender, with the patterns and types of violence illustrating the persuasive inequalities between men and women (Bond and Phillips 2000). To begin to look at why a gendered definition is pertinent to the issue of violence we first need to look at the concept of gender.

What is gender?

Second wave feminism questioned the supposedly innate and natural differences that have been used to justify the divisions between men and women such as the dichotomous relationship between 'male aggression' and 'female passivity'. Such dichotomies have informed what Butler (1990) termed the 'bipolar gender that positioned men and masculinity as the norm and in opposition to 'the other' (de Beauvoir 1949).

Within this framework, gender is understood as a social construction and as a set of social relations. For the purposes of this chapter, gender refers to the range of socially constructed roles, behaviours, positions, responsibilities and expectations that are ascribed to men and women that inform ideas of how they are meant to act and behave. It does not refer to men and women *per se* but to the relationships between and among them. Gender is constructed discursively through language and performances and institutionally through people's positioning of their own identities in relation to social and cultural structures. Locating gender within wider cultural and historical contexts enables the mediation of other social factors such as class, sexualities, 'race' and ethnicity, thus conceptualising gender as a socially produced, continuously contested category that is perpetuated and negotiated at both ideological and institutional levels.

Connell (2000) stresses the importance of gender relations and the construction of a gender regime for understanding violence, and in particular men's violence. This view is echoed by Dragiewicz and Lindgren:

> ...it is critical to view domestic violence within the context of sex discrimination in order to reframe the issue as one of societal and political concern rather than simply a private matter of interpersonal relationships. (Dragiewicz and Lindgren 2009, p.233)

To explore this further the concept of gender order as defined by Connell (1987) is examined before going on to discuss 'masculinities' and the social construction of violence.

The gender order

Connell (1987) argues that different organisations and institutions have gender regimes that interact or conflict with each other, generating a 'gender order'. The gender order changes over time, highlighting gender as transient and socially constructed. Therefore the gender order is maintained through both behaviour and practice. Within this order, differing forms of masculinity and femininity are ranked, with the most powerful and dominant at the top.

Connell invites the view that masculinity is a discourse to be accessed by, and imposed upon, both men and women, and not a character type or a label to describe men:

> 'Masculinity', to the extent that the term can be briefly identified at all, is simultaneously a place in gender relations, the practices through which men and women engage that place in gender and the effects of these practices in bodily experience, personality and culture. (Connell 2005, p.34)

Connell's (1995, 2005) theorisation of hegemonic masculinity as 'the cultural dynamic by which a group claims and sustains a leading position in social life' (Connell 2005, p.77) has proved of critical importance as a way to understand the construction of gender identity and the valorisation of violence. Connell's term refers to the most dominant (and dominating) form of masculinity which structures power relations among and between other masculinities and femininities and legitimates the use of power and control (see also Kimmel 1987).

It is important to note here that although not all men are equally privileged within or by patriarchal relations, all benefit from what Connell terms 'the patriarchal dividend' – the advantage men in general gain from the overall subordination of women (2001, p.40). Whilst hegemonic masculinity is not necessarily the most common form of masculinity given it is 'a question of relations of cultural domination, not of head counts' (Connell 1993, p.610), nor is it the most attainable, it is, however, the most dominant. Connell asserts that power is the defining feature of hegemonic masculinity and that this power is symbolised through enactments of violence.

Violent masculinities

Violence is predominantly perpetrated by men and this has led to competing theorisations about the creation of a gendered (male) identity through the perpetration of violence. Yet this crude view of violence as a simplistic means to accomplish masculinity has been disputed (Gadd 2002). Therefore when analysing violence the focus needs to be upon men and their behaviour, rather than viewing it as an act that is constitutive of masculinity. Otherwise, masculinity is theorised as deterministic and resistant to change and men as violent because their masculinity constitutes their actions. This conceptual shift has succeeded in attributing the violence to men and removing the assumption of biological inevitability whilst acknowledging the plurality of men's violences (Hearn 1998, 2001).

Whilst it is crucial to identify that most violence is committed by men (from situations of war through to violence within families) it is equally important to recognise that not all men are violent (Connell 2000, p.215). Indeed, if all men were labelled as violent this would simply be perpetuating the taken for granted nature of sex differences discussed at the outset of this chapter. As such it is critical to acknowledge that men are not violent because of their 'biology', rather they exist in a culture where certain forms of masculine identities are esteemed above others. Connell's hegemonic masculinity is 'the successful claim to authority, more than direct violence, that is the mark of hegemony (although violence often underpins or supports authority)' (Connell 1987, p.39). However, such an ideology of masculinism sustains and perpetuates power on the basis of supposed biological difference securing the domination of men and the subjugation of women (Brittan 1989). It is pertinent however to acknowledge that the regularity and prevalence of men's violence constitutes 'acceptable' forms of normative masculinity. It is also often encapsulated by society's understanding of 'normal' interaction between men and women:

> [men's violence against women] is something that normal, ordinary men do routinely on a very substantial scale because they want to, because they think they have a right to and because nothing effective is done to stop them. (Itzin 2000, p.378)

As such, 'violence is not a deviant act; it is a conforming one' (Hatty 2000, p.1). Masculine identities are social constructions, with violent behaviour understood as a means chosen by some men, and boys, to demonstrate this. In this way, much of men's violence needs to be understood as conscious, deliberate actions and as forms or examples of particular masculinities (Hearn 1998).

Why does gender matter in an analysis of violence?

In this context, in any study of violence it is crucial to analyse the role of gender. Hearn (1998) argues that all violence is gendered whether it is violence that is experienced, perpetrated or witnessed. We live in a society where the dominant social construction of masculinity rewards aggression (Connell 1987, 2005; Brownmiller 1975) and femininity is often constructed as passive, fearful and dependent (Connell 2005) which go on to inform stereotypes and myths around violence (Soothill and Walby 1991; Worrall 2004).

Stanko (2006) insists that gender matters in experiences of violence, in how we understand it and also in how people receive help and support as 'victims'. By ignoring gender, Stanko (2006, p.551) maintains that we risk 'impoverishing' any analyses of violence as gender is integral to 'the way we speak, conceptualise and challenge violence.' Research tells us that gender is the most significant risk factor for domestic abuse (Dobash and Dobash 2004; Johnson 1995, 2005; Stark 2007) which means that women are more likely to experience violence from their intimate (or estranged) partners than men are. It does not mean, however, that all perpetrators are men and all victims are female. What it indicates is that the intimate violence is taking place within wider structures of gender inequality. Gender is important in any analysis of violence because men and women use violence in different ways and have different motivations for doing so (Hester 2009).

Skinner, Hester and Malos (2005) maintain that 'gender violence' is a more inclusive term than 'violence against women' as it does not restrict itself to women but engages with the theoretical connection between violence and gender relations thus including gay and lesbian people as well as children and young people. The term gender violence also incorporates a wider definition of abuses and violations including prostitution and trafficking as well as violence where women are the perpetrators (Skinner *et al.* 2005, p.3). Gender also matters because violence is so often treated as gender-neutral through terms such as 'spousal abuse', 'date rape', 'sexual harassment', 'marital rape', 'battery' and 'child sexual abuse' (Hague and Malos 1998).

So what about the men?

Some commentators (e.g. Archer 2006; Straus, Gelles and Steinmetz 1980) and also men's rights groups have questioned the use of a gender-based definition of domestic abuse arguing that it excludes men in general, and male victims in particular. However, using a gendered analysis means taking into consideration the *differences* in men and women's lives, experiences and opportunities because of the socially ascribed roles of gender. It does not mean focusing solely upon women. It also provides a way to examine how the different social, economic and political structures impact men and women differentially because of gender-based stereotypes, abuses and inequalities.

The increase in attention to men as victims of domestic abuse has coincided with an increase or 'rising tide' of hyperbole on women's criminality more generally (Batchelor 2001 cited in Burman 2004; Batchelor 2007). The common-sense assumption perpetuated, in particular by the media (Burman, Brown and Batchelor 2003), is that women's violence is equal to that of men's (both in ferocity and occurrence). Such a view also propagates the biological view of violence as innate and as stemming from aggression thereby labelling 'violent women' as unnatural. Women's violence against men is much more anecdotal, not (as some of its supporters would argue) because of the shame silencing male victims (see Whiting's Chapter in this volume) but because it happens less frequently and on a much, much smaller scale (Gadd *et al.* 2002, 2003). Indeed, Gadd *et al.* (2003, p.113) warns against allowing anecdotal evidence to 'negate the vast body of social research that has demonstrated the motivatedness of perpetrators' accounts and the gendered power dynamics intrinsic to most abusive relationships.'

In terms of general victimisation, men are more likely to be victims of crime than women but the risk and pattern of violent victimisation is very different for men and for women (McMillan 2010, p.92). Indeed, McMillan goes on to argue:

> Women are the primary victims of violence and abuse in the home and within intimate relationships and are those most likely to be sexually victimised, most often by the men they know. The risk for women, then, is the men they love, live with, are related to and work with. (McMillan 2010, p.106)

Are women as violent as men?

There have been numerous studies that have looked at 'interpersonal' violence seeking to label men and women as equal combatants (Gelles 1983, 1987, 1993, 1997; Straus et al. 1980) undertaking 'mutual acts of aggression' (Fergusson, Horwood and Ridder 2005, p.1116) and endorsing women as being as violent as men (see Steinmetz 1977).[1]

Family violence research is most closely associated with the work of American sociologists Straus and Gelles (1986) who argue that violence is built into family life. Straus and Gelles developed the 'Conflict Tactics Scale' (CTS) to measure the controlling and abusive tactics couples may use against each other. Using this scale to measure results, Straus and Gelles conducted The National Family Violence Survey (NFVS) in 1975 and again in 1985 with a representative sample of married heterosexual couples in the USA. Their results showed that similar levels of partner violence were experienced and perpetrated by men and women. In half the cases, both partners were equally combative (violent) and in the remaining sample, the role of the primary perpetrator was divided equally between the sexes. From these results, Straus and Gelles claimed that the dominant family member uses violence in order to legitimise their position. They maintained that violence and/or conflict within the family arose from stress (from unemployment, health issues and financial insecurity) or as a means to 'solve' conflict (e.g. the smacking of children).

Family violence research has come under heavy criticism (Gadd et al. 2002; Gadd et al. 2003; Hester 2009; Johnson 1995; Kelly and Johnson 2008; Stanko 2006; Stark 2007). Although the dynamic of power is included in the analysis by Straus and Gelles, it is at an individualistic level, that is, particular to each family. It is also agendered research that does not take account of the gendered power dynamics that exist within the home. For example, the research has been criticised for interviewing respondents whilst other family members were present. It also under-sampled those women whose victimisation was likely to be more severe (separated and divorced women and those residing in refuges).

Whilst the NFVS showed that women sustained more injuries than men (Gelles 1993; Flood 1997) it did not include forms of victimisation women are more likely to experience such as sexual assault, suffocating and stalking (Gadd et al. 2002). The quantitative nature of the NFVS also

---

1 Steinmetz' (1977) study has since been discredited by several academic studies (Dobash et al. 1992; Kurz 1989; Straus 1999; Yllo 1988 cited in Johnson 2005, p.1129) but it is important to mention as it is often used as evidence (mainly by men's rights groups) that women are 'as violent' as men.

meant that the subjectivities and nuances of the encounters could not be determined (Renzetti 1999). The context, motivations and meanings of violence are crucial factors in feminist research into violence (Gadd *et al.* 2003; Hester 2009) and must be taken into account if a realistic understanding of violence in general and men's violence against women in particular is to be understood. Research continually contradicts the gender-symmetric view of violence evidenced in the NFVS as well as disputing the role of women as equal aggressors (Gadd *et al.* 2002; Johnson 2005; Stark 2007). The work of Johnson (1995, 2005) and Kelly and Johnson (2008) has been influential in highlighting the limitations of the Conflict Tactics Scale.

According to Johnson (1995, 2005) and Kelly and Johnson (2008) the differences in terms of intimate violence can be divided into two types: situational couple violence and coercive controlling violence (or intimate terrorism). Situational couple violence is when an argument escalates. It could be a one-off incident or more frequent, but there is not a desire to control the other partner. Intimate terrorism describes patterns of coercive control (see Stark, this volume) by one partner over the other, where physical violence may be one of the methods used to control. The differences between these forms of violence are critical. For example, Kelly and Johnson maintain that:

> when family sociologists and/or advocates for men claim that domestic violence is perpetrated equally by men and women, referring to the data from large survey studies, they are describing Situational Couple Violence, not Coercive Controlling Violence (…) these two types of violence differ in significant ways, including causes, participation, consequences to participants, and forms of intervention required. (Kelly and Johnson 2008, p.481)

In asking the question 'What about male victims?' there is a supposition that men and women experience violence in similar ways and in similar numbers, which fails to take account of the gendered nature of violence:

> Thus, although situational couple violence is nearly gender symmetric and not strongly related to gender attitudes, intimate terrorism (domestic violence) is almost entirely male perpetrated and is strongly related to gender attitudes (…) men's violence produces more frequent and more severe injuries, thereby producing a fear (or even terror)

> that is quite rare when women are violent toward their
> male partners. My intention is not to justify or minimize
> women's violence but to recognize it for what it is (mostly
> situational couple violence or violent resistance). (Johnson
> 2005, pp.1128–1129)

Kelly and Johnson (2008) list the reasons for this as, firstly, down to a
man's physical size and strength and, secondly, individual misogyny and
gender traditionalism (supported by research into children's attitudes to
violence against women; see Lombard 2010). Thirdly, the meaning of
violence differs greatly depending upon the gender of the perpetrator;
and fourthly, heterosexual relationships are rooted in patriarchy and as
such validate men's power. Finally, the broader social context in which
the violence takes place is crucial. Women are unequal in violence because
they are unequal in society, in terms of the resources and opportunities
they can access (Stark 2007). Therefore to understand violence, we also
need to take account of the wider social contexts:

> Violence is not, of course, a homogeneous phenomenon
> (…) Violence is (…) manifested within the wider
> framework of hatred towards specific groups, whether on
> grounds of sexual, religious or other forms of prejudice.
> Tackling violence in its varied forms, and dealing with its
> consequences, requires an understanding of its motivation
> and its wider social contexts. (Scottish Government 2003,
> p.11)

Whilst men can and do experience forms of domestic abuse, research has
demonstrated that they experience it in a way that is different to that of
women. This is illustrated below using two case studies which support a
gender-based definition of violence.

Case studies
Male domestic abuse in Scotland

As was noted in the introduction to this chapter, the social and political
context of Scotland is unique as it is the only country in the UK to
recognise and facilitate a gender-based definition of domestic abuse.
The gender-based definition used by the Scottish government has been
subject to criticism from men's rights groups and other proponents of a
gender-neutral definition, initially in 2000 and again in 2010. One of
the strategies of men's rights groups in Scotland was to quote figures

from the 2000 Scottish Crime Survey (SCS) as 'proof' that men and women experienced similar levels of domestic abuse. The survey data shows that 19 per cent of women and 8 per cent of men had experienced either 'threats' or 'force' from their partners or ex-partners at some point in their lives (MVA 2000). The Scottish Executive commissioned research to examine these figures (see Gadd *et al.* 2002) and to look more generally at the context in which the domestic abuse occurred. The research team re-contacted[2] the men who had taken part in the Scottish Crime Survey, asking them to participate in an hour-long interview. The research found that one in four of the men had 'inaccurately reported experiences of force or threats from a partner in the SCS 2000 self-completion questionnaire' (Gadd *et al.* 2002, p.55). Some men had misinterpreted the question and had taken domestic abuse to mean any form of violence (or indeed a skirmish) within the home; for example a domestic burglary of a bicycle or a fist fight with a male relative in the garden.

The findings also revealed that men who reported being victims of abuse could be grouped into one of four categories: primary instigators; equal combatants; retaliators; or non-retaliatory victims (n indicates the number of men in this category):

- *Primary Instigators*: These are men who admitted that they instigated most of the abuse in their relationships (n = 1).

- *Equal Combatants*: These men argued that their relationships were equally abusive on both sides (n = 4).

- *Retaliators*: These men admitted having been abusive to their partners, but argued that this abuse occurred in the context of more prolonged or serious levels of abuse perpetrated against them by their partners (n = 8).

- *Non-Retaliatory Victims*: These men said they were victims of their partner's abuse, but had never retaliated and had only used force to restrain partners who were physically attacking them (n = 9).

(Gadd *et al.* 2002, p.38)

Many of the men who had identified themselves as victims in the survey were less likely than women to have been repeatedly victimised

---

2 The men had provided their contact details and agreed to being re-contacted at a later date.

or suffered serious injury. Also Gadd *et al.* (2002) identified that the majority of the men they spoke to 'did not consider themselves to be either "victims" of "crime" or of "domestic violence", although many were embarrassed by the abuse they had experienced' (2002, p.56). While there were a very small minority of men who maintained that they 'lived in fear' it was more common that the men interviewed were:

> more upset and/or angry about the *breakdown* of relationships in which abuse had occurred than the actual abuse itself. Separations between abused men and their partners occasionally resulted in distressing disputes over child custody, the family home and shared finances. (Gadd *et al.* 2002, p.56)

The results of this study highlighted that a number of the men interviewed were also perpetrators of the abuse, leading to the conclusion that '[d]ifferentiating perpetrators from victims in these cases is an irreconcilably contentious task' (Gadd *et al.* 2002, p.44). This finding substantiated previous work where men depicted themselves as victims of violence to exonerate themselves from blame (Gondolf 1988; Hearn 1998; Wolf-Light 1999 cited in Gadd *et al.* 2002, p.3). Also while men may be victims of domestic abuse they do not experience it in the same way as women. That is, men are less likely to live in fear of violence against them and it does not impact upon their daily lives as it does with female victims. Crucially, it was highlighted that specific services for male victims were not necessary (in terms of numbers and need); however, there was a lack of services and provision for gay men who were identified as victims of domestic abuse and in need of support. Gadd *et al.* (2003) state that:

> …there are many comprehensible reasons why the incidents of domestic abuse against men detected in crime surveys do not get reported to the police. Sometimes the incidents are trivial, non-criminal and/or inconsequential. Often domestic abuse against men is not repeated and hence victims prefer not to involve criminal justice practitioners. Sometimes male victims of domestic abuse are also perpetrators who fear incriminating themselves. (2003, p.112)

Who does what to whom?

The second case study draws upon the work of Hester (2009) which tracked cases of domestic violence over a period of six years. Hester states that a longitudinal study such as this reflects the pattern of domestic abuse over time rather than focusing upon single incidents. Hester argues that crime figures cannot be looked at in isolation. When presented with police data on domestic abuse we need to look beyond the numbers to see the whole picture of who experiences what. Hester maintains that to understand who is affected by domestic violence/abuse we need to ask about prevalence, incidence and impact. Prevalence helps us to see how many people experience certain behaviours but not if they have any effect; incidence helps us to measure intensity and possibly severity; and impact allows us to see what effect and consequences the behaviours have and to see if services are needed (Hester 2011). In her analysis of police and interview data Hester found that the nature of incidents, levels of repeat perpetration and arrest and conviction could be differentiated by gender (Hester 2009, p.7). The arrest practices rates were in line with Association of Chief Police Officers ACPO guidelines which advised police officers to identify one perpetrator and one victim in each incident. Hester also found that men were significantly more likely to be repeat perpetrators and to use physical violence, threats and harassment (Hester 2009, pp.7–8). This confirmed earlier research by Gadd *et al.* (2002):

> The infrequency with which male victims appeared in Scottish recorded crime statistics relative to women was mostly due to gender differences in patterns of victimisation and not differential reporting patterns or police recording priorities. (2002, pp.21–24 cited in Gadd *et al.* 2003, p.99)

In addition, Hester also found that women were more likely to use a weapon (often for protection) and, because of this, were more likely to be arrested. However, such actions were not likely to induce fear; rather it was 'men's violence [that] tended to create a context of fear, and related to that, control. This was not similarly the case where women were perpetrators' (Hester 2009, p.8). Hester's research consolidates earlier research (Gadd *et al.* 2002; Johnson 2005; Stark 2007) which identifies that men and women use and experience violence in differing ways. Her findings also illustrate that while both men and women may come to the attention of the police, they may refuse to co-operate for different reasons; women out of fear and men because they were perpetrators (Hester 2009, p.19).

Hester identified that in examining domestic abuse we also need to look at the motivations and consequences of such behaviour on the 'victim'. Available survey data illustrates that the rate and the severity of domestic abuse against women is greater than that experienced by men (Dobash *et al.* 1992; Gadd *et al.* 2002, 2003; Hester 2009). It is critical to look at incidence but also beyond this at the effect of those incidences; what Hester terms the impact of the violence. It is the impact of such violence that is more easily understood within a gendered analysis as women disproportionately experience it. For example, violence is more detrimental to their health, life and general wellbeing and this dictates the gendered nature of violence.

Gadd *et al.* (2003) maintain that of the men they interviewed, 'very few of the men's accounts lent support to the idea that there are substantial numbers of men living with the kinds of fears for their own safety' (2003, p.110). Time and time again, research studies identify that the impact of violent and abusive behaviour is most keenly experienced by women and girls (Barter and McCarry, this volume; Gadd *et al.* 2002; Hester 2009; Hoyle 2007; Lombard 2010). They stress that such violence is not 'incidence based', but rather it focuses upon repeat victimisation and the context of fear and control that is particular to women's victimisation by men.

Conclusions and implications for social work practice

The aim of this chapter has been to examine the reasons for gender-based definitions of domestic abuse. The purpose has not been to argue that all women are victims of domestic abuse and all men are perpetrators. Rather, by introducing a gender analysis to understand violence social workers can examine the complexities of the situation by looking beyond the particular incident and looking at the wider context. There is a need to recognise that our everyday understanding of men's and women's violence is informed by, and based upon, our perceptions of gender. Women's violence is often judged to be 'unnatural' and as going against traditional notions of femininity (Burman 2004; Edwards 1984; Worrall 2004). Men are framed by cultural understandings of what it is to be a man with physical prowess, protection, anger and entitlement all bound up in expectations of men and masculinity.

When encountering cases of domestic abuse in the course of social work practice individual practitioners use their existing knowledge and understandings to interpret what is being said, and by whom. Whilst their presence that day may be as the result of a particular occurrence of domestic abuse, that one 'incident' should always be framed by the wider context of gender-based abuse and within a framework of fear and inequality. A woman's agency and the choices she makes need to be respected. Practitioners cannot simply advise a woman to leave. She will be scared of the repercussions – what he may do to her, the children, whether her children will be taken from her. Her situation is complex and multifarious; it is not just a simple question of her moving out.

Related to this is the assumption that it is the woman's responsibility to stop the violence by leaving. Within this gendered framework of abuse the question that needs to be asked is not 'Why doesn't she leave?' but 'Why doesn't he stop?' It is frustrating for social workers (and others) to continue to see a woman remain but her reasons for doing so need to be located within a gendered analysis of her situation that emphasise her possible lack of access to material and social resources as well as the situation of fear and control she is living within.

Often practitioners dealing with domestic abuse may suggest that within a family, the couple are 'both as bad as each other' or question 'But what about the men?' Whilst some men may experience violence within the home and women may be perpetrators of that violence it is argued here that such an assertion needs to be examined critically within a gendered analysis to fully understand the context, motivations and impact of the violence upon the man and the woman involved.

References

Archer, J. (2006) 'Cross-cultural differences in physical aggression between partners: A social-role analysis.' *Personality and Social Psychology Review 10*, 2, 133–153.

Batchelor, S. (2007) '"Getting Mad wi' it": Risk-seeking by Young Women.' In K. Hannah-Moffat and P. O'Malley (eds) *Gendered Risks*. London: Glasshouse Press.

Bond, J. and Phillips R. (2000) 'Violence Against Women as a Human Rights Abuse.' In C. Renzetti, J. Edleson and R. Bergen (eds) *Sourcebook on Violence Against Women*. London: Sage Publications.

Brittan, A. (1989) *Masculinity and Power.* Oxford: Blackwell.

Brownmiller, S. (1975) *Against Our Will: Men, Women and Rape*. London: Penguin.

Burman, M. (2004) 'Breaking the Mould: Patterns of Female Offending.' In G. McIvor (ed.) *Women Who Offend*. London: Jessica Kingsley Publishers.

Burman, M., Brown, J. and Batchelor, S. (2003) 'Taking it to Heart: Girls and the Meanings of Violence.' In E.A. Stanko (ed.) *The Meaning of Violence*. London: Routledge.

Butler, J. (1990) *Gender Trouble: Feminism and the Subversion of Identity*. London: Routledge.

Connell, R.W. (1987) *Gender and Power.* Stanford: Stanford University Press.

Connell, R.W. (1993) 'The big picture: Changing masculinities in the perspective of recent world history.' *Theory and Society 22*, 5, 597–623.

Connell, R.W. (1995, 2005) *Masculinities.* Cambridge: Polity Press.

Connell, R.W. (2000) *The Men and The Boys.* Cambridge: Polity Press.

Connell, R.W. (2001) 'The Social Organisation of Masculinity.' In S.M. Whitehead and F.J. Barrett (eds) *The Masculinities Reader.* Cambridge: Polity Press.

de Beauvoir, S. (1949) (translated 2009) *The Second Sex*. Trans. Constance Borde and Sheila Malovany-Chevallier. Random House: Alfred A. Knopf.

Dobash, R.P. and Dobash, R.E. (2004) 'Women's violence to men in intimate relationships: Working on a puzzle.' *British Journal of Criminology 44*, 3, 324–349.

Dobash, R.P., Dobash, R.E., Wilson, M. and Daly, M. (1992) 'The myth of sexual symmetry in marital violence.' *Social Problems 39*, 1, 71–91.

Dragiewicz, M. and Lindgren, Y. (2009) 'The gendered nature of domestic violence: Statistical data for lawyers considering equal protection analysis.' *American University Journal of Gender, Social Policy & the Law. The first annual American Bar Association Domestic Violence Commission and Journal of Gender, Social Policy and the Law domestic violence dedicated section 17*, 2, 229–268.

Edwards, S. (1984) *Women On Trial*. Manchester: Manchester University Press.

Fergusson, D., Horwood, J. and Ridder, E. (2005) 'Partner violence and mental health outcomes in a New Zealand birth cohort.' *Journal of Marriage and Family 67*, 5, 1103–1119.

Flood, M. (1997) *Responding to Men*. Available atwww.xyonline.net/content/responding-mens-rights-groups, accessed on 14 October 2012.

Gadd, D. (2002) 'Masculinities and violence against female partners.' *Social & Legal Studies 11*, 1, 61–80.

Gadd, D., Farrell, S., Lombard, N. and Dallimore, D. (2002) *Domestic Abuse Against Men in Scotland*. Edinburgh: Scottish Executive Central Research Unit.

Gadd, D., Farrell, S., Lombard, N. and Dallimore, D. (2003) 'Equal victims or the usual suspects? Making sense of domestic abuse against men.' *International Review of Victimology 10*, 2, 95–116.

Gelles, R.J. (1983) 'An Exchange /Social Control Theory.' In D. Finkelhor, R.J. Gelles, G.T. Hotaling and M.A. Straus (eds) *The Dark Side of Families: Current Family Violence Research*. London: Sage Publications.

Gelles, R.J. (1987) *Family Violence Research*. London: Sage Publications.

Gelles, R.J. (1993) 'Through A Sociological Lens: Social Structure and Family Violence.' In R.J. Gelles and D.R. Loseke (eds) *Current Controversies on Family Violence*. London: Sage Publications.

Gelles, R.J. (1997) *Intimate Violence in Families*. London: Sage Publications.

Gondolf, E. (1988) 'Letters "Continued Debate": The truth about domestic violence.' *Social Work 33*, 2, 109.

Hague, G. and Malos, E. (1998) *Domestic Violence: Action for Change*. Cheltenham: New Clarion Press.

Hatty, S.E. (2000) *Masculinities, Violence and Culture*. London: Sage Publications.

Hearn, J. (1998) *The Violences of Men: How Men Talk and How Agencies Respond to Men's Violences Against Women*. London: Sage Publications.

Hearn, J. (2001) 'Men organizing and working against men's violence to women: campaigns, programmes, development.' *Development: the Journal of the Society for International Development 44*, 3, 85–89.

Hester, M. (2009) *Who Does What to Whom? Gender and Domestic Violence Perpetrators*. Bristol: University of Bristol in association with the Northern Rock Foundation.

Hester, M. (2011) 'Gender Analysis and Domestic Abuse.' Presentation to the Cross Party Group on Violence Against Women, Edinburgh, 23 February 2011.

Hoyle, C. (2007) 'Feminism, Victimology and Domestic Violence.' In S. Walklate (ed.) *Handbook of Victims and Victimology*. Cullompton, Devon: Willan Publishing.

Itzin, C. (2000) 'Gendering Domestic Violence: the Influence of Feminism on Policy and Practice.' In J. Hamner and C. Itzin with S. Quaid and D. Wigglesworth (eds) *Home Truths About Domestic Violence: Feminist Influences on Policy and Practice: A Reader*. London: Routledge.

Johnson, M. (1995) 'Patriarchal terrorism and common couple violence: Two forms of violence against women.' *Journal of Marriage and Family 57*, 2, 283–294.

Johnson, M. (2005) 'Domestic violence: It's not about gender – Or is it?' *Journal of Marriage and Family 67*, 5, 1126–1130.

Kelly, J.B. and Johnson, M.P. (2008) 'Differentiation among types of intimate partner violence: Research update and implications for interventions.' *Family Court Review 46*, 3, 476–499.

Kimmel, M. (1987) 'Rethinking Masculinity: New Directions in Research.' In M.S. Kimmel (ed.) *Changing Men: New Directions in Research on Men and Masculinity.* London: Sage Publications.

Kurz, D. (1989) 'Social science perspectives on wife abuse: Current debates and future directions.' *Gender Society 3*, 4, 489–505.

Lombard, N. (2010) *It's Wrong for a Boy to Hit a Girl Because the Girl Might Cry: Investigating Young People's Understandings of Men's Violence Against Women.* Unpublished PhD thesis, Glasgow Caledonian University.

McMillan, L. (2010) *Gender, Crime and Criminal Justice in Scotland.* In Croall, H., Mooney, G. and Munro, M. (eds) *Criminal Justice in Contemporary Scotland.* Cullompton: Willan Publishing.

MVA (2000) *The 2000 Scottish Crime Survey: First Results.* Crime and Criminal Justice Research, Finding No. 51. Edinburgh: Scottish Executive.

Renzetti, C. (1999) 'The Challenge to Feminism Posed by Women's Use of Violence in Intimate Relationships.' In S. Lamb (ed.) *New Versions of Victims: Feminists Struggle with the Concept.* New York: New York University Press.

Scottish Executive (2000) *National Strategy to Address Domestic Abuse in Scotland.* Edinburgh: Stationery Office.

Scottish Executive (2001) *Preventing Violence Against Women: Action Across the Scottish Executive.* Edinburgh: Stationery Office.

Scottish Government (2003) *Crime and Criminal Justice Research Agenda.* Available at www.scotland.gov.uk/Resource/Doc/47021/0025178.pdf, accessed on 17 July 2012.

Skinner, T., Hester, M. and Malos, E. (eds) (2005) *Researching Gender Violence: Feminist Methodology in Action.* Cullompton, Devon: Willan Publishing.

Soothill, K. and Walby, S. (1991) *Sex Crime in the News.* London: Routledge.

Stanko, E.A. (2006) 'Theorizing About Violence Observations From the Economic and Social Research Council's Violence Research Program.' *Violence Against Women 12*, 6, 543–555.

Stark, E. (2007) *Coercive Control: How Men Entrap Women in Personal Life.* Oxford: Oxford University Press.

Steinmetz, S. (1977) 'The battered husband syndrome.' *Victimology 2*, 3-4, 499–509.

Straus, M.A. (1999) 'The Controversy Over Domestic Violence by Women: A Methodological, Theoretical, and Sociology of Science Analysis.' In X. Arriaga and S. Oskamp (eds) *Violence in Intimate Relationships.* Thousand Oaks, CA: Sage.

Straus, M.A. and Gelles, R.J. (1986) 'Societal change and change in family violence from 1975 to 1985 as revealed by two national surveys.' *Journal of Marriage and Family 48*, 465–479.

Straus, M., Gelles, R. and Steinmetz, R. (1980) *Behind Closed Doors: Violence in the American Family.* New York: Doubleday/Anchor.

Wolf-Light, P. (1999) 'Men, Violence and Love.' In J. Wild (ed.) *Working with Men for Change.* London: UCL Press.

Worrall, A. (2004) 'Twisted Sisters, Ladettes, and the New Penology: The Social Construction of "Violent Girls".' In C. Adler and A. Worrall (eds) *Girls' Violence.* New York: State University of New York Press.

CHAPTER 11

Effecting Operational Change Through Training
Challenges and Approaches

Nel Whiting

Introduction

This chapter will focus on the challenges to delivering effective learning opportunities on the topic of violence against women to social work practitioners. The discussion will draw on research about these challenges as well as theorising on how most effectively to frame the issue to make it pertinent to social work practice. Utilising work undertaken in Scotland as a case study, the specifics will be from a Scottish content but the general themes and concerns are transferable across Western nations. The chapter will highlight some of the pragmatic challenges experienced when translating theory and research into practice-driven training. The role of training in supporting safe and effective intervention will be explored as will the importance of keeping survivors' voices central to the learning experience.

Scottish policy context

In 2000 the publication of *The National Strategy to Address Domestic Abuse in Scotland* recognised 'a need to challenge and change attitudes which perpetuate domestic abuse, which *cannot be tackled effectively without education and training*' (Scottish Executive 2000, p.13).[1]

Subsequently in March 2004 the Scottish Executive launched the National Training Strategy acknowledging that 'training is essential to enable staff to provide a good service' to those affected by domestic abuse (Scottish Executive 2004, p.1). The strategy aimed to ensure 'that all workers who come into contact with women, children and young people who have experienced domestic abuse, and men who have used violence, have the knowledge, understanding and skills required' (Scottish Executive 2004, p.4).

Henceforth, then, training on domestic abuse was to be viewed as core business throughout the voluntary and statutory sectors. More importantly, as the strategy makes explicit, the focus of any training was to be *attitudinal change* as well as skills development. This dual approach is vital when domestic abuse is understood as 'social entrapment' (Ptacek 1999) whereby the systems of agencies and the attitudes of workers within them reinforce the perpetrator's tactics to socially isolate a woman. Examples of this are overly rigid appointment booking systems, limited opening hours, 'dry' refuges and questioning a woman about abuse in front of a perpetrator.

From the outset the Scottish Executive applied a gendered analysis to its understanding of domestic abuse, viewing it as both a cause and consequence of gender inequality and intrinsically linked to women's historical and current subordinate position in society:

> Domestic abuse is associated with broader gender inequality and should be understood in its historical context, whereby societies have given greater status, wealth, influence, control and power to men. It is part of a range of behaviours constituting male abuse of power,

---

1   Domestic abuse, as opposed to domestic violence, has been the preferred policy term in Scotland for over a decade. The semantic development was made in recognition of the fact that physical violence is only one of a range of controlling behaviours utilised by perpetrators. Thus in Scotland, domestic abuse is defined as that which 'can be perpetrated by partners or ex-partners and can include physical abuse (assault and physical attack involving a range of behaviour), sexual abuse (acts which degrade and humiliate women and are perpetrated against their will, including rape) and mental and emotional abuse (such as threats, verbal abuse, racial abuse, withholding money and other types of controlling behaviour such as isolation from family or friends)' (Scottish Executive 2000, p.4).

and is linked to other forms of male violence. (Scottish Executive 2000, p.5)

As such, domestic abuse was set within a theoretical framework which acknowledged the influence of gender on men's and women's lives: the decisions they may make, the status accorded them and the relationship between them. Importantly it placed domestic abuse within a continuum of violence against women which crosses both public and private space and is underpinned by ideas about women's position in society (Kelly 1988). In light of this understanding, the scope of the original domestic abuse strategy was extended in 2005 to cover other forms of violence against women. Where government policy leads, however, local policy and individual practice does not always follow and in Scotland some resistance to the gendered analysis of domestic abuse and the 'true' prevalence of violence against women still exists. It is what Hearn and McKie describe as the 'the averted gaze to the gendered nature of violence' (2010, p.137). This 'averted gaze', and the other training challenges, is explored in the next section.

Training challenges
The gender question

Perhaps the single greatest challenge in providing training addressing domestic abuse and other forms of violence against women is the still pervasive issue of its gendered nature. This takes a variety of forms: confusion as to what is meant by 'gender' leading to a misunderstanding of the phrase 'gender-based abuse'; outright denial of, and hostility to, gender as a shaper of men's and women's lives; and/or a general denial of the scale and scope of the issues being discussed. Sometimes these issues are separate challenges but usually they intertwine to form multi-layered resistance. That this is so is perhaps unsurprising; as Hearn and McKie maintain, the definitions of an issue 'provide parameters in discourses as to what may, or may not, be considered' (2010, p.138). In other words if you deny gender as a framework which sets expectations for lived experience you will inevitably find it hard to accept that violence against women is a serious social issue as you will be unable to find any reason for it being so.

Gender is complex. As it is socially constructed, and as individuals we are actively engaged with it at all times, it is always open to contestation, constantly evolving, culturally and temporally specific, and thus inherently unstable (Connell 2002). As it is 'social practice', that is as individual identity, performative interaction and socio-cultural ordering (Connell 1987), then it is multifarious and nebulous. What a volatile thing to describe in a training room! How much more so in the face of hostility or apathy from those who only want to know 'what to do' when faced with disclosure or how to 'fix' a broken client. A balance needs to be struck in training, therefore, between providing delegates with an understanding of what is meant by gender, and by extension gender-based abuse, and getting bogged down in philosophical debates which are too abstract or esoteric to be of practical use when working with a client. In other words theory must be actualised, or humanised, rooted in the experience of clients and shown to be of absolute pertinence to practice. Where a discussion about gender may seem abstract, discussion about the rules which govern a female client's life and how these shape her experiences of violence can bear fruit. Hence forming a set of questions for group discussion can be useful, questions that from the outset are rooted in real life:

- What does a given society say it means to be a 'real man'/'real woman'?
- What does that look like in your client group?
- How will it shape experiences of violence?

In setting up this discussion it is vital to take cognisance of its sensitivity: it is a discussion which goes to the heart of an individual's sense of themselves as men and women and their place in society. As Connell argues, gender is 'a key dimension of personal life, social relations and culture' (2002, p.vii). Furthermore, gender is so normalised/naturalised that it has often been previously invisible to delegates and if one is thinking about it for the first time discomfort can arise. Space and reassurance needs to be provided to make this process safe.

A more light-hearted, and therefore possibly a safe, approach to initiating this gender discussion can be the use of images, such as those from contemporary advertising campaigns, where delegates are asked to discuss what messages the images are promoting. Such an approach has the threefold benefit of highlighting that gender as social control sets boundaries around what men are allowed to do and has detriments for them as well as for women; stressing how messages can be naturalised through repetition; and highlighting the increasing normalisation of sexualised imagery, often violent sexualised imagery, that surround our multi-media existence. The step then to discussing forms of violence against women is but a small one as the 'conducive context' (EVAW 2008) for such violence has been established.

Most commonly, delegates' perception of gender on entering the training room is that it is another word for 'sex'; this is entirely understandable given that the words are frequently used interchangeably or conflated in everyday speech and official documents. It remains important, however, in distinguishing between sex and gender not to separate them completely; sexed bodies remain central to gender rules. As Connell argues:

> Society *addresses* bodies and puts reproductive difference into play. There is no fixed 'biological base' for the social process of gender. Rather, there is an arena in which bodies are brought into social processes, in which our social conduct does something with reproductive difference... gender concerns the way human society deals with human bodies, and the many consequences of that 'dealing' in our personal lives and our collective fate. (Connell 2002, p.10)

In other words, what one is allowed to do with one's body, the amount of space one is able to occupy, how one decorates it, and significantly in discussions about violence against women how that sexed body is valued, denigrated, objectified and/or punished, remain not just pertinent but fundamental. Hence a discussion about gender divorced from the sexed body is merely abstraction for the purposes of practice-based training for social workers; it is essential that a trainer helps the delegates understand the very practical impact that gender and gender-based abuse has on the bodies of the clients they are working with. For example, the sexed body of a woman experiencing domestic abuse may be bruised, denied food, expected to wear certain clothing or locked away in what Stark describes as the perpetrator's 'microregulation of everyday behaviours associated with stereotypic female roles, such as how women dress, cook, clean, socialize, care for their children, or perform sexually' (Stark 2007, p.5).

Another prevalent belief amongst delegates is that gender means 'woman', in the sense that gender issues means women's issues. Both together and separately these convictions lead to a conceptualisation of 'gender-based abuse' or violence as meaning something that is done to women by men, or by all men to all women. In this way, 'gender-based abuse' comes to mean men are bad and women are good. The most effective definition I have identified in countering this assumption is that of James Lang (2003) who argues, 'gender-based violence is any form of violence used to establish, enforce or perpetuate gender inequalities and keep in place gendered orders. In other words, gender-based violence is a policing mechanism.'

A reason why this definition proves so effective in training is that it asks us not to concentrate on who is doing what to whom at an individual level, and what the sex of either the 'perpetrator' or 'victim' is, but what motivates the action. The motivation, in Lang's definition, lying in upholding society's expectations of what it means to be a man or a woman and punishing those who break the rules. In this way, gender-based abuse can be perpetrated by individuals, groups or states; it can be carried out by familiars or strangers. The definition counters the widely held belief that to talk about gender-based abuse is discriminatory as it excludes men's experiences of abuse as it is a definition which holds that men and women can both perpetrate and experience gendered violence. It questions, however, the purported neutrality of a 'gender-neutral' approach and emphasises the proportionality of a gendered analysis (Hester 2009; Johnson 2008; Kimmel 2002).

Furthermore, this definition enables a global and structural discussion; rape in war, trafficking, domestic abuse no longer appear disparate but can now be connected in a continuum of violence, underpinned by the cultural and historical values and attitudes which drive them. In turn, this allows discussion of the intersection of culture and class with gender without the need to resort to stereotypes. So, for example, I am less likely to be trafficked as a white, middle-class British woman than a poor working class Bosnian woman or Pakistani girl caught up in the flood disaster not because it is less acceptable in 'my' culture but because I live in a situation where the context is less conducive to such a thing occurring. Again, such discussion allows the theory to be connected to everyday practice; it highlights that all women can experience violence against women while acknowledging risk factors and vulnerabilities. By extension this leads to consideration of the risk factors and vulnerabilities in clients' lives, issues central to safe working practice.

Most frustrating of all for a trainer in this context is facing a gendered argument to deny the gendered analysis, an irony usually missed by the asserter. Hence the argument is forwarded that there are 'as many men experiencing domestic abuse as women but men don't report it because it would be too shameful'. When asked why the men would find it 'shameful' the delegate responds that 'a man wouldn't feel like a "real" man if he gets beaten up by a woman'. It is vital here to acknowledge that men can and do experience violence in their intimate relationships, that domestic abuse occurs in same-sex relationships and that all those experiencing abuse should receive sensitive and appropriate support. However, research carried out by Dobash and Dobash (2004) suggests that it is less shame that holds men back from reporting violence and more that they are less likely to experience fear as a result of a partner's violence and therefore not feel the need to report the matter as they are not looking for 'help'. Furthermore, analysis of calls to the Men's Advice Line (a helpline for men affected by domestic abuse) suggests that male perpetrators of abuse against female partners may claim victim status for themselves identify as victims of abuse due to 'thwarted entitlement' – that is, not having their gendered expectations met by their partner (Respect 2010). Hester's recent research with Northumbria police (2009) also highlights that often where police are called to a domestic incident and a woman is identified as a primary perpetrator on one occasion she is very likely to have been the victim on several occasions and is using violence as self-protection or in retaliation to assault, what Johnson terms as 'violent resistance' (2008). In many senses, however, the lack of academic research to back up an assertion such as 'women are as bad as men but men don't report it' is less to the point than the continuing 'averted gaze to the gendered nature of violence' (Hearn and McKie 2010, p.138). Such an averted gaze makes a practitioner less likely to believe a woman is experiencing abuse, more likely to label a woman using 'violent resistance' as a perpetrator of abuse, unlikely to distinguish between a man perpetrating and experiencing abuse, and unable to respond sensitively or appropriately when a man experiencing abuse presents to our service. Making such discussion even more challenging is the absolute need for sensitivity to survivors in the room who can find denial of the issue frustrating or distressing.

A sensitive and private matter

Sensitivity to survivors in a training room is paramount at all times. Statistically in a training room of 12 people you are likely to be joined by at the very least two survivors and this increases incrementally with the number in the room. An assumption should not be made that survivors will necessarily find discussions troubling or re-traumatising, but ground rules must be established at the outset to promote safety. This safety applies to all delegates. Some may be new to the topic and find it shocking and possibly distressing. Others may be touched in a way that they had not expected; for example experienced practitioners who deal with such issues daily but whose professional 'armour' slips in the training environment.

The trainer must be aware not only of potential sensitivity to the nature of the issue but to the attitudes of other delegates that others, and survivors in particular, might find distressing. These may take the form of denying the seriousness of the issue, pathologising or stereotyping the 'victims' or 'perpetrators' or victim-blaming statements. It needs to be recognised that for some, holding onto the belief that violence against women 'happens over there' or 'happens to that sort of woman' is about safety. If it happens over there, it can't happen to me and I am safe. Victim-blaming can also be the result of feeling overwhelmed by the issue: 'I feel I should be able to help you but I can't think how, you're making me feel hopeless, I can't help you therefore it's your fault.' The role of training in this instance is to help build self-efficacy and this, in part, is achieved by working with the practitioner to re-frame the issue; a client is not someone to fix but someone to work with.

Conversely, occasionally it can also prove challenging to have a survivor on a training course. S/he may be unable to see beyond her/ his own experiences and relate everything back to her/himself. Others in the group may constantly defer to her/him or become frustrated that the discussion seems self-centred. Sensitive but firm facilitation is needed to validate the individual's experiences whilst, at the same time, ensuring that momentum is retained and learning objectives stuck to. A trainer may need to remind the group of safety ground rules established at the beginning of the course, remind the group of the learning outcomes, identify the topic as something that belongs in another training course or introduce other case studies into the discussion. Sometimes it is necessary to speak privately to the survivor and suggest the need for self-care.

To theorise or not to theorise?

Despite the emphasis in Scotland's national strategy on developing a robust and uniform theoretical understanding of the nature of violence against women, it has become a common-place amongst practitioners that a theoretical knowledge is less important than knowing 'what to do' or 'what to say' on receiving a disclosure. And it is not just front line staff that hold this view; recent research (Payne 2008) suggests that theoretical perspectives on domestic abuse were rated low on a staff need-to-know basis by their supervisors. Again, 'what to do' was valued more highly. As Payne says, many academics and educators 'regard theory as the backbone of their disciplines' (2008, p.1210) and cannot conceive of training on an issue without placing it within a robust theoretical framework. A challenge is therefore faced by trainers trying to bridge the gap between what practitioners and their supervisors say they want and what they as educators (and, in Scotland at least, strategy) highlight as appropriate.

Theory or practice is not a nil sum game. The primary reason for providing a theoretical perspective in training is to provide a framework for understanding the issue in hand, a framework that in turn enables safer practice. Put simply, if one does not understand the dynamics of an issue, one is unable to practise safely and indeed one might inadvertently make a situation less safe for a client. This is often described in the context of child protection as 'professional dangerousness'. Reder and Duncan (1999) define professional dangerousness as:

> the process by which individual workers or multi-disciplinary networks can, mostly unwittingly, act in such a way as to collude with, maintain or increase the dangerous dynamics of the family in which abuse takes place. (Cited in Calder 2008, p.65)

It is a concept I extend to domestic abuse interventions and it usefully highlights the idea that risks can be service-generated as well as created by an individual perpetrator or a 'victim's' vulnerabilities and that reflection on our own attitudes and how they shape our responses to issues is vital. So, for example, if one's construction of domestic abuse is of a series of violent incidents, one is likely to look for physical indicators of abuse (black eyes, moving with difficulty) in a client but not look out for emotional or behavioural indicators. An opportunity is then lost to speak with a client about the issue. I would term this as professional dangerousness through inaction. If one does not understand the dynamics of domestic abuse as rooted in power and control, the sole focus of one's engagement of the issue with a client may be to encourage her to leave a relationship without appropriate support in place. I would deem this to be professional dangerousness through inappropriate action. If, on the other hand, one understands the dynamics of domestic abuse one understands why leaving is a time of increased risk of physical violence, including death, for her and her children and one will work accordingly.

The value of training is often found in the time and space to reflect on individual practice within newly encountered theoretic frameworks and exchange experiences with other practitioners. A key part of the training I undertake is to invite delegates, in small groups, to consider how their own framing of domestic abuse could lead to professional dangerousness and what systems in their own agency create service-generated risks for clients. To enable this discussion to be safe, delegates are not asked to feed back their discussions but to frame the feedback by highlighting one thing the training has helped them acknowledge they do well in their work with those experiencing domestic abuse and one thing they've learned/may wish to change in their practice.

Of peripheral significance

If a desire for de-theorised, and thus many educators would argue de-contextualised, training is a challenge, it pales into insignificance compared with denial that training is needed at all. Research undertaken in Scotland by Hurley *et al.* (2007, p.2) found that 'according to the relevant professional bodies, skills and understanding in dealing with violence against women are not a necessary prerequisite to be recognised as a doctor, teacher or social worker. There was no indication from any professional body that they would wish to move to change this situation.' This may mean that those wishing to offer training in this area will face apathy or hostility. Practitioners may then feel justified in arguing that it is 'not my job' to deal with issues of violence against women and may not be receptive to receiving such training as a result. The challenge for trainers then is to establish the significance of the issue to individual practice. Prevalence statistics, such as those which highlight that the Scottish police recorded 59,847 domestic incidents in 2010–2011 (with 54% of these recorded as a crime), which equates to the police receiving a domestic abuse related call every 10 minutes (Scottish Government 2012), can help highlight just how many clients are likely to be living with violence/abuse. But this can only ever be part of the answer; it is possible to acknowledge the extent of the problem, even to acknowledge that a large number of female clients are living with the issues, and still hold on to the idea that 'it is not my job'. In this way the needs of clients are portioned out amongst different practitioners like the pieces of an orange with no one engaging with the complex whole. The challenge then is to establish the relationship between different forms of violence against women and what a practitioner has identified as his or her priority. For example, to establish that if a client is drinking as a way of self-medicating to cope with experiences of domestic abuse this experience (and the potential risks of detoxification) needs to be factored in to any harm reduction programme embarked upon; indeed that the programme is unlikely to be safe or successful without it being factored in. The role of training is therefore to help practitioners understand that they are not being asked to take on additional work, or do someone else's job, but that an understanding of both the dynamics of violence against women and its impacts on those experiencing it enables them to undertake their key role with clients more effectively and more safely.

Case studies can be an excellent way of addressing some of these issues. There are no right and wrong answers, and practitioners challenge each other or share good practice or advice around solutions they have successfully implemented. An occasional criticism of case studies can be that not enough information is given for the delegates to work with, making them 'not real'. I would argue that this is, in fact, a case study's strength, not its weakness; it is entirely 'real' for a practitioner to work without all the information about a client's life and information is offered up gradually or sporadically. This is possibly even more the case where a woman is living in fear due to abuse; how far she can trust a practitioner and the potential detriments to giving too much information away is paramount in her mind. A useful first question then when working through a case study in a training room is 'What information do you need in order to work safely and effectively with this client?' before considering options and interventions. An interesting approach to case studies is to let delegates create their own. Delegates are divided into small groups, with the bare bones of information such as makeup of the family, names, ages and situation and are then given five minutes to create a case study, drawing on their own professional experiences, for a different small group to work through. They are expected to respect the confidentiality of clients they're working with by creating a composite of many situations they have experienced. This approach creates a sense of authenticity and rootedness in practice for those attending the training.

If support to women experiencing different forms of violence is seen as marginal to mainstream social work, issues related to perpetrators are even more so. It is vital to the safety of women, children and young people that the perpetrator is made visible in all training and, at the very least, practitioners understand the importance of not colluding with a perpetrator. Questions in training are often framed in ways that make the perpetrator invisible; for example 'Why doesn't she leave?' which places emphasis on the woman to change rather than the perpetrator and ignores the perpetrator's ongoing actions to make leaving difficult or unsafe. By keeping the perpetrator visible in the training it is possible to explore the very fact that precisely because he is feeling powerless at her decision to leave, he becomes a greater risk to her. Hence powerlessness becomes not the antithesis of power but its dangerous bed-fellow. Power and powerlessness are engaged in a macabre pas-de-deux and they can be joined by the unsuspecting uninformed practitioner and/ or the inflexible, non-understanding system. Another common example of evidence of the perpetrator disappearing from practitioner view is when a woman experiencing domestic abuse is blamed for 'failing to protect her children' (from the violence perpetrated by her abusive, and hidden, partner). However, there are ways to challenge this invisibility. An example is a dvd, funded by the Scottish government, which has been created by CHANGE, Falkirk SACRO and Edinburgh's Domestic Violence Probation Project, three projects with long histories of working with perpetrators. The dvd consists of scenarios which allow the facilitator to explore the motivations of a perpetrator whilst at the same time considering the impact of abusive behaviour on a range of family members.

Theoretical concepts that work

Intrinsically bound up with the concept of 'professional dangerousness' (Reder and Duncan 1999) is the fact that one's world view shapes one's understanding of an issue which, in turn, shapes one's response to clients facing that issue. Thus professional thresholds are fundamentally connected to private attitudes. The private views delegates bring to the training about the relationships between men and women, including in intimate relationships, the role alcohol plays in 'causing' violence, all shape responses to client's experiences. The challenge then for a trainer can be how to re-structure deeply held belief systems to enable safer practice and offer alternative, theorised rather than intuitive, frames of reference. In this section I highlight how the work of one theorist, featured elsewhere in this book, has been translated into practice-based training.

Reframing domestic abuse as coercive control

In many ways one of the greatest challenges faced by domestic abuse trainers is the framing of the problem as episodic bouts of physical violence. While there is acknowledgement of the mental/emotional and sexual abuse experienced, it is the physical violence which is fore-grounded in practice. While in Scotland the government's definition attempts to rectify this with a definition of *domestic abuse* as an ongoing pattern of controlling behaviours (see footnote 1), definitions of *domestic violence* used elsewhere in the UK which focus on *incidents of violence* situated in the *domestic* setting, exacerbate the problem for trainers. Evan Stark's theorising of domestic abuse as *coercive control* has proved very illuminating for delegates, focusing as it does on domestic abuse experienced as ongoing rather than as episodic; as the white noise against which women experiencing abuse live their lives.

What this brings for delegates is an understanding that domestic abuse does not just happen at home, that it is not *domestic* but crosses social space. A perpetrator does it in work when he calls and texts to monitor his partner's movement; a woman experiences it in the supermarket when she doesn't buy a piece of meat because the voice in her head shouts 'I'm not eating this shit'; a child experiences it in the classroom when he doesn't raise his hand to answer a question he knows the answer to because in his head he hears, 'Don't be stupid, you're just as pathetic as your mother.' Significantly for practice, this brings an understanding that a client experiencing domestic abuse brings it to the meeting with the practitioner, that it shapes the interaction with the practitioner. In this way, domestic abuse is understood not as living with violence but living in fear. Experiential learning can be useful to highlight this. An instructive exercise can be to utilise a balloon to simulate on a micro-level the experience of living in fear. Delegates are invited to close their eyes and wait, and are informed that within five minutes the trainer will burst the balloon. (Obviously for safety no one is made to do this.) The trainer then walks around and amongst the delegates squeaking the balloon, changing the pace of the squeaking, allowing periods of silence and so on. After about a minute the delegates are asked to open their eyes (the balloon is never burst) and to share the feelings and thoughts they experienced. Amongst these are usually: racing hearts, sweaty hands, following the trainer around the room with their ears, the quiet bit as bad as, or worse than, when the squeaking was ongoing, wanting the balloon to burst to get it over with, and anger.

In the debrief which follows, the trainer states that all of these are similar to feelings that women living with domestic abuse can feel: physical responses, hyper-vigilance, and even when there is no violence/ confrontation she cannot relax as she wonders when it's all going to start again. Analogy can be also be drawn between the delegates' desire for the balloon to burst and the way that sometimes women say they 'provoke' their partner into hitting them as they can't cope with the tension any longer. Taken out of context that might seem like they like the violence or are as bad as the partner, but in the context of fear and lack of control it is more understandable.

Another strength of this framing of domestic abuse in the training room is that it enables delegates to envision domestic abuse less as a crime of violence and primarily as a *liberty crime* (Stark 2007, p.13). This in no way plays down the level or breadth of violence of those experiences but reshapes the purpose; in this framing, violence is a means not an end, it is a tool, not necessarily a goal. It is a tool that is used alongside others such as the micro-regulation of everyday life, the rules that must be obeyed, threats and degradation. If domestic abuse is framed as a crime of violence, the impact on the woman is a broken bone and the resulting desire from service intervention is to get her away from the violence. If domestic abuse is framed as a liberty crime the impact on the woman is that her agency is diminished, she experiences a lack of space for action. In order to make this practical and real to participants it can be helpful to ask delegates to make lists of the rules (using Stark's headings of mothering, socialising, dress-code, home-making and as a sexual partner) that clients must live by, followed by some of the consequences of not doing so. This can make visible the often invisible and 'mundane' constraints a client is operating within.

Such a framing does not place the woman as a passive victim but acknowledges her continuing agency; she is still trying to live her life and manage her situation, mother her children, but these attempts are being blocked by the perpetrator and his rules. I attempt to get this message across visually through a performance or dance whereby I act out my 'space for action' in which I can wear what I want, go where I want and so forth. I then shout out the rules, the demands, the threats, the curses, that occur when living with domestic abuse (using those drawn up by participants if this exercise has been undertaken) while simultaneously gradually constraining my movements until I am totally 'blocked', blocked but still trying to move. It is an emotive performance but one that feedback suggests actualises the idea of a 'lack of space for action'. It leads to a discussion about what the practitioner's role is in working with a woman to broaden her space for action, identifying the woman's strengths and working with these. This then allows discussion about safety planning with a client. It can be a weight lifted from a practitioner's shoulders; they no longer feel the need to fix the situation or the client but to work with her on safety and exploring options.

Survivors' voices heard

As has been reiterated throughout this chapter, in practice-based training theory cannot appear as something dry and dusty from the academy but must be rooted in lived experience and resonate with practitioners' experiences of working with clients. One way of ensuring that is to obtain and utilise the testimonies, words and pictures of survivors. Of course it is essential that in so doing there is a specific, practical purpose and that it is not voyeuristic or gratuitous. However, part of the authenticity of violence against women training is and always has been, and this is true of much feminist and pro-feminist theorising, its connectedness with survivors. It has been gleaned from and shaped around survivors' stories. It asks practitioners not to assume that they know best but to listen to, to truly hear, survivors' voices. This integration of survivors' voices leads to training that has at one and the same time intellectual and visceral appeal; it is both understood and felt. Increasingly, certainly with regard to domestic abuse, it is possible to integrate the voices of perpetrators as more research and theorising is taking place with them (research that is in no way an apologia but which seeks to understand in order to address what is raised).

Conclusion

Scotland's policy documents are not alone in placing training at the centre of strategy, with a fundamental role to support the implementation of practice change. Indeed, it is difficult to find such a document where training is not accordingly placed. For example, the Joseph Rowntree Foundation funded report (Humphreys *et al.* 2000, p.3) which mapped domestic violence services across the UK, stated training 'to raise awareness, explore values and develop skills is a further element in the development of effective intervention'. Major reviews following child deaths, and indeed in other contexts, also usually focus heavily on training of staff; for example Lord Laming's recommendations following the death of Baby Peter (2009).

This is both positive and problematic. It is positive that reports and strategies acknowledge that training can provide practitioners with understanding, knowledge, skills and improved self-efficacy. The problems tend to arise less in this principle and more in its practical implementation; as Horwarth suggests, all too often training is adopted by organisations 'as a panacea to cure all ills' (2001, p.33). It is often the most tangible recommendation, the most easy to implement; unfortunately this means often training takes the form of a box ticked, a job done, a milestone achieved by management rather than the integrated step in organisational change that was envisioned. It is carried out in isolation from organisational policies, procedures are not in place to support the implementation of learning, ineffective support and supervision exists to embed it in practice; all of which means that training is actually offered in a vacuum. It is possibly for this reason that research reports the mixed success of training in this area, often highlighting lasting increased awareness, (semi)temporary increased self-efficacy and difficulties in following through on skills learned (Minsky-Kelly *et al.* 2005).

Until this challenge is tackled head on with an integrated approach that joins up pre-qualification training with post-qualification continuing professional development, supported by employers and relevant professional bodies, training will never achieve its capacity-building potential. This position will remain to the frustration of many practitioners and to the (sometimes fatal) detriment of service users. It is a challenge trainers and educators have a role to effect change in, but cannot achieve alone; managers, policy-makers and strategists need to take on a robust leadership role and move training from the decorative periphery, where it is burdened with weight of expectation, to the heart of policy. This means not just policy as written but as practised and implemented.

Despite the commonplace belief that theory is not important for practitioners who just need to know how to 'do', the contrary is true: the challenge for trainers is to make relevant theory accessible and applicable. Translating research into practice-driven training, drawing on a range of active, reflective and experiential training techniques, is vital to ensure practitioners have a true understanding of the causes and consequences of violence against women. This understanding of the dynamics of the issue is a vital first step to ensuring safe and effective intervention and is the foundation stone for building skills, knowledge and confidence. Once that foundation has been laid, further training can provide the opportunity to consider and practise further skills development. Without it the client's situation may be misjudged, the need for safety overlooked, the client blamed for making the 'wrong' decisions or inappropriate advice offered. Thus theory provides not just the backbone to practice but a framework for safe working practice.

References

Calder, M. (2008) 'Professional Dangerousness: Causes and Contemporary Features.' In M. Calder (ed.) *Contemporary Risk Assessment in Safeguarding Children*. Dorset: Russell House Publishing.

Connell, R.W. (1987) *Gender and Power*. Stanford, CA: Stanford University Press.

Connell, R.W. (2002) *Gender*. Cambridge: Polity Press.

Dobash, R.P. and Dobash, R.E. (2004) 'Women's violence to men in intimate relationships: Working on a puzzle.' *British Journal of Criminology 44*, 3, 324–349.

EVAW (2008) See www.endviolenceagainstwomen.org.uk, accessed on 27 July 2012.

Hearn, J. and McKie, L. (2010) 'Gendered and social hierarchies in problem representation and policy processes: "Domestic violence" in Finland and Scotland.' *Violence Against Women 16*, 136.

Hester, M. (2009) *Who Does What to Whom?: Gender and Domestic Violence Perpetrators*. Bristol: University of Bristol in association with the Northern Rock Foundation.

Horwarth, J. (2001) 'Child care practice innovations: Using a model of change to develop training strategies.' *Child Abuse Review 10*, 1, 18–30.

Humphreys, C., Hester, M., Hague, G., Mullender, A., Abrahams, H. and Lowe, P. (2000) *Working with Families Where There is Domestic Violence*. Report No. 830. York: Joseph Rowntree Foundation.

Hurley, N., Kennedy, K., Wilson, L. and Henderson, S. (2007) *Mapping of Education and Training Addressing Violence Against Women*. Research Findings No. 35. Edinburgh: Scottish Executive.

Johnson, M.P. (2008) *A Typology of Domestic Violence: Intimate Terrorism, Violent Resistance, and Situational Couple Violence*. Boston: Northeastern University Press.

Kelly, L. (1988) *Surviving Sexual Violence*. Cambridge: Polity Press.

Kimmel, M. (2002) 'Gender symmetry in domestic violence: A substantive and methodological research review.' *Violence Against Women 8*, 11, 1332–1362.

Lang. J. (2002) *'Men, Masculinities and Violence'*. Available at www.vawpreventionscotland.org.uk/resources/presentations/men-masculinities-and-violence-james-lang, accessed on 15 October 2012.

Lord Laming (2009) *The Protection of Children in England: A Progress Report*. London: House of Commons.

Minsky-Kelly, D., Hamberger, L.K., Pape, D.A. and Wolff, M. (2005) 'We've had training, now what? Qualitative barriers to domestic violence screening and referral in a health care setting.' *Journal of Interpersonal Violence 20*, 1288.

Payne, B.K. (2008) 'Training adult protective services workers about domestic violence: Training needs and strategies.' *Violence Against Women 14*, 1199.

Ptacek, J. (1999) *Battered Women in the Courtroom: The Power of Judicial Responses*. Boston: Northeastern University Press.

Reder, P. and Duncan, S. (1999) *Lost Innocents: A Follow-up Study of Fatal Child Abuse*. London and New York: Routledge.

Respect (2010) *Respect Practice Guidance: Values, Purposes and Methods of Identifying Who is Doing What to Whom in Intimate Partner Violence (IPV)*. Available at www.respect.uk.net/data/files/resources/16/27th_may_2010_final_respect_practice_guidance_on_value_and_purpose_of_identifying_who_is_doing_what_to_whom_in_ipv.pdf, accessed on 27 July 2012.

Scottish Executive (2000) *The National Strategy to Address Domestic Abuse.* Edinburgh: Scottish Executive.

Scottish Executive (2004) *Domestic Abuse: A National Training Strategy.* Edinburgh: Scottish Executive.

Scottish Government (2012) *Domestic Abuse Recorded by Police in Scotland.* Available at www.scotland.gov.uk/Publications/2012/10/domestic-abuse30102012, accessed on 27 July 2012.

Stark, E. (2007) *Coercive Control: How Men Entrap Women in Personal Life.* Oxford: Oxford University Press.

CHAPTER 12

Partnership Working and Tackling Violence Against Women
Pitfalls and Possibilities

Kirstein Rummery

Introduction

There is a growing realisation that violence against women is a complex issue that cannot be tackled by one profession or organisation working in isolation. Partnership working and collaboration in tackling violence against women is therefore an increasingly important part of the daily work of social workers and other practitioners. However, if you take a look at the different agencies and professionals involved in tackling violence against women, it is clear that a fairly complex picture emerges of people working in different organisations, all with their own different values, aims and ways of working. Working in partnership to tackle violence against women can therefore be a challenge.

This chapter will give an overview of some of the theoretical and policy context that shapes partnership working and collaboration in general. What does it mean to work in partnership? When is it useful to work in partnership? It will then look at the way the different professionals involved in tackling violence against women work, and how these ways of working influence how they might work in partnership or collaboration with each other. Drawing on examples of different projects across the world, it will look at some of the possibilities opened up and some of the dangers to be avoided. It will finish up with some key issues that practitioners need to consider when considering which partners to work with, and how to go about it.

The theory and policy of partnership working

In a previous research volume in this series, *Collaboration in Social Work Practice,* Whittington (2003) helpfully sets out the background to what he called a 'powerful policy case for collaboration and partnership' in welfare (Whittington 2003, p.18). These include: a history of inquiries where systematic failures of inter-agency co-ordination and inter-professional communication were implicated in the death or harm of children and vulnerable adults (see e.g. the Laming report following the deaths of Victoria Climbié in 2000 and Peter Connelly in 2007); the need to overcome fragmentation caused by constant service reorganisation; the drive for efficient and effective services in the face of resource constraints; the commitment to user involvement; and a recognition by practitioners themselves of the need to involve other agencies and individuals in tackling complex social problems and effectively support individuals. My own research echoes Whittington's assertions: in a recent review of partnership programmes across health and social care, I found that:

> Partnership working, both between public and other sectors, and between different areas of the public sector, is held up as being a way of achieving improved services for users where there is a commonality of interest between the partners, and a history of failing to co-ordinate services effectively by other means. (Rummery 2009, p.1797)

The Audit Commission (1998, p.8) describes partnership as a joint working arrangement whereby the partners:

- are otherwise independent bodies
- agree to co-operate to achieve a common goal
- create a new organisational structure or process to achieve this goal

- plan and implement a joint programme, and

- share relevant information, risks and rewards.

This framework implies that the partners involved have a degree of autonomy to be able to co-operate and implement a programme. It also implies that there is a common goal to be achieved. Because the policy case for collaboration and partnerships seems to be powerful and persuasive across different contexts, partnership working has moved from the margins to the mainstream of social policy. Statutory organisations now often have to demonstrate that they are working in partnership (with other statutory organisations, with the voluntary and/or private sector, and with users/carers) in order to meet their own performance targets. For example, in Scotland the National Strategy to Address Domestic Abuse (2000) has clear guidelines which tie together policies and practices concerning tackling violence against women with those concerning children's safety from harm and abuse (see *Getting It Right for Every Child*, Scottish Executive 2005), and there are numerous examples of collaborative projects in the field of violence against women, some of which are discussed in this chapter.

Because partnership working is so central to policy, there is no shortage of guidance on 'how to' work in partnership and collaborate across agencies. For example, Hardy and colleagues have drawn up a 'Partnership Assessment Tool' that enables organisations to map whether their partnership working will be successful or not. It is based on six principles: the acknowledgement of the need for partnership; clarity and realism of purpose; commitment and ownership; development and maintenance of trust; establishment of clear and robust partnership arrangements; and monitoring, review and organisational learning (Hardy, Hudson and Waddington 2000). I have discussed elsewhere (Rummery 2002) that what distinguishes partnerships from other ways of joint working are interdependence (that the partners involved need each other to achieve their own aims) and trust (that the partners involved trust each other to deliver on jointly held objectives).

However, if we look at tackling violence against women, we can see that several issues emerge as being problematic when we think about partnership working. Who are the real and potential 'partners' involved in tackling violence against women? Do they acknowledge that they need to work in partnership with each other? Are they clear about what they want to achieve, and committed to achieving it together? Are they interdependent, and do they trust one another? The next section of this chapter will explore some of these questions in more detail.

Partnership working and tackling violence against women
Who are the partners? Do they share goals? Do they need to work in partnership?

Understanding *who* might be involved in tackling violence against women relies in part on an understanding of the complex social issues involved. There has been a significant shift in emphasis since groundbreaking studies revealed the extent of violence against women in the UK (e.g. Dobash and Dobash 1992; Pahl 1987). This has involved a growing acceptance of the problem as a *public* rather than a *private* issue, necessitating a social policy response. The nature of that response has also changed over time, involving different professionals and agencies from different sectors. For example, Walby (2004) used Home Office methods for costing crime to show that violence against women costs the UK state (in the form of services in the criminal justice system, health, social services, housing and civil legal services) in the region of £3.1 billion a year, whilst the estimated cost to the economy (in terms of lost output due to injuries) is £2.3 billion. She breaks the costs down as follows:

- *Criminal Justice System*: The cost of domestic violence to the criminal justice system (CJS) is around £1 billion a year. This is nearly one-quarter of the CJS budget for violent crime. The largest single component is that of the police. Other components include prosecution, courts, probation, prison, and legal aid.

- *Health Care*: The cost to the NHS for physical injuries is around £1.2 billion a year. This includes GPs and hospitals. Physical injuries account for most of the NHS costs, but there is an important element of mental health care, estimated at an additional £176 million.

- *Social Services*: The annual cost is nearly £0.25 billion. This is overwhelmingly for children rather than for adults, especially those caught up in the co-occurrence of domestic violence and child abuse.

- *Housing*: Expenditure on emergency housing includes costs to Local Housing Authorities and Housing Associations for housing those homeless because of domestic violence, housing benefit for such emergency housing, and, importantly, refuges. This amounts to £0.16 billion a year.

- *Civil Legal*: Civil legal services cost over £0.3 billion, about half of which is borne by legal aid and half by the individual. This includes both specialist legal actions such as injunctions to restrain or expel a violent partner, as well as actions consequent on the disentangling of marriages and relationships such as divorce and child custody.

- *Economic Output*: Lost economic output accounts for around £2.7 billion a year. This is the cost of time off work due to injuries. It is estimated that around half of the costs of such sickness absences is borne by the employer and half by the individual in lost wages.

(Walby 2004, p.1)

Moreover, Walby also estimates that the costs of violence against women borne by the victims amount to around £17 billion per year. There are therefore real economic imperatives that explain why different sectors and organisations would have a stake in tackling violence against women: it is often these imperatives, rather than 'justice' arguments, that drive policy-makers and practitioners to take action (Stanko 2007).

Research has shown that it is often women's relative economic insecurity and their financial reliance on abusive partners which traps women into violent relationships (Brush 2004). It is estimated that up to 65 per cent of women welfare recipients are experiencing, or have experienced, abuse (Tolman and Raphael 2000). If we accept that tackling women's poverty and women's risk of violence go together, this means that welfare advice/advocacy organisations are potential 'partners' to be considered (Postmus and Hahn 2007). Recent research has also highlighted the links between violence against mothers and child abuse and neglect: for example, it is estimated that at least 30–60 per cent of families experiencing violence against women or children will also experience another form of violence (Edleson 1999), and violence against mothers is present in at least one-third of the families involved in child protective services (Findlater and Kelly 1999). An understanding that violence against women is a complex social issue needing collaborative 'joined-up' approaches between various agencies has led to calls for a 'community-coordinated' approach bringing together key stakeholders (Findlater and Kelly 1999; Fleck-Henderson 2000; Pennington-Zoellner 2009; Saathoff and Stoffel 1999) particularly with regard to protecting women *and* children from violence.

The sector with the longest history of involvement in tackling violence against women is that of women's organisations in the voluntary sector, whose motivation has often been characterised as being drawn from a feminist commitment to recognising violence as a 'sociocultural phenomenon, reflecting women's powerlessness in society, rather than simply as a feature of private interpersonal relationships' (Saathoff and Stoffel 1999, p.98). They often encompass a philosophical and practical commitment to support and empower victims, and have grown out of a voluntary response to the perceived failure of the state to adequately prevent and tackle violence against women (Schow 2006).

The Scottish government provides a useful example of partnership working in the area of tackling violence against women. Following the publication of the National Strategy to Address Domestic Abuse, the (then) Scottish Executive worked in close collaboration with the violence against women sector to draw up a policy framework which was rooted in a multi-agency partnership context. The resulting strategy, Safer Lives (Scottish Government 2009), gave a specific role to multi-agency partnerships to prioritise and tackle violence against women, holding them accountable through policy instruments such as the Gender Equality Duty, and committing specific funding totalling over £44 million (Scott 2006). Moreover, Pennington-Zoellner (2009) has argued persuasively that such initiatives should go wider and include employers, as a way of tackling the economic cost of violence against women.

TABLE 12.1 MAPPING OF SOME OF THE DIFFERENT POTENTIAL PARTNERS INVOLVED IN TACKLING VIOLENCE AGAINST WOMEN

	Sector	Goals	Values	Power	Organisation
VAW[1]	Voluntary	Protection and empowerment of women	Woman-centred	No coercion –voluntary compliance and participation	Democratic
Criminal Justice	Public	Prosecution of offenders	Punitive	Coercion	Hierarchical, formal
Health	Public	Treatment of victims Treatment/rehabilitation of offenders	Universal access	Low coercion – usually voluntary compliance	Hierarchical, formal
Social Services	Public	Protection of children Prevention of abuse Tackling social problems Addressing individual behaviour Family support	Child protection User empowerment	Some coercive powers	Formal
Housing	Public and private	Provision of shelter	Responding to user need	No coercion	Formal Profit
Civil Legal	Public	Dispute resolution	Legal protection	Coercion	Formal, hierarchical
Employers	Private	Maximise profits Employer protection	Profit protection	Low coercion, but economic sanctions	Various

1 Referred to in the literature variously as domestic violence, violence against women, domestic abuse, intimate partner violence, family violence.

Clarity of goals

Although a fairly simplistic summary, Table 12.1 reveals that on the face of it there is very little substantial overlap in the core goals of each of the potential partners. Indeed, some partners may have divergent, or even conflicting, goals. For example, the criminal justice system is primarily concerned with the prosecution of offenders. Whilst at first sight this is not contradictory to the goal of protecting victims, it becomes complex when the victims of violence include children. Within many legal systems, for example, there is an established precedent that mothers who fail to protect their children from abuse can be held culpable for that abuse. Contact with the criminal justice system (e.g. police and courts) may therefore place a woman who is the victim of violence in the position of being a potential offender. For similar reasons, if a mother is the victim of violence and is simultaneously seen as 'failing to protect' her children from violence, child protection and VAW services may have completely opposite goals. On a related note, if social services are working to support and preserve the family that may well place a victim, or potential victim, of violence in danger.

The differing professional and organisational values which drive each partner may also mitigate against working in partnership and lead to a lack of clarity about goals. For example, contact with sections of the public sector that have coercive powers (such as criminal justice and social services) can be seen to be replicating the kind of coercion a victim of violence may experience from a perpetrator (Lessard *et al.* 2006). Although coercion can be used for ostensibly positive and protective purposes (e.g. the mandatory arrest of perpetrators of violence), it may not be the choice of the victim, or lead to positive outcomes. Moreover, even where organisations do not use coercive powers, the fact that they might places them in a relatively powerful position over non-coercive organisations AND over victims of violence. Fleck-Henderson (2000) argues that the goal and value of 'family preservation' may be in conflict with the goal of victim safety (whether victims are women or children), but both are explicit goals of child protection services. This highlights the fact that the *internal* aims of different organisations may themselves be contradictory – similar arguments can be made with regard to *prevention of crime* and *punishment of perpetrators* within different branches of the criminal justice system. This can affect how clear and meaningful values and goals can be when working with outside partners.

If the goals are not clear, it will be confusing to establish just how interdependent the different actors are. For example, if the goal is 'preservation of the family', who is the 'family'? Fleck-Henderson points out that:

> Child protection agencies are mandated to assure that children are safe and that the family is, if possible, preserved. Women's advocates have argued that in situations of domestic violence it is the unit of children and non-abusive parent that should be preserved, while the non-abusive parent is helped to protect herself and her children. (Fleck-Henderson 2000, p.337)

Fleck-Henderson (2000) has posited that in order for child protection agencies and women's advocacy organisations to work effectively in partnership, both agencies would have to accept that safety for women AND children is the goal, and that assailants, not the abused, are accountable for their abuse. This may seem on the face of it unproblematic, but it would in fact involve a shift in goals, values and priorities for both agencies. This may involve a shift of emphasis and resources away from primary or core goals and values. Investing in partnership work makes sense if the parties can, by working in partnership, achieve what Huxham (2000) calls the 'collaborative advantage'. That advantage may be lost if the partners have to forgo their core aims and values to achieve the partnership.

Interdependence and trust in tackling violence against women

Whilst clearly there needs to be some degree of interdependence between partners to make working in partnership a necessity, the degree of interdependence can vary significantly according to the sector of the partners (Rummery 2002). If the public sector is mandated to work 'in partnership' it will become one of the targets upon which its performance is measured. So, for example, within Scotland, the Safer Lives policy places both the criminal justice system and the child protection system under a duty to work 'in partnership' within multi-agency partnerships, and thus partnership working, in itself, becomes an objective. Agencies can clearly demonstrate that they rely on each other to meet their core objectives if these core objectives include working in partnership with the other agency. However, this is not so clearly the case when government cannot 'set' the objectives of agencies in this way, as is the case with the private and voluntary sector.

Whilst the private sector may rely on some elements of the public sector to meet its core objectives (e.g. it may rely on funding and government contracts to carry out its business), it will not often be the case that simply working in partnership will be one of its 'core' goals. It would only work in partnership if by doing so it achieved its own objectives (e.g. made a profit). Pennington-Zoellner (2009) argues that formal 'community coordination' collaborations to address violence against women should work with a wider concept of 'community' than simply different parts of the public and voluntary sector:

> Not only does community need to expand to include the other formal service organizations that are not currently involved in the response to [violence against women], it also needs to include informal networks like family, friends, and coworkers... Employers can play a pivotal role in the community coordinated response to [violence against women] because they have the resources to address [violence against women] in ways that seem to have eluded traditional models of community coordination. (Pennington-Zoellner 2009, pp.542–543)

She argues that many women experiencing violence see employment as part of a strategic plan to escape, and thus employers form an important part of survivors' networks. Moreover, as violent partners often target women at their place of employment, in the interests of employee safety as well as lost economic output, employers have an interest in tackling violence against women. However, this interest does not translate necessarily into an interdependence on the other agencies involved, particularly if those agencies do not share the goals of employee safety and avoiding lost profits. Moreover, workers in the public and voluntary sector may not see collaboration with employers in the private sector as one of their core objectives. Differing values and ways of working can act as a significant barrier to partnership working (Rummery 2006) and if there is not a shared interdependence to give the partners a significantly strong reason to overcome these barriers, partnerships involving the private sector in tackling violence against women are unlikely to succeed.

Trust can be said to be the one of the defining characteristics of partnership working (Rowe and Devanney 2003; Rummery 2002). It has many dimensions, including a shared history, and its absence is an indication that partnerships will not prove sustainable or achieve their goals. The different agencies and professions involved in tackling violence against women may well have a shared history and experiential basis for trust, but the discussion of the three different case studies outlined in the next section indicates that this is by no means always the case. There may well be very good reasons *not* to trust other agencies and professions, particularly when you are aware that their values and goals may be very different from yours. As was discussed above, agencies and professionals who have coercive powers may well be able to use those powers against the interests of vulnerable women (Lessard *et al.* 2006). For example, social services in the USA have regularly used legislation to prosecute women who were themselves the victims of violence for 'failing to protect' their children from violence and abuse. The history of using such powers mitigates against trust.

The following section will look at examples of three projects which were designed to develop partnerships in tackling violence against women to examine how some of these dilemmas and contractions manifest themselves in practice.

Examining the possibilities and pitfalls of partnership working
Case study 1: Building co-ordinated services in a rural community

My own review of the outcomes of partnership working across several sectors indicated that joint working can be particularly effective at enabling the delivery of services which have been poorly served by traditional services (Rummery 2009). This is particularly the case with rural services, where the physical and geographical challenges associated with designing and delivering services can be significant. With regard to tackling violence against women, there is an additional challenge associated with providing services where expertise may be thinly spread across generalist service providers. In addition, issues around confidentiality and safety can be challenging in remote, tightly knit communities, leaving violent relationships can be problematic in very geographically isolated areas, and gaining access to finances can be difficult for victims of violence in rural and farm-based economies where assets are tied up in property and livestock.

In this context, Wendt (2010) carried out a qualitative, interpretive study involving face-to-face semi-structured interviews with 20 human services workers and two women who had experienced domestic and family violence. The aim of the project was to examine the barriers to co-ordination and to visualise a local response to enabling partnership work. The fieldwork was carried out in an area called Murray Bridge, 80 km east of Adelaide, with a population of 16,500, including 695 Indigenous people. The research was commissioned by a service provider who had won funding under a competitive tendering process, which had in itself produced feelings of frustration and negativity in the community. Wendt explains:

> Early meetings held in Murray Bridge indicated that human service workers had different and competing understandings of domestic and family violence and this was a potential factor hindering a co-ordinated response. For example, anecdotal evidence showed that workers had debated over time the extent to which domestic and family violence should be understood as a gendered issue in their community. Another issue that emerged during early meetings was a perceived lack of understanding about what each agency was responsible for in the community and, consequently, this was creating frustration, suspicion and misrepresented innuendos about each other. (Wendt 2010, p.49)

Barriers to co-ordination included a lack of awareness of agency roles, loss of specialised knowledge in broad generalised services, and the differing theoretical positions held by different workers on how they understood domestic and family violence. Wendt found that:

> Holding your own personal, strong ideologies about how to work in the field of violence was named as a barrier to co-ordination and as impacting on service delivery... The differences were identified as mainly being those who held feminist positions and those who did not, or, alternatively, those who argued domestic violence as being gendered and those who did not. However, the interviews found that the majority of workers...supported feminist and gendered perspectives but, despite this, the perception that workers being closed to a range of understandings became so dominant that it created suspicion amongst workers. (Wendt 2010, pp.54–55)

One example where real ideological divisions were apparent was in tensions between Aboriginal and non-Aboriginal workers' perceptions of family violence, with Aboriginal workers placing great importance on holistic and contextual understandings, as exemplified by this example:

> if you had a domestic dispute with your partner, it won't just be with the partner, but with the whole family or the extended family get involved and so it is hard to pull yourself out of that. (Aboriginal worker quoted in Wendt 2010, p.55)

Entrenched ideological positions can mitigate again the development of trust, which is such a vital component of partnership working. However, the workers in Wendt's study did think it was possible to overcome mistrust and develop a collective response to tackling violence against women, not least because of the perception of gaps in services and highlighting what resources were needed. Collaborative responses were also viewed as being a way to engage with the community and to establish mainstream provision, and a way of overcoming past prejudice and mistrust. Wendt quotes the following Aboriginal worker: 'We need white and black men and women working in partnerships and managers of programmes and agencies saying I am happy to be involved in that' (Wendt 2010, p.59).

Case study 2: Child protection and VAW services

There has been a body of research which has highlighted how violence against women is an important issue for child protection services, and vice versa. As was highlighted above, reviews of both formal case reports and self-reports in child abuse cases indicate that in 30–40 per cent of cases domestic violence is an issue, and that in up to 60 per cent of cases men who commit violence against female partners also abuse their children (Edleson 1999). Moreover, even where there is no evidence of direct violence to themselves, there is clear evidence that witnessing violence against their mothers is detrimental to children (Malik, Ward and Janczewski 2008). However, as Findlater and Kelly found:

> A significant obstacle to collaboration has been the tension caused by the different historical developments and missions of the domestic violence and child welfare movements…the domestic violence movement began less than 30 years ago in order to provide safety to battered

> women because public institutions were not doing so...
> when domestic violence was identified, [child protection]
> workers have often misunderstood its dynamics and held
> battered mothers responsible for ending it. (Findlater and
> Kelly 1999, p.87)

As acknowledgement of both the need to engage in partnership working, and the barriers preventing this, the American National Council of Juvenile and Family Court Judges published a list of recommendations in 1999 which came to be known as the *Greenbook*. This led to six pilot projects across the USA being given funding to 'help the [child welfare] system, [domestic violence] service providers, and the dependency courts collaborate, exact system change, and develop policies to keep families safe' (Malik *et al.* 2008, p.935). The programme evaluators used a participatory action research design to examine how domestic violence agencies were involved in the leadership of projects, and how they collaborated with other agencies to remove the barriers to joint working and achieving *family* safety.

The evaluators found that the participants from the domestic violence sector were involved in the leadership of the *Greenbook* initiative pilot programmes. However, just how much weight their voices carried was an issue for concern. Malik and her colleagues found that:

> Many [domestic violence] stakeholders reported feeling
> that because of limited resources, philosophical differences
> regarding consensus versus hierarchy, and systematic
> differences related to being the one system outside the
> authority of the state, their voice was less powerful than
> the voices of others, particularly with regard to the courts.
> (Malik *et al.* 2008, p.948)

This imbalance of power has been found across other partnership initiatives involving state and non-state partners (Rummery 2002), and demonstrates clearly that there can be significant barriers to partnership working where one side has less power to define the objectives and ways of working than the other. However, a history of difficult relationships does not necessarily sound the death knell for partnership working. As one participant in Malik's study pointed out:

> the [domestic violence] community is highly vocal, and
> we're not afraid to step on toes. So if people didn't know
> that before, they certainly know it more now. But I think

we see that as our responsibility [in] our role as advocates. (Domestic violence agency manager quoted in Malik *et al.* 2008, p.949)

Moreover, numerous studies have shown that the experience of working together can in itself help overcome historical and philosophical obstacles, as the partners involved develop trust and an awareness of their interdependence. This was clearly shown in some of the *Greenbook* initiative projects, who recognised a need for cross-training and the use of screening instruments for domestic violence in child protection agencies and the courts. These initiatives themselves led to increased co-ordination around risk assessment and better information sharing.

However, the impact of the *Greenbook* initiative projects on the actual practice within domestic violence services was minimal, with most sites reporting little practice innovation to make their policies, procedures and premises more amenable to child welfare issues. Malik and colleagues reported that:

> [Domestic violences services] participants were neutral in their assessments of the ways in which they developed policies and informed mothers of policies related to [child maltreatment], as well as in terms of assisting mothers with reporting [child maltreatment] to the [child welfare] system…[domestic violence] stakeholders and frontline workers were also relatively neutral in their assessment of how well they provided services to children and maltreating mothers and how well they engaged in referrals for services or separate safety planning for mothers and children. (Malik *et al.* 2008, p.950)

One area that Malik's study did not explore was how far the priorities, values and goals of the domestic violence partners influenced the development of services and policies in the more powerful state sector. However, other studies of partnership working do not give us much reason to be optimistic about the extent to which less-powerful partners can change or influence the behaviour of more-powerful partners. There is little evidence to suggest that working in partnership will enable the voices of the victims of violence against women, or their advocates, to be heard and acted upon in the face of other, more powerful voices.

Case study 3: Welfare and advocacy

One of the key issues in tackling violence against women is attempting to understand and address the link between women's socio-economic status and their risk, and experience, of violence. This is particularly complex in the case of women experiencing violence from their partners. Although not universal, there is an established link between women's financial dependence on violent partners, their risk of poverty, and their ability to leave abusive relationships (Brush 2004). It is estimated that up to 65 per cent of welfare recipients have experienced domestic violence (Tolman and Raphael 2000). In recognition of this, the Family Violence Option (FVO) of the Personal Responsibility and Work Reconciliation Act of 1996 gave states in the USA the flexibility to offer more time for women experiencing domestic violence to seek safety before welfare penalties were imposed. Kansas created the Orientation, Assessment, Referral and Safety programme (OARS), which gave contracts to advocacy organisations to provide on-site services for women who qualified for the FVO. Postmus and Hahn (2007) undertook a study looking at the inter-agency collaboration on OARS by carrying out focus groups with women who had self-identified as being victims of domestic violence and had received an eligible welfare benefit within the last six months.

The women reported mixed experiences. On the one hand, they highlighted the importance of receiving benefits: 'If it wasn't for [welfare benefit] I wouldn't be pulling myself out just right now. I wouldn't be sitting here asking myself just how did I get away from the past' (quoted in Postmus and Hahn 2007, p.478).

However, a lack of awareness of issues concerning domestic violence was highlighted as a problem for benefits recipients:

> ...the bad part, they don't want to hear about it. They want to hear about everything is hunky dory, we just need money right now, blah, blah blah. They don't want to hear that I got beat up last night and I ain't ate in four days. They don't want to hear that. (Quoted in Postmus and Hahn 2007, p.479)

Postmus and Hahn found that the inter-agency collaboration which led to key workers being appointed as advocates showed real benefits for the women concerned:

> 'Since I have been with OARS, it has made me feel a little bit safer...'

'Helping us not rely on the abuser. For money...'

'When you are with [the advocate] they don't mess with you. I had some problems at first and my social worker was after me, "You need to do this" and my [advocate] said I don't. She was like "oh, okay." And that was it: okay. They hear that name, and that's all it takes.'

(Quoted in Postmus and Hahn 2007, pp.480–481)

However, there were problems with the OARS programme, including an unwillingness on the part of benefits workers to accept input from OARS workers, and a reluctance on the part of women to share information about sexual or physical abuse. In some cases, having another agency involved served to complicate matters and led to concerns about confidentiality, rather than providing additional relief and support.

Conclusions and practice guidelines for working in partnership

A case for collaboration, not partnership?

The evidence suggests that partnerships can be sustainable, and there can be clear benefits for both partners, if there is an element of *trust* and *interdependence* between those involved (Rummery 2002). The partners need to acknowledge the need for partnership, have clear goals, and be committed to the partnership (Hardy *et al.* 2000). Practitioners who are working to tackle violence against women therefore need to consider carefully whether those key elements are in place before they start working in partnership with other professionals and agencies. Fleck-Henderson (2000) argues persuasively that in the case of violence against women and child protection agencies, a more realistic goal for practitioners may be working in *collaboration* rather than *partnership*. Individual agencies and professionals have different ideological perspectives and different goals, and this is sometimes to be welcomed. She asserts that:

> Whatever the form, consultation and collaboration should contribute to a double perspective that allows the assumptions and knowledge of the Battered Women's Movement and the assumptions and knowledge of the Child Protection Movement to inform each other. (Fleck-Henderson 2000, p.351)

My own research into health and social care partnerships indicates that 'successful' partnerships do involve changing the values and goals of the other organisation (Rummery 2009). It may be that practitioners working to tackle violence against women may want to revise their goals (e.g. to tackling violence against families, or tackling violence against women AND children, or to tackling violence AND poverty) in order to collaborate successfully with partners. It may also be that they wish to retain their focus, ideological commitments and values but wish their partners to share those goals and values. The implications, benefits and pitfalls of both strategies would need to be carefully considered before working in collaboration or partnership with another agency.

There are, therefore, several things to be considered before embarking on working in partnership with another organisation, or individual. What are your core goals, values and commitments? What goals, values and commitments are you willing to adapt, or compromise? You then need to consider what the core goals, values and commitments of the agency or individual you are hoping to work with are, and are they willing to adapt, or compromise? Do you both need to work together to meet your own core goals?

If you do need to work together, then you need to think whether you can trust each other – and if not, can you work to develop that trust? What would the benefits be to working together – and do you agree on what those benefits are? What would the dangers be of working together, and are there any ways you can reduce those dangers?

Perhaps most important, you need to ask yourself what do women who have experienced violence themselves think about the above questions? What are their values, goals and commitments? Am I serving them best by working in partnership, or is there a better way to achieve this?

References

Audit Commission (1998) *A Fruitful Partnership: Effective Partnership Working.* London: Audit Commission.

Brush, L.D. (2004) 'Battering and the poverty trap.' *Journal of Poverty 8*, 3, 23–43.

Dobash, R. and Dobash, R. (1992) *Women, Violence and Social Change.* London: Routledge.

Edleson, J.L. (1999) 'Responsible mothers and invisible men: Child protection in the case of adult domestic violence.' *Journal of Interpersonal Violence 13*, 2, 294–298.

Findlater, J.E. and Kelly, S. (1999) 'Child protective services and domestic violence.' *Domestic Violence and Children 9*, 3, 84–96.

Fleck-Henderson, A. (2000) 'Domestic violence in the child protection system: Seeing double.' *Children and Youth Services Review 22*, 5, 333–352.

Hardy, B., Hudson, B. and Waddington, E. (2000) *What Makes a Good Partnership? A Partnership Assessment Tool.* Leeds: Nuffield Institute for Health.

Huxham, C. (2000) 'The challenge of collaborative governance.' *Public Management 2*, 3, 337–357.

Lessard, G., Lavergne, C., Chamberland, C., Dmanat, D. and Turcotte, D. (2006) 'Conditions for resolving controversies between social actors in domestic violence and youth protection services: Toward innovative collaborative practices.' *Children and Youth Services Review 28*, 5, 511–534.

Malik, N.M., Ward, K. and Janczewski, C. (2008) 'Coordinated community response to family violence: The role of domestic violence service organizations.' *Journal of Interpersonal Violence 23*, 7, 933–955.

Pahl, J. (ed.) (1987) *Private Violence and Public Policy: The Needs of Battered Women and the Response of the Public Services.* London: Routledge and Kegan Paul.

Pennington-Zoellner, K. (2009) 'Expanding "community" in the community response to intimate partner violence.' *Journal of Family Violence 24*, 8, 539–545.

Postmus, J.L. and Hahn, S.A. (2007) 'The collaboration between welfare and advocacy organisations: Learning from the experiences of domestic violence survivors.' *Families in Society: The Journal of Contemporary Social Services 88*, 3, 475–484.

Rowe, M. and Devanney, C. (2003) 'Partnership and the governance of regeneration.' *Critical Social Policy 23*, 3, 375–397.

Rummery, K. (2002) 'Towards a Theory of Welfare Partnerships.' In C. Glendinning, M. Powell and K. Rummery (eds) *Partnerships, New Labour and the Governance of Welfare.* Bristol: Policy Press.

Rummery, K. (2006) 'Partnerships and collaborative governance in welfare: The citizenship challenge.' *Social Policy and Society 5*, 2, 293–303.

Rummery, K. (2009) 'Healthy partnerships, healthy citizens? An international review of health partnerships and user outcomes.' *Social Science and Medicine 69*, 12, 1797–1804.

Saathoff, A.J. and Stoffel, E.A. (1999) 'Community-based domestic violence services.' *Domestic Violence and Children 9*, 3, 97–110.

Schow, D. (2006) 'The culture of domestic violence advocacy: Values of equality/behaviours of control.' *Women and Health 43*, 4, 49–68.

Scott, M. (2006) *Partnership, Power and Policy: A Case Study of the Scottish Partnership on Domestic Abuse.* Unpublished PhD thesis, University of Edinburgh.

Scottish Executive (2000) *The National Strategy to Address Domestic Abuse in Scotland.* Edinburgh: Scottish Executive.

Scottish Executive (2005) *Getting it Right for Every Child. Proposals for Action.* Edinburgh: Scottish Executive.

Scottish Government (2009) *Safer Lives: Changed Lives.* Edinburgh: Scottish Government.

Stanko, B. (2007) 'From academia to policy making: Changing police responses to violence against women.' *Theoretical Criminology 11*, 2, 209–219.

Tolman, R.M. and Raphael, J. (2000) 'A review of research on welfare and domestic violence.' *Journal of Social Issues 56*, 4, 655–682.

Walby, S. (2004) *The Cost of Domestic Violence.* London: Women and Equality Unit.

Wendt, S. (2010) 'Building and sustaining local co-ordination: An Australian rural community responds to domestic and family violence.' *British Journal of Social Work 40*, 44–62.

Whittington, C. (2003) 'Collaboration and Partnership in Context.' In J. Weinstein, C. Whittington and T. Leiba (eds) *Collaboration in Social Work Practice.* London: Jessica Kingsley Publishers.

CHAPTER 13

Taking Stock
Theory and Practice in Violence Against Women

Nancy Lombard and Lesley McMillan

Introduction

This volume has brought together a number of theoretical, empirical, policy-related and practice-related contributions all of which illuminate our understandings of men's violence against women. One of the foremost results of this book project has been to illustrate the range of violence women experience throughout their lifetimes and to exemplify the centrality of gender in all forms of violence. In this concluding chapter we will draw out and discuss some of the thematic areas that have emerged from the book in relation to theory, policy and practice.

Theoretical underpinnings

The aim of this book has been to draw together current theory and practice in the areas of domestic abuse, sexual violence and exploitation. The theories drawn upon in this volume all place gender as central to contextualising and understanding abuse. Stark's highly influential coercive control thesis illustrates that all such abuses take place within a framework of gendered inequality. They occur, continue and persist because women are unequal to men. Stark's model of violence is cited by several of our contributors. This highlights not only the salience of this work but also the continuing need to reframe violence to enable us to better understand women's experiences. Such a model builds upon earlier feminist work that sought to redefine men's violence(s) against women as part of the gendered system of men's power (Hearn 1998, 1999; Lovenduski and Randall 1993; Rowland and Klein 1990) which is propagated through embedded social (and gendered) practices and institutions. This system of patriarchal relations perpetuates, legitimates and sustains the powerful position of men, both as a group and as individuals. This highlights the need to explain the social problem of men's violence against women on a societal scale, rather than individualise it (Connell 1995, 2002; Dobash and Dobash 1979, 1998).

Stark's theory of coercive control shifts the attention from solely physical abuse to the tactics used to generate and sustain women's continued subordination within intimate relationships. It was in response to the focus upon physical violence and also the graded scale of impact and injury that Radford (1987) suggested the 'circular spiral of violence' and Kelly (1988) devised her 'continuum'. Kelly's 'continuum of violence' discouraged the creation of a hierarchy of forms of violence and abuse and many contributors in this volume have drawn upon it to highlight the range of abuses women face. As a theoretical framework, it also succeeded in merging the dichotomous spheres of the public and the private by illustrating that men's normative behaviour and women's oppression crossed these spatial boundaries. Kelly sought to highlight that these examples of male behaviour, however commonplace for men and women, were not normal or acceptable and needed to be named and challenged as wrong. In doing so, the continuum facilitated the labelling of apparently normal behaviour as part of men's ability and choice to control, conceptualising commonalities experienced by many women and girls in their day-to-day lives by 'enabl[ing] women to make sense of their own experiences by showing how "typical" and "aberrant" male behaviour shade into one another' (Kelly 1988, p.75). Our authors draw upon Kelly's continuum to highlight the breadth of victimisation women experience every day whilst also illustrating its continued relevance with the field of violence against women almost 25 years after its original inception. In addition authors use Stark's theory to explain the specific nature of coercion and control which, crucially, are not always accompanied by physical violence. It also provides academics, policy-makers and social workers with a context to further understand violence and abuse within an intimate relationship.

What these theoretical models of violence illustrate is the need to continually frame and reframe violence to highlight changes in both its conception and application. As Stark notes, many forms of violence against women are illegal, whilst other forms, because of their perpetration within an intimate relationship, are not. There are of course differences between Stark's American examples and ones from the UK. Indeed there are also discrepancies between how different women are treated (see Phipps, Gill, and Lombard and Scott, this volume). Definitions and meanings of violence, however, are dependent upon the individual's position or standpoint as violated, violator or witness (Burman, Brown and Batchelor 2003; Hearn 1998) and also the present legal context in which it occurs as well as the cultural setting (incorporating different traditions, beliefs and violations). Whilst we are at present living in a time and a culture where many aspects of men's violence against women are outwardly condemned and are subject to consequences, we also exist alongside a historical legacy (of the UK and other Western countries) evidenced through religious, legal and social and political examples where men's right to control and physically chastise their wives and children was accepted, endorsed and legalised.

The condemning of some acts of violence over others is in part due to changes in legislation and practice but is also mediated by the multiple forms of identity that women have and the intersections of oppressions that they experience (see Heywood and Drake 1997). The term 'intersectionality' describes the 'intersections' of various identities – generally in relation to oppression (see Hill Collins 2000). In this volume the concept is used by contributors to explore how gender intersects with multiple identities which all impact upon how women experience violence and abuse. It is also appropriated to highlight the further disadvantages some women may experience because of their age, ethnicity and class especially when seeking help or interacting with agencies.

As part of the reframing of violence we also need to examine the changing dynamics of institutions and agencies that are involved in generating the provision and continued protection for women and children affected. Hester's three planet model allows us to conceptualise the failure of many agencies to work holistically with women, children and men when violence is evident in relationships. The notion of planets provides a mental image of how agencies separate the areas of domestic violence, child abuse and child contact and encapsulates the divisive ways in which agencies focus upon children and then women, ignoring the men who have perpetrated the violence. Hester notes that until agencies learn to work within a gendered model of understanding that incorporates the links between all of these fields, providing an integrated response, women and children will continue to be failed by systemic divisions.

Work with, and for, women experiencing abuse cannot be conducted in a theoretical vacuum. This argument is made by Whiting in her chapter on training. The commonalities of the theories explored and drawn upon in this volume are gender and inequality. The violence is perpetrated against, and experienced by, women. Women's oppression originates from the inequities of power between men and women, and men's violence against women is a manifestation and consequence of this power.

Invisibility

A significant theme of this volume has been the invisibility of violence against women, and in particular certain violent practices and the experiences of certain groups of women. The invisibility of violence against women has been a long-standing problem (Department of Health 2000; Henderson 1992; McGarry and Simpson 2011; Mooney 1993; Painter 1991; Strümpel and Hackl 2011) but one that the feminist movement has challenged specifically, and it is the case that knowledge about the continuum of abuses that women are subjected to (Kelly 1988), and the legislative and policy attention paid, is thanks to decades of feminist campaigning. Whilst it is the case that many aspects of men's violence against women are outwardly condemned, it is sadly the case that much is tolerated or explained away (see Amnesty International 2005; Lombard 2011; McCarry 2010).

Whilst it is the case that increased attention over the last four decades has resulted in violence against women no longer being as 'hidden' or 'invisible' as it once was (McKie 2005), nevertheless, the experiences of particular groups of women can remain hidden or be marginalised (Cook, Bessent and Chenoweth 1997; Donovan et al. 2007; Finnbogadóttir and Dykes 2012; Hague, Thiara and Mullender 2011) and it is clear from the contributions to this volume that aspects of invisibility do remain problematic. Stark highlights that the absence of physical violence in a relationship is seen as a 'litmus test' for relationship integrity, but that this focus on the physical aspects of domestic abuse have distracted attention from the wide repertoire of abusive practices that men may employ in an abusive relationship, and the extent to which they can adapt and develop such repertoires. It is for this very reason that some jurisdictions (Scotland) have sought to define violence in intimate relationships as domestic *abuse* as opposed to domestic *violence*. And it is undoubtedly the case that violence against women has received considerably more attention since the 1970s – so it is certainly less invisible and less hidden than it used to be – but as the contributors to this volume have noted, the experiences of many women, and especially particular groups of women, need to be brought to the fore. For example, Scott and Lombard have drawn attention to the invisibility of older women in the domestic abuse field in terms of theory, policy and practice. In addition, other aspects of the life course may also be neglected, for example young people's experience of relationship violence as discussed by Barter and McCarry. Phipps also highlights the invisibility of the violence sex workers experience, McMillan highlights the under-reporting of rape and how most women do not disclose to anyone, and Gill aptly illustrates that BMER (black, minority ethnic and refugee) women are further hidden because they are already considered 'other'. Collectively these chapters show that whilst we have moved on significantly in the field of violence against women there is still some way to go in terms of turning the spotlight on violence against women and subjecting it to the scrutiny it requires.

Impact

This leads us to the impact of violence against women, another theme that is repeatedly echoed throughout this volume. There are two concurrent messages here. Firstly, virtually all of the contributors highlight the impact that violence has upon women's lives. One of the arguments for a gendered analysis of violence made by Lombard draws upon the differential impact of violence experienced by women. This factors in not only their experiences of the abuse but also situates it within the wider social structures of society. This argument is also made by Stark who positions his thesis of coercive control alongside women's differential life chances, maintaining that the impact of the abuse is greater for them because of this.

Barter and McCarry's study clearly highlights the gendered nature of impact. In what they term 'negative impact' there is a clear gender divide between how the teenage boys and girls they interviewed attributed 'seriousness' to their victimisation. Their conclusions illustrate that violence does not affect boys' welfare in the same way as it does to girls.

Hester's and Radford's chapters look at the impact of domestic abuse upon children. Hester looks particularly at how expectations of gender may impact upon decisions made by professionals. That is, whilst recognising the impact of domestic violence upon women, professionals also judge the continuing victimisation to be partly the responsibility of the mother and see her as failing to protect her children. This highlights the intersections of gender, violence and care. The same links are made by Radford in her discussion of child contact and the continuing impact of abuse that is perpetuated by state agencies insisting upon contact with both parents.

The second message related to impact challenges the assumption that violence has less impact upon certain groups of women than others. This relates particularly to the intersections of different forms of inequality. For example, several of the contributors challenge the stereotypes that are often presented whereby certain women are judged to be 'less violated' or 'less victimised' than other groups of women. Phipps in her chapter examines how sex workers find it difficult to disclose or report rape because of preconceptions agency workers have about the impact such violence would have on them, instead seeing rape as 'part of the job description'. This theme is also addressed by McMillan in her discussion of how some 'victims' are being judged by the system as more credible, or 'deserving', than others. Lombard and Scott argue that the term 'elder abuse' has deflected attention away from older women who are experiencing domestic abuse. Instead, by negating gender, the impact of violence upon this group of older women is seen as based on their own vulnerabilities and frailties. Gill also draws upon the intersections of different forms of inequality that impact upon women's lives, highlighting specific examples from BMER communities.

Whiting's chapter brings together both forms of impact, looking at the constitutive impact upon individual women and their families and how this needs to be addressed in training. She also highlights how viewing abuse in different ways impacts upon how we understand, interpret and intervene in violence.

What are the best interventions?

A central aspect of this volume has been discussion of interventions in the violence against women field, and highlighting of the aspects and issues that should inform interventions when women do engage with services, both statutory and non-statutory. It has been argued by authors in this book that service interventions should seek to increase women's empowerment and agency, maximise choice and facilitate decision-making. Disempowerment of women is a significant consequence of violence against women and interventions that seek to restore a woman's capacity for free and independent decision-making are likely to be most helpful. This is not to say that all women who experience men's violence are always disempowered, and indeed we have seen from a number of contributors that women's capacity for resistance, agency and survival is noteworthy. For example, Phipps' discussion of the range of self-protection strategies employed by sex workers and their informal policing practices to create a safer working environment for themselves and other women. Additionally, Barter and McCarry highlight that young women do not simply passively accept the violence they experience but react to it as active agents and respond to it in a number of ways. Similarly, McMillan and Gill also document women's capacity to resist and survive. We must also be careful not to assume that women's decision not to engage with statutory agencies is always because they are unable to do so, or have no personal power to engage; we must recognise that their decision may represent resistance and agency and the desire to deal with their situations in their own ways.

This volume has also highlighted the need for interventions to provide safety for women experiencing violence. In some situations where social work is involved, a woman's relationship with the perpetrator of violence may be over and social work may be required in the aftermath of the incident(s) to work on mitigating the impact of the violence and abuse (discussed above). However, in some circumstances, as evidenced by Stark, Phipps, Scott and Lombard, and Gill, an ongoing relationship with the perpetrator or perpetrators may exist, and even when it does not, violence may still be a serious risk. This is evidenced by a number of authors in the volume who drew attention to the high levels of violence from known men, some of whom may be former partners. Such interventions may include help for women in building support networks, as a significant impact of violence is the isolation it can engender for those who experience it (Lewis Herman 1992). It is also clear that well-organised, co-ordinated interventions create safety for both women and children. Previous research (Laming 2009) and contributors in this volume (Hester, Radford, Rummery) have outlined the potential benefits of multi-agency and partnership working for providing cohesive yet differentiated responses that create safety for adults and children. Additionally, it is not only about the safety of the individual who may experience violence directly, but the safety that can be facilitated around a child's contact with a violent parent (see Radford). It is also argued by Whiting that for any intervention to be safe and effective, it must be based on a solid training base that, in itself, is located in a theoretical framework that allows an understanding of why such violence and abuse occurs.

In addition, it is also of vital importance that interventions are *sensitive*. We know from the discussion of the impact of violence against women that those seeking help, or those who agencies may have referred to them, may have experienced very traumatic incident(s), and may also have the cumulative effects of trauma and violence. These issues may be compounded by other social or demographic issues which make circumstances more challenging for certain groups of women (e.g. age, additional vulnerabilities, marginalised ethnic and cultural groups). It is therefore of paramount importance that all interventions with women, children and families are sensitive to the situation they find themselves in. As such, interventions themselves, and those intervening, need to be free from judgement about cultural preferences, lifestyle choices, family practices and ways of living – women who experience violence face challenge enough, without the additional burden of insensitive treatment.

It is also incredibly important that all interventions in the area of violence against women are *gender sensitive*. In order to achieve this, any interventions need to reflect the distinct experiences that women and men, and girls and boys, have in relation to the instigation and impact of violence. To be gender sensitive we also need to challenge stereotypes and assumptions about violence, for example that there is gender symmetry in perpetration and victimisation which has been shown by a number of authors in this volume (including Gilchrist, McMillan and Lombard) not to be the case. We also need to challenge assumptions that particular groups of women will experience violence in particular ways, and that the impact for some groups might not be 'as bad' as for others. It is also important to challenge assumptions that some women are credible and plausible victims whereas others are not. For example, Phipps, Gill and McMillan all draw attention to these processes highlighting how sex workers are generally regarded as implausible complainants by criminal justice agencies, rape victims are treated as problematic or their cases treated sceptically if they do not meet certain standards, and BMER are likely to be seen as lacking credibility and as such receive a different level and quality of service from statutory agencies. This is also further complicated by the fact that many survivors of men's violence may be reluctant witnesses or participants in state processes.

Given this potential reluctance to engage with state agencies and processes, and many women's reluctance to disclose, it is important (as many contributors have reiterated) to ask women and girls about their experiences of violence. Barter and McCarry and Lombard and Scott draw attention to this in particular for younger and older women respectively, but the importance of asking *all* women in social work contexts should be reiterated. We know that women may be reluctant to engage with state services or to seek help for violence but regular, sensitive asking of women may increase disclosure and help-seeking, and may also challenge the silence around violence against women that Lewis Herman (1992) argues is akin to cultural psychosis.

Knowledge is power

Additionally, this silence can also be challenged through an increase in knowledge, and the willingness to use that knowledge. People in authority have been accorded the 'power of naming' (Foucault 1980) and consequently have been positioned so as to define the issue for others. Bacchi (1999, p.165) argues that it is not simply the 'definition' or 'definer' that is of most relevance but how these labels function in conceptualising the issue further. We can see how power pervades not only violence and its perpetration, but also its conceptualisation. Some social workers will be accorded with this power of 'naming' or helping to name violence for others. The more knowledge one has about violence, the more able you are to contribute to its naming and its prevention (Stanko 2003, p.11).

Prevention is one of the core elements of the strategy to address men's violence against women (Cabinet Office 1999; Scottish Executive 2001). Whiting's recommendations highlight the continued prevalence of the three 'p' model – protection, provision and prevention – and Rummery addresses the need for collaboration to meet these targets. The Scottish government has since included the fourth 'p' of participation to encourage the active engagement of all in eliminating violence against women (see Scottish Government 2009). Protection of women and children can be achieved to some extent through criminal and civil laws and agents of the criminal justice system such as the police. Provision deals more generally with the entitlements for help and care such as housing provision (including refuge space) and advocacy.

Feminist academics and activists have always advocated prevention as the ultimate 'answer' (Kelly 1999) but policies that meet with the least resistance (Charles 1995) often have more chance of wider governmental approval (Boneparth and Stoper 1988). Whilst, previously, feminists have sought to challenge violent behaviour and promote positive role change within wider social contexts where men's violence is tolerated, the UK government at Westminster has remained focused on providing individual women and children with immediate (and more quantifiable) protection and provision (Cabinet Office 1999). The Scottish Executive (2000, 2001) developed a prevention strategy that included education and awareness-raising. The aims of education strategies are to increase awareness, change patterns of behaviour and develop the understanding that all violence is wrong (Smaoun 2000). Yet unless there is transformative equality, any actions will simply result in normalisation rather than resistance (Kelly 1999).

Gender, inequality and social transformation

It is to this need for transformative equality that we now turn. We began this book by talking about the importance of gender to any analysis of violence against women and it is on this same topic that we will end. Throughout the volume contributors have drawn attention to the myriad ways gender 'matters' in relation to violence against women. It is clear that the link between gender and violence against women is of paramount importance, and this understanding moving forward helps frame future research, policy, practice and interventions. However, it is not enough to only have policies, practices and interventions – a wider social transformative project is required, and many contributors to this volume argue for this. If we do not challenge stereotypes and common-sense understandings of violence, of victims/survivors, and of the impact on individuals, families and society as a whole, then we continue to work within restrictive and flawed constructions of gender. We must recognise that specific gendered harms occur within a general framework of gender inequality that supports violence against women, and it is only by challenging, and ultimately transforming, that framework that we will see real and lasting change.

References

Amnesty International (2005) *Sexual Assault Research Summary Report.* London: Amnesty International United Kingdom.

Bacchi, C. (1999) *Women, Policy and Politics: The Construction of Policy Problems.* London: Sage Publications.

Boneparth, E. and Stoper, E. (eds) (1988) *Women, Power and Policy.* Oxford: Pergamon Press.

Burman, M., Brown, J. and Batchelor, S. (2003) '"Taking it to Heart": Girls and the Meanings of Violence.' In E.A. Stanko (ed.) *The Meaning of Violence.* London: Routledge.

Cabinet Office (1999) *Living Without Fear: An Integrated Approach to Tackling Violence Against Women.* London: The Women's Unit.

Charles, N. (1995) 'Feminist politics, domestic violence and the state.' *Sociological Review 43,* 4, 617–640.

Connell, R.W. (1995, 2005) *Masculinities.* Cambridge: Polity Press.

Connell, R.W. (2002) *Gender.* Cambridge: Polity Press.

Cook, S., Bessant, J. and Chenoweth, L. (1997) 'Violence and Women with Disabilities: Silence and Paradox.' In S. Cook and J. Bessant (eds) *Women's Encounters with Violence: Australian Experiences.* Newbury Park, CA: Sage.

Department of Health (2000) *Domestic Violence: A Resource Manual for Health Care Professionals.* London: Department of Health.

Dobash, R.E. and Dobash, R.P. (1979) *Women, Violence and Social Change.* London: Routledge.

Dobash, R. and Dobash, R.E. (1998) 'Violent Men and Violent Contexts.' In R. Dobash and R.E. Dobash (eds) *Rethinking Violence Against Women.* London: Sage Publications.

Donovan, C., Hester, M., Fahmy, E., Holmes, J. and McCarry, M. (2007) *Comparing Love and Domestic Violence in Heterosexual and Same Sex Relationships: Full Research Report.* Swindon: ESRC.

Finnbogadóttir, H. and Dykes, A.K. (2012) 'Midwives' awareness and experiences regarding domestic violence among pregnant women in southern Sweden.' *Midwifery 28,* 2, 181–189.

Foucault, M. (1980) '"Body/Power" and "Truth and Power".' In C. Gordon (ed.) *Michel Foucault: Power/Knowledge.* Hemel Hempstead: Harvester.

Hague, G., Thiara, R. and Mullender, A. (2011) 'Disabled women, domestic violence and social care: The risk of isolation, vulnerability and neglect.' *British Journal of Social Work 41,* 1, 148–165.

Hearn, J. (1998) *The Violences of Men: How Men Talk and How Agencies Respond to Men's Violences Against Women.* London: Sage Publications.

Hearn, J. (1999) 'A Crisis in Masculinity or New Agendas for Men?' In S. Walby (ed.) *New Agendas for Women.* London: Macmillan.

Henderson, S. (1992) *Hidden Findings: The Edinburgh Women's Safety Survey.* Edinburgh: The City of Edinburgh Council.

Herman, L.J. (1992) *Trauma and recovery: The aftermath of recovery.* New York: Basic Books.

Heywood, L. and Drake, J. (1997) *Third Wave Agenda: Being Feminist, Doing Feminism.* Minnesota: University of Minnesota Press.

Hill Collins, P. (2000) *Black Feminist Thought: Knowledge, Consciousness, and the Politics of Empowerment* (2nd ed.). New York: Routledge.

Kelly, L. (1988) *Surviving Sexual Violence.* Oxford: Polity Press.

Kelly, L. (1999) 'Violence Against Women: A Policy of Neglect or a Neglect of Policy?' In S. Walby (ed.) *New Agendas for Women.* London: Macmillan.

Laming, H. (2009) *The Protection of Children in England: A Progress Report.* London: The Stationery Office.

Lewis Herman, J. (1992) *Trauma and Recovery: From Domestic Abuse to Political Terror.* London: Pandora.

Lombard, N. (2011) *Young People's Attitudes about Violence.* Briefing 54. Edinburgh: Centre for Families and Relationships, University of Edinburgh. Available at www.crfr.ac.uk/reports/briefing%2054.pdf, accessed on 27 July 2012.

Lovenduski, J. and Randall, V. (1993) *Contemporary Feminist Politics.* Oxford: Oxford University Press.

McCarry, M. (2010) 'Becoming a "proper man": Young people's attitudes about interpersonal violence and perceptions of gender.' *Gender and Education 22,* 1, 17–30.

McGarry, J. and Simpson, C. (2011) 'Domestic abuse and older women: Exploring the opportunities for service development and care delivery.' *The Journal of Adult Protection 13,* 6, 294–301.

McKie, L. (2005) *Families, Violence, and Social Change.* Buckingham: Open University Press.

Mooney, J. (1993) *The Hidden Figure: Domestic Violence in North London.* London: Islington Police & Crime Prevention Unit.

Painter, K. (1991) *Wife Rape, Marriage and Law: Survey Report, Key Findings and Recommendations.* Manchester: Manchester University Department of Social Policy and Social Work.

Radford, J. (1987) 'Policing Male Violence – Policing Women.' In J. Hanmer and M. Maynard (eds) *Women, Violence and Social Control.* Atlantic Highlands, NJ: Humanities Press International.

Rowland, R. and Klein, R.D. (1990) 'Radical Feminism: Critique and Construct?' In S. Gunew (ed.) *Feminist Knowledge: Critique and Construct.* London: Routledge.

Scottish Executive (2000) *National Strategy to Address Domestic Abuse in Scotland.* Edinburgh: Stationery Office.

Scottish Executive (2001) *Preventing Violence Against Women: Action across the Scottish Executive.* Edinburgh: Stationery Office.

Scottish Government (2009) *Safer Lives: Changed Lives. A Shared Approach to Tackling Violence Against Women in Scotland.* Edinburgh: Scottish Government.

Smaoun, S. (2000) *Violence Against Women in Urban Areas: An Analysis of the Problem from a Gender Perspective.* Urban Management Working Paper Series 17. Nairobi: United Nations Centre for Human Settlements (UN-Habitat).

Stanko, E.A. (2003) 'Conceptualising the Meaning of Violence.' In E.A. Stanko (ed.) *The Meaning of Violence.* London: Routledge.

Strümpel, C. and Hackl, C. (2011) 'The Breaking the Taboo projects – raising awareness of, and training staff in community health and care services on violence against older women within families.' *The Journal of Adult Protection 13,* 6, 323–335.

The Contributors

Christine Barter is a NSPCC Senior Research Fellow at the School for Policy Studies, University of Bristol. Christine has published on a range of child welfare issues, including *Peer Violence in Residential Children's Homes* (Palgrave). Her most recent work has focused on teenage violence in intimate relationships, undertaking the first UK-wide study in this area. Her work has received substantial media, public and policy interest. She has acted as a consultant for the Home Office on their two teenage relationship abuse campaigns. Christine has recently co-edited a book on young people and peer violence, *Children behaving badly?* (Wiley).

Professor Liz Gilchrist is a Registered Forensic Psychologist and Professor in Forensic Psychology at Glasgow Caledonian University. Her primary research interest is in the area of domestic violence, with particular focus on risk assessment. She is recognised as an expert in the area of domestic violence and child protection. She is a member of the Research Advisory Group for the Risk Management Authority, a Scottish organisation set up following the MacLean committee to manage serious risk/violence in Scotland, a member of the Parole Board for Scotland and was recently appointed to the Scottish Advisory Panel on Offender Rehabilitation.

Dr Aisha K. Gill is a Reader in Criminology at University of Roehampton. She has been involved in addressing the problem of violence against women at the grassroots level for the past 14 years. Dr Gill has extensive experience of providing expert advice to the government, Ministry of Justice, Scotland Yard, Crown Prosecution Service and the voluntary sector on legal policy issues related to 'honour' killings and forced marriage. Dr Gill is a media commentator on forced marriage, violence against women and so-called 'honour' killings and writes for mainstream popular as well as academic audiences.

Marianne Hester is Professor of Gender, Violence and International Policy in the School for Policy Studies, University of Bristol, where she heads the Centre for Gender and Violence Research. She has conducted groundbreaking research on many aspects of violence and abuse, with key studies on domestic violence, children and contact, domestic violence and the criminal justice system, and domestic violence across heterosexual and same-sex relationships.

Nancy Lombard is a Lecturer in Social Policy at Glasgow Caledonian University. She recently completed her PhD on what 11- and 12-year-olds think about men's violence against women, which received considerable academic and media interest. Nancy was part of the research team commissioned by the Scottish Executive to investigate male domestic abuse in Scotland. Before returning to academia in 2003 Nancy worked in the third sector and was Deputy Manager at North Kensington Women's Aid in London. She has been a volunteer, researcher and activist within the violence against women movement for 15 years. She lives in Glasgow with her partner and their three children.

Melanie McCarry has been involved in the area of violence against women as an academic and activist for many years in both Glasgow and Bristol. Melanie has recently completed a number of high profile research projects including a collaborative project with the NSPCC on violence and exploitation in young people's relationships. Melanie was also the lead researcher on a project investigating violence against women in rural and urban areas commissioned by the Women's Institute. Melanie's previous research has investigated forced marriage within the UK's south Asian community, domestic violence in same-sex and heterosexual relationships, and young people's views of gender constructions and domestic violence.

Dr Lesley McMillan is Reader in Sociology and Criminology at Glasgow Caledonian University. Her main areas of research are gender inequalities, feminism, gendered and sexual violence, and in particular the statutory and non-statutory response to sexual violence. Recently she has been interested in the criminal justice response to rape and sexual assault looking at all aspects of the justice process including policing, medico-legal interventions, prosecution and trial/court stage. She has recently completed a large ESRC-funded study seeking to understand why so many rape cases are lost from the justice process, titled *Understanding Attrition in Rape Cases*. She has published in a number of outlets and is author of *Feminists Organising Against Gendered Violence* (Palgrave, 2007).

Alison Phipps is Director of Gender Studies and Senior Lecturer in Sociology at the University of Sussex. She is primarily interested in the politics of the body, in particular as they play out around issues to do with gender and health. Her current research focuses on debates about sex work and other controversial subjects such as sexual violence, childbirth and breastfeeding, and abortion. She is working on a monograph bringing all these topics together, under contract with Polity Press. Her most recent papers have been focused on sexual violence and published in *Sociology*, *Critical Social Policy*, and *Gender and Education*. She is particularly interested in violence against women students, and the experiences of students working in the sex industry.

Lorraine Radford, PhD, is an independent violence prevention researcher. She has over 30 years of grassroots experience working within the feminist and child violence prevention voluntary sector and almost as long an involvement in antiviolence research. She is author (with Marianne Hester) of the book *Mothering Through Domestic Violence* (2006) and solo author of the new book *Re-Thinking Children Violence and Safeguarding* (2012). She previously worked as head of research at the NSPCC, on violence prevention research in the Department of Health and as a university-based researcher/academic, her last post being Reader in Criminology at Roehampton University. She is mother of three daughters, now grown, who are also proud feminists.

Kirstein Rummery is Professor of Social Policy at the University of Stirling, a member of the Scottish Women's Budget Group and on the Board of Directors of Engender, a Scottish feminist organisation. Her recent work includes inter-professional and partnership working in the welfare state, an analysis of the gendered impacts of care policy, the costs of personalisation and self-directed support in social care, and a gendered analysis of economic, social policy and constitutional change in Scotland.

Marsha Scott is a feminist activist, researcher and practitioner and has advocated, volunteered, researched, and worked in the violence against women sector in the United Kingdom, the United States and Europe for 20 years. She is Convener of Engender, a national feminist organisation in Scotland, and the UK Expert delegate to the EWL's European Observatory on Violence Against Women.

Evan Stark is a forensic social worker and award-winning researcher with an international reputation for his work on the legal, policy and health dimensions of interpersonal violence. A founder of one of the first shelters for abused women in the USA, in the 1980s Dr Stark co-directed the Yale Trauma Studies with Dr Anne Flitcraft, research that documented the significance of domestic violence for female health. The findings from these studies appeared in *Women at Risk: Domestic Violence and Women's Health* (Sage 1996). His book *Coercive Control: The Entrapment of Women in Personal Life* (Oxford 2007) was named the best social science book published in 2007. Dr Stark is a Professor Emeritus of Public Administration, Public Health and Women and Gender Studies at Rutgers University in New Jersey.

Nel Whiting is Learning and Development Co-ordinator with Scottish Women's Aid, where she has worked since September 2003. Her role takes her throughout Scotland providing learning opportunities which explore the dynamics of domestic abuse to a range of professionals in the voluntary and statutory sector. She is committed to providing high quality training which reflects the practical concerns of delegates and is underpinned by a solid theoretical understanding of the issues. Nel is a regular lecturer at the Scottish Police College, the Scottish Prosecution College and Queen Margaret University.

Subject Index

adolescent girls
  age of 119
  coercive control against 113–17
  family violence against 117–19
  help for 120–1
  partner age 119–20
  peer violence against 117–19
  research methodology 104–6
  sexual violence against 109–12
  violence against 106–9
Adoption and Children Act (2002) 40, 41, 61
anonymous acts
  as form of coercive control 25

black and minority ethnic women
  female genital mutilation 14
  and forced marriage 143–6
  and 'honour'-based violence 146–9
  and intersectionality 142–3
  social work implications 150–5

child contact
  and domestic violence 45–8
  next steps in 64–6
  pro-contact stance 54
  process of 60–1
  safe contact approach 55–7
  safety in 61–4
  and 'three planets model' 45–9
  and wellbeing 57–60
child protection
  and domestic violence 36, 39–40
  and 'three planets model' 40–5
Children Act (1989) 40, 61, 64
Chldren Act (2004) 40
Children and Adoption Act (2006) 61, 63
Children (Contact) and Adoption Act (2005) 46
Children and Family Court Advisory Service
  (CAFCASS) 45, 46, 61
Children's Hearing (Scotland) Act (2011) 65
Common Assessment Framework (CAF) 41
Co-ordinated Community Response (CCR) 35,
  38
coercive control
  and adolescent girls 113–17

description of 17–18, 21–2
forms of 22–7
intimidation 23–7
prevalence of 18–19
technology of 21–2
training for 207–9
and violence 19–20, 22–3
control
  deprivation 29–31
  description of 27
  exploitation 29–31
  isolation 27–9
  regulation 29–31
criminal justice system
  and rape 80–3

Danger Assessment instrument 166
degredation
  as form of coercive control 26
deprivation
  as form of control 29–31
domestic violence
  and child contact 45–8
  and child protection 36
  men as victims of 177–91
  and older women 125–38
  and 'three planets model' 38–40
Domestic Violence, Crimes and Victims Act
  (2004) 39, 40

Every Child Matters 41
exploitation
  as form of control 29–31

Family Law Act (1996) 41–2
Family Law (Scotland) Act (2006) 65
female genital mutilation 149
forced marriage 143–6

gender
  bias in family courts 60–1
  description of 179–80
  importance of in violence 8–9, 178–9, 182,
    183–6
  and perpetuators of domestic violence 162–3
  and training 197–201

Getting It Right for Every Child (Scottish Executive)
    215
'honour'-based violence 146–9

Independent Domestic Violence Advisors (IDVAs)
    38, 40, 46, 62
intersectionality 142–3
intimidation
    as form of coercive control 23–7
isolation
    as form of control 27–9

masculinity
    and violence181–2
men
    as perpetuators of domestic violence 159–71
    as victims of domestic violence 177–91
Multi-Agency Risk Assessment Conferences
    (MARACs) 38, 40

National Domestic Abuse Delivery Plan for Children
    (Scottish Government) 65
National Strategy to Address Domestic Abuse in
    Scotland (Scottish Executive) 178, 196,
    215, 218

older women
    barriers to help 132–4
    data on 130
    and dependence 134–5
    description of 126–8
    form of abuse 128–30
    impact of abuse 135–6
    practice implications 136–8
    and shame 131–2
    and younger women's experiences 130–1

partnership working
    case studies in 223–9
    goals of 220–1
    and interdependence 221–3
    membership of 216–19
    theory and policy of 214–15
perpetuators of domestic violence
    behaviour explanations 161–5
    differences between 164–5
    focus on 160
    interventions for 169–71
    risk assessments 166–9
    risk factors 165–6
Policing and Crime Act (2009) 89–90
*Preventing Violence Against Women: Action Across the
    Scottish Executive (Scottish Executive)* 178
pro-contact stance 54

rape
    characteristics of reported 74–5
    and criminal justice system 80–3
    disclosure of 75–80

impact of 72
prevalence of 72
research methodology 73
regulation
    as form of control 29–31
risk assessments 166–9

safe contact approach 55–7
Scotland
    child contact in 65
    importance of gender in 178–9
    male domestic abuse in 186–8
    older women in 128
    sex work in 90
    training in 196–211
Separation, Pregnancy, Escalation, Cultural Issues,
    Stalking and Sexual Assault (SPECSS)
    screening tool 166–7
sex workers
    growth in demand for 88
    prevalence of 88–9
    prevalence of violence against 90–3
    preventing violence against 95–8
    violence against 87–8, 93–5
sexual violence *see* rape
shaming tactics
    as form of coercive control 26–7
Spousal Assault Risk Assessment (SARA) 166,
    168–9, 176
stalking
    as form of coercive control 25–6

'three model planet'
    child contact 45–9
    child protection 40–5
    description of 35–8
    domestic violence 38–40
training
    and coercive control 207–9
    and gender 197–201
    importance of 204–6
    and privacy 201–2
    in Scotland 196–211
    theoretical knowledge for 202–4, 206

UN Convention on the Rights of the Child 45,
    58

violence against women
    and coercive control 19–20, 22–3
    and gender 8–9, 178–9, 182, 183–6
    impact of 237–8
    interventions for 238–41
    invisibility of 236–7
    knowledge of 241–2
    language used 10–11
    and masculinities 181–2
    pervasiveness of 9–10
    theory of 233–6

Author Index

Abdo, N. 146
Acierno, R. 130, 132
ACPO 96, 97
Adams, D. 22
Agnew-Davies, R. 17
Agustín, L. 92
Aitken, L. 135
Alexander, C. 148
Allen, J. 55, 75, 143
AMICA 59
Amnesty International 9, 10, 236
Anitha, S. 146, 147, 148, 151
Archer, J. 54, 163, 183
Aris, R. 62
Aronson, J. 129
Arriaga, X.B. 106, 118
Audit Commission 214

Babcock, J.C. 169, 170, 171
Bachar, K. 72
Bachman, R. 76, 81
Bagley, C. 94
Baig, A. 151
Baker, L.M. 97
Bancroft, L. 65
Band-Winterstein, T. 130
Barford, A. 129
Barker, C. 17
Barkan, H. 93
Barkham, M. 17
Barter, C. 28, 103, 105, 106, 111, 122, 190
Basile, S. 54
Batchelor, S. 183, 235
Batsleer, J. 152
Beaulaurier, R.L. 133
Beck, C.J.A. 18
Beek, M. 59
Beichner, D. 80
Belfrage, H. 166, 167
Bennett, C.G. 93
Bennett, G. 127
Bennett, L.W. 163, 164
Benson, C. 90
Bergman, L. 113

Berliner, L. 72
Berridge, D. 105
Bernstein, E. 88
Bessant, J. 236
Blevins, K.R. 95
Blood, I. 125, 133
Bond, J. 9, 179
Boneparth, E. 242
Bookwala, J. 118
Bouffard, J.A. 160
Bouffard, L.A. 160
Bourdieu, P. 37, 147
Bowen, E. 169, 170
Brah, A. 143
Brandon, M. 55
Bream, V. 60
Brents, B.G. 88
Brittan, A. 181
Brockopp, K. 103
Brown, J. 183, 235
Brown, L. 169
Browning, J.J. 163
Brownmiller, S. 182
Brush, L.D. 217, 228
Bryman, A. 73
Buchanan, A. 60
Burman, M. 183, 190, 235
Busch, N.B. 90
Butler, S. 179
Buzawa, E. 29
Bybee, D. 80
Byers, S. 113
Byrne, C.A. 80

CAADA 42
Cabinet Office 241, 242
CAFCASS 61
Calder, M. 203
Callahan, J.E. 118
Campbell, J.C. 18, 166
Campbell, R. 72, 80, 81, 84, 90, 91, 92, 95, 96, 97
Capaldi, D.M. 164
Carter, D.J. 97, 98

Carter, H. 87
Cassidy, D. 55
Cavanagh, K. 55
Cawson, P. 109
Chantler, K. 146
Charles, N. 242
Chenoweth, L. 236
Chesney-Lind, M. 80
Chetwynd, S.J. 91
Chew, E. 103
Chisholm, R. 64
Chung, D. 112
Church, S. 90, 92
Clark, S. 164
Cleaver, H. 35, 42
Cohen, S. 78
Coleman, S. 90
Collin-Vézina, D. 113
Collins, P. 143
Connell, R.W. 21, 159, 178, 179, 180, 181,
        182, 198, 199, 234
Connolly, J. 59
Conservative Party 54
Cook, D. 39
Cook, S. 236
Cooke, D.J. 168
Cooper, L. 10
Cornell, D. 26, 159
Council of Europe 144
Coy, M. 38, 155
Craig, J. 62
Cram, F. 106
Crenshaw, K. 143, 155
Creswell, J.W. 104
Cusick, L. 89

Dalla, R.L. 97, 98
Daly, J. 170
Daly, M. 55, 129
Davey, S. 55
Davies, C. 58
Davis-Frenzel, E. 80
Day, S. 90
de Beauvoir, S. 179
Department of Children, Schools and Families
        (DCSF) 41
Department of Health 236
Devaney, C. 222
Devanney, J. 43
Dicker, R. 127
Dobash, R.E. 9, 55, 128, 129, 129, 160, 162,
        163, 166, 170, 171, 182, 190, 201, 216,
        234
Dobash, R.P. 9, 55, 128, 160, 163, 182, 201,
        216, 234
Dominy, N. 10
Donder, L. 129
Donovan, C. 121, 236

Dragiewicz, M. 179
Drake, J. 130, 235
Duncan, S. 203, 206
Dupont, I. 143
Dustin, M. 147, 151, 152
Dutton, D.G. 163, 164, 165
Dworkin, A. 92
Dye, M. 164
Dykes, A.K. 236

Eade, J. 146
Eckhardt, C. 164
Edleson, J.L. 55, 64, 65, 218, 225
Edwards, R. 90
Edwards, S. 190
Ehrensaft, M.K. 162
Eisikovits, Z. 130
Eisler, R. 164
Ellison, L. 150
Equal Parenting Alliance 54
Eriksson, M. 48
European Parliament 127
EVAW 199
Evers, H. 127

Falik, M. 72
Farley, M. 93
Farmer, E. 41, 42, 44, 58, 63
Fatherhood Institute 54
Faulk, M. 163
Featherstone, B. 54
Fekete, L. 148
Felson, R. 81
Fennell, G. 127
Fergusson, D. 184
Fick, N. 93, 94, 95
Findlater, J.E. 218, 225, 226
Finnbogadóttir, H. 236
Fisher, B. 127, 136
Fitzclarence, L. 9
Fleck-Henderson, A. 218, 220, 221, 229
Flitcraft, A. 17, 19
Flood, M. 54, 184
Folaron, G. 97, 98
Foord, J. 155
Forte, J.A. 27
Foshee, V.A. 106, 118
Foucault, M. 241
Franchina, J.J. 164
Frankel, S.L. 161
Frey, T. 30
Frohmann, L. 80

Gadd, D. 159, 178, 181, 183, 184, 185, 187,
        188, 189
Gamache, D. 106
Gamble, N. 80, 84
Gangoli, G. 121, 146

Gelles, R.J. 19, 162, 166, 183, 184
Gilchrist, E. 160, 162, 164, 165, 169, 170
Giles, J. 160
Gill, A. 13, 59, 146, 147, 148, 149, 151, 152, 153, 154, 235
Giobbe, E. 93
Giovanninni, E. 58, 62
Glaser, D. 60
Glass, N. 18
Goergen, T. 125
Goldsmith, C. 148
Gondolf, E. 188
Grace, S. 81
Graham-Kevan, N. 171
Grant, S.R. 166
Greenfield, L. 74, 77
Griffin, G. 135
Gullette, M.M. 127
Gupta, T. 150, 151

Hackl, C. 134, 236
Hague, G. 132, 182, 236
Hahn, S.A. 217, 228, 229
Halpern, T.C. 113
Hamberger, L.K. 163, 165
Hamby, S. 56
Hamill, R. 169, 170
Hardy, B. 215, 229
Harne, L. 64
Harocopos, A. 90
Harris, G.T.166
Harris, J. 81
Harris, S. 129
Harrison, C. 62
Hart, S.D. 166, 168, 169
Harvey, M.R. 72
Hastings, J.E. 163
Hatty, S.E. 181
Hausbeck, K. 88
Hearn, J. 181, 182, 188, 197, 201, 234, 235
Henderson, S. 10, 236
Henning, K. 168
Heslet, L. 74, 77
Hester, M. 20, 35, 39, 40, 41, 42, 43, 44, 45, 46, 48, 56, 57, 59, 63, 90, 121, 129, 178, 181, 184, 185, 188–90, 200, 201, 235, 236, 239
Heyman, R. 169
Heywood, L. 130, 235
Hightower, J. 129, 130, 133
Hill Collins, P. 235
Hilton, N.Z. 166
Hinchcliff-Smith, K. 127
Hird, M.J. 113
Hisashima, J. 166
HM Government 97
HMICA 46, 62
Holdford, R. 168

Holt, T.J. 95
Holzworth-Munroe, A. 164, 165
Home Affairs Select Committee 38
Home Office 38, 89, 94, 96
Horvath, M. 142
Horwarth, J. 210
Horwood, J. 184
Hossain, S. 146
Hotaling, G. 29
Hotaling, N. 91
Hough, M. 90
House of Commons 63, 64
Howarth, E. 38, 40, 45, 62
Hoyle, C. 190
Hubbard, P. 90, 91, 95
Hudson, B. 80, 215
Hughes, D. 30
Humphreys, C. 36, 42, 62, 209
Hunt, J. 58, 59, 60, 62
Hurley, N. 204
Husseini, R. 147
Huxham, C. 221

Itzin, C. 181

Jackson, L.A. 93, 94, 95
Jackson, S.M. 106
Jaffe, P. 57, 60, 64
Janczewski, C. 225
Jeal, N. 90, 91, 94, 95
Jeffreys, S. 92
Jezl, D. 113
Johnson, M. 11, 17, 22, 92, 127, 160, 178, 182, 184, 185, 186, 189, 200
Johnson-Reid, M. 164
Jones, A. 17
Jordan, A. 148

Kaganas, F. 53
Kaspiew, R. 64
Kaufmann, J. 170
Kazimirski, A. 144
Kebbell, M. 162
Kelly, J. 160, 185
Kelly, L. 9, 10, 38, 76, 79, 81, 127, 128, 142, 155, 197, 218, 234, 242
Kelly, S. 225, 226
Kenway, J. 10
Kerstetter, W.A. 80
Kessler, R.C. 72
Khanum, N. 143, 144
Kilpatrick, D.G. 80
Kimmel, M. 180, 200
Kinnell, H. 89, 91, 92, 95, 96, 97
Kistenmacher, B.R. 170
Klaus, P. 19
Klein, R.D. 9, 234
Knight, I. 87

Koss, M.P. 72, 74, 77
Koss, P.G. 72
Kropp, P.R. 166, 169
Kunitz, S.J. 164
Kurz, D. 184

Lackey, C. 164
LaFree, G. 80
Laming, H. 40, 49
Laming, Lord 209
Lane, G. 163
Lang, J. 200
Langlands, R. 170
Lapierre, S. 36, 42
LeBlanc, K. 127, 136
Lepper, J. 64
Lessard, G. 223
Levesque, F. 170
Lewis Herman, J. 239, 241
Lindgren, Y. 178
Lindholm, C. 147
Lischick, C.W. 19
Local Government Association 43
Lombard, N. 119, 185, 190, 235, 236
Lovenduski, J. 234
Lovett, J. 81
Lutman, E. 58, 63

Macdonald, G.S. 47
Macdonald, L.O. 132
Macleod, A. 60, 62
Madigan, L. 80, 84
Magdol, L. 164
Malik, N. 64, 65, 225, 226, 227
Malkin, B. 87
Malos, E. 39, 182
Manganello, J. 18
Maris, C. 147
Martin, P.Y. 80
Martinez, E. 103
Martinsson, R. 168
Masson, J. 62
Matoesian, G.M. 80
Matthews, R. 96
May, T. 90
McCarry, M. 28, 104, 190, 236
McCollum, E. 169
McElroy, W. 92
McGarry, J. 127, 132, 133, 136, 236
McGee, C. 58
McGibbon, A. 10
McKie, L. 77, 126, 127, 128, 129, 131, 134,
     197, 201, 236
McMahon, S. 71, 72
McMillan, L. 9, 72, 73, 79, 81, 83, 90, 130, 183
McMurran, M. 164
Meadows, A. 170
Mears, J. 126, 129, 134, 135

Meloy, M.L. 38, 160
Meltzer, H. 55
Michie, C. 168
Miller, S.L. 38, 160
Ministry of Justice 63, 64
Minsky-Kelly, D. 210
Mirza, H. 143
Mitra-Kahn, T. 148
Moffitt, T.E. 174
Mojab, S. 146
Molidor, C. 113
Montminy, L. 126, 130, 132
Monto, M.A. 89, 91, 92
Mooney, A. 58
Mooney, J. 19, 236
Moore, T.M. 164
Morgan Disney and Associates 126, 130, 135,
     136, 137
Morran, D. 170
Morrison, F. 58
Mrsevic, S. 30
Muftic, L.R. 160
Mullender, A. 59, 236
Munro, V. 150
Murphy, C.M. 170
Myhill, A. 75

NAGALRO 64
Narayan, U. 150
Neidig, P. 169
New, M. 72
Nixon, K. 167
Njambi, W. 149

Ofsted 46, 47
Ogg, J. 127
O'Keefe, M. 103, 118
Okun, L. 17
O'Leary, D. 169
Oliver, C. 58
ONS 58
Ortner, S. 146

Pahl, J. 29, 216
Painter, K. 75, 236
Paré, P. 81
Parker, M.L. 19
Paymar, M. 160, 170
Payne, B.K. 203
Peacey, V. 58, 59
Pearce, J. 48
Pearson, C. 56
Peckover, S. 54
Pelowski, S. 170
Pence, E. 160, 162, 170
Penfold, C. 90, 91, 93, 96
Penhale, B. 135, 137
Pennington-Zoellner, K. 218, 222

Philips, L. 130
Phillips, A. 147, 151
Phillips, R. 9, 179
Phillipson, C. 127
Phipps, A. 91, 96, 235
Phoenix, A. 143
Phoenix, J. 94
Piepmeier, A. 127
Piispa, M. 19
Pillemer, K. 135
Piper, N. 146
Plano Clark, V.L. 104
Plichta, S.B. 72
Plumridge, E.W. 91, 92
Postmus, J.L. 217, 228, 229
Povey, D. 42, 55
Powell, M.R. 80
Press Association 87
Price, L. 113
Prochaska, J. 98
Pryor, J. 57
Ptacek, J. 196

Radford, J. 9, 234, 239, 240
Radford, L. 10, 42, 45, 46, 48, 55, 57, 59, 61, 65
Raghavan, C. 18
Rand, M. 19
Randall, V. 234
Raphael, J. 93, 217, 228
Razack, S. 151
Reder, P. 203, 206
Reed, A. 91
Rees, A. 17, 22, 23, 24, 26–7, 28, 29, 30
Regan, L. 76, 81
Regan, S. 127, 136
Renzetti, C. 185
Rice, M.E. 166
Richards, L. 166
Ridder, E. 184
Rivett, M. 63
Roberts, C. 58, 59
Robinson, A.L. 40
Rodgers, B. 57
Roe-Sepowitz, D. 97
Romero-Daza, N. 93, 94, 95
Roscoe, B. 118
Rosen, K. 169
Rosenfeld, B.D. 170
Rowe, M. 222
Rowland, R. 9, 234
Rummery, K. 214, 215, 221, 222, 223, 226, 229, 230, 239
Russell, D. 72
Russell, T. 163
Rying, M. 167

Saathoff, A.J. 218
Saharso, S. 147
Salisbury, C. 90, 91, 94, 95
Samad, Y. 146
Sanders, T. 89, 90, 91, 92, 94, 95, 96, 97
Sapnara, K. 150, 151
Sargent, M. 129
Saunders, D. 163, 169, 170
Saunders, H. 55
Sayer, S. 59
Schaffer, J. 137
Schechter, S. 17
Schein, E. 17
Schneier, I. 17
Schow, D. 218
Schwartz, R. 71, 72
Scott, M. 126, 127, 129, 130, 131, 132, 133, 134, 135, 137, 138, 218
Scottish Executive 128, 178, 179, 196, 197, 215, 218, 241, 242
Scottish Government 65, 90, 170, 178, 186, 204, 241
Scourfield, J.B. 171
Sears, H. 113
Seaver, C. 129, 135, 137
Sedger, R. 129
Sen, P. 149
Seymour, F.W. 106
Shapiro, D.L. 93
Sharpe, K. 97
Shaw, A. 146
Sidebotham, P. 55
Silverman, J. 65
Simons, R.L. 164
Simpson, C. 127, 132, 133, 136, 236
Singer, M. 93
Skinner, T. 39, 182
Slack, J. 144
Smaoun, S. 242
Smedslund, G. 170
Smith, M. 58
Snow, D.L. 160
Sokoloff, N.J. 143
Sonkin, D.J. 163
Soothill, K. 182
Southall Black Sisters 152
Sowinski, B.A. 93
Spivak, G. 143
Spohn, C. 76, 80
Stanko, E. 72, 74, 77, 81, 82, 182, 184, 217, 241
Stanley, N. 36, 40, 41, 43, 44, 61, 63
Stark, E. 11, 17, 18, 19, 30, 39, 57, 113, 178, 181, 184, 186, 189, 199, 208, 233–4
Steinmetz, S. 183
Stith, S. 164, 169, 170
Stoffel, E.A. 218
Stoper, E. 242

Stover, C.S. 170
Straka, S. 126, 130, 132
Straus, M.A. 162, 166, 183
Strümpel, C. 134, 236
Stuart, G.L. 165
Sturge, C. 60
Sugarman, D.B. 161
Sullivan, B. 91
Surratt, H.L. 94, 95
Swan, S.C. 160
Sweeney, J. 150

Teske, R.H. 19
Thiara, R. 13, 42, 59, 62, 236
Thoennes, N. 26
Thomas, M. 79, 81, 83
Thornewell, C. 129
Timms, J. 63
Tjaden, P. 26
Tolman, R. 17, 24, 26, 28, 29, 163, 164, 217,
    228
Torkington, P. 90
Treister, L. 118
Trellis, K. 76
Trinder, L. 45, 46, 47, 59, 62
Tulle, E. 127
Turkat, I. 54
Tweed, R.G. 165

UK Network of Sex Work Projects 91, 98
Ullman, S.E. 75
UNICEF 10, 72
United Nations 9
Utting, W. 103

Vinton, L. 135, 136

Waddington, E. 215
Wade, J. 58, 63
Waigandt, A. 72
Walby, S. 55, 75, 130, 143, 182, 216, 217
Walker, A. 55
Walker, L. 160
Waltz, J. 165
Wangmann, J. 164
Ward, A. 97
Ward, H. 58, 90
Ward, K. 225
Ward, T. 170
Wasoff, F. 64
Weber, J. 90
Weeks, L.E. 127, 136
Weeks, M. 93
Weir, K. 54
Weitzer, R. 92
Welchman, L. 146
Wendt, S. 223, 224, 225
Westmarland, N. 20, 48, 90

White, T. 113
Whitehead, T. 90
Whittaker, K. 129, 135
Whittington, C. 214
Wilke, D. 135, 136
Williams, E. 72, 74, 80, 81, 83
Williams, K. 129, 164, 166
Williams, S.E. 103
Williamson, C. 97, 98
Williamson, E. 44
Wilson, M. 55, 170
Wolf-Light, P. 189
Women's Aid 130, 131, 137
Wood, M. 105
Woodruff, J. 72
World Health Organisation 72, 129
Worrall, A. 182, 190

Yllo, K. 11

Zink, T. 126, 127, 134, 137